The Lost Se

A SPIRITUAL JOURNEY

LOOKING FOR MORE THAN CONVENTIONAL CHRISTIANITY?
DISCOVER THE *NON-HOW TO* WAY THAT UNLOCKS GOD'S POWER.
A WORLD OF LOVE, BLESSINGS, AND FULFILLED DESTINY AWAITS!

The Lost Secret

Archaeological Adventure Map

SVR

ÆQVATOR

Potoſi.
Plata.
Sierra del Potoſi.

GRAD. Siue Latitudo. MERIDIONALIS.

Timana   Carthago

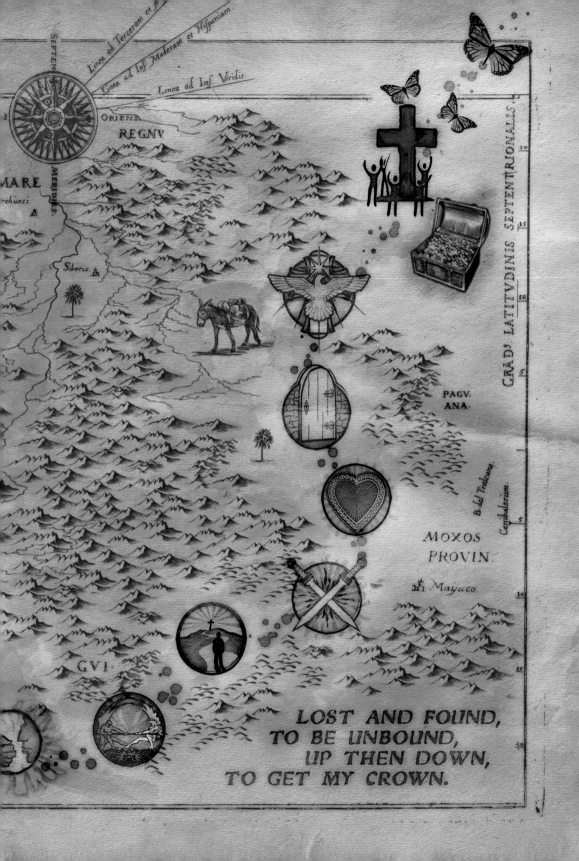

LOST AND FOUND,
TO BE UNBOUND,
UP THEN DOWN,
TO GET MY CROWN.

The Lost Secret

by Rick Suarez

Published by
Fresh Start Ministries
P.O. Box 35217
Canton, Ohio 44735
www.lostsecret.org | info@lostsecret.org

Unless otherwise noted, all Scripture quotations
are taken from the New King James Version of the
Bible. Copyright © 1982 by Thomas Nelson, Inc.,
publishers. Used by permission.

Scripture marked NIV are taken from the Holy
Bible, New International Version. Copyright
© 1973, 1978, 1984 by International Bible
Society. Used by permission of Zondervan Bible
Publishers. All rights reserved.

Scripture marked NASB are taken from the New
American Standard Bible. Copyright © 1960,
1962, 1963, 1968, 1971, 1972, 1973, 1975, 1977,
1995 by The Lockman Foundation. Used by
permission. All rights reserved.

Scripture marked Amplified are taken from The
Amplified Bible, Expanded edition. Copyright
© 1987 by The Zondervan Corporation and The
Lockman Foundation. All rights reserved.

Scripture marked Phillips are taken from J.B.
Phillips: The New Testament in Modern English.
Copyright © 1958, 1960, 1972 by J.B. Phillips.
Copyright © renewed 1986, 1988 by Vera M.
Phillips. Permission by Macmillan Publishing
Company.

References consulted:

Strong's Exhaustive Concordance of the Bible by James
Strong, S.T.D., L.L.D. Copyright © 1979 by
Thomas Nelson Inc., Publishers. All rights
reserved.

The Merriam-Webster Dictionary. Copyright © 1998
by Merriam-Webster, Incorporated. All rights
reserved.

Webster's New World Dictionary. Copyright © 2002 by
Wiley Publishing, Inc. All rights reserved.

ISBN 978-0-615-19597-1

Printed in China

It's not just a book…it's a journey.

INTRODUCTION: Are you a Christian who loves God but has left church? Do you still go to church, maybe you're even a minister, but you know deep in your heart that something is missing? You may not be a born-again Christian, but are you searching for God and yet convinced conventional Christianity isn't where you're going to find Him? Finally, are you sincerely seeking God through one of the many religions around the world? No matter who you are, is the cry of your heart to God, "Where's the love and where's the power?" If so, *The Lost Secret* may be for you.

OUR GOD GIVEN BIRTHRIGHT: There are two things that every human being wants and needs—to be loved unconditionally and to have access to God's power to be blessed and have the ability to bless others. God gave this birthright to Adam and Eve in the Garden of Eden. They lived in this world of love with God and each other. And they were given power and dominion for rulership over the entire earth…but their fall caused them to lose it.

In 33 AD Jesus died on the cross and was raised from the dead in order to buy our birthright back. During the first century, believers lived in a wonderful two-dimensional world. They had supernatural love, joy, and peace even in the midst of their persecutions and trials. They also had access to God's power for victory over sin, Satan, and curses—to be blessed and fulfill their destiny to bless others with signs and wonders following. But then something happened, and their world was lost.

THE SECRET WAS LOST: During the second and third centuries, things began to slowly change with believers. And in 313 AD, the emperor Constantine legalized Christianity. This appeared to be a move that would help the church flourish, but instead, things took a turn for the worse. Once the church became organized, it began to take on many of the characteristics of worldly organizations. When this happened, the secret to God's love and power was lost. Since then, sincere Christians have gone through a lot of religious motions that have produced little love and supernatural power in the church. But now that the lost secret has been found, the time for change has come.

THE UN-BOOK: Many good books have been written on how to tap into God's love and power by giving people a formula, or a set of rules to follow. This book is not a how to formula. In fact, in that sense it could be called "the unbook." I don't have it all figured out, but I'm in the process of having my life transformed by the lost secret, and more and more I'm experiencing His love, joy, peace, and power.

In this unbook, I hope to open up a conversation among Christians and ministers who long for more than what conventional Christianity has to offer. I also believe people who have not accepted Jesus as Lord and Savior will be attracted to Him as they see Christianity in a different light.

I share my spiritual journey and some concepts and principles the Lord has shared with me. I also ask many questions for individuals to ask themselves and for groups to discuss together. The Lord is the one with the answers. My prayer is that He might use this book as part of a dynamic process in our lives as we seek to move beyond conventional Christianity into a world of love and power.

JOIN THE JOURNEY: Refer to the archaelogical adventure map in the front of the book and join the journey to this lost world. As you read each chapter, you will understand what each icon symbolizes, and in the end be able to decipher the riddle on the map. On your journey, you will find the secret that has been lost for 1,600 years and discover how to make it part of your life. We're about to get back everything that was lost!

Let the journey begin...

Rick Suarez

The Author's Journey

A Parable of Grace

CHAPTER 1

The Author's Journey

A PARABLE OF GRACE

COULD AN AVOWED ATHEIST become a minister of the gospel of Jesus Christ crucified? Could the son of a blue-collar worker become a millionaire at the age of twenty-three? Could a multi-millionaire lose almost everything and yet, through such loss, gain the one thing he really needed? This is my journey, and as you read it, you will find out that yes, these things are possible.

I call my testimony a "parable of grace" because God's grace is really what it's all about. His lavish grace—and severe mercy—are the themes of my life. Like Greek theater, my makeup and actions have been so extreme at times that it may seem an exaggeration—just a story told to make a point. Well, it's not an exaggeration, and the point is that God is full of grace. At times my life has been as bad as it could get, and yet His grace and mercy were enough even then—especially then—to redeem me. I guarantee you, if Jesus never gave up on Rick Suarez, He'll never give up on you.

I was born and raised Catholic, the son of a blue-collar worker, in Canton, Ohio. In first grade, at St. Benedict's Catholic School, I felt a call on my life to be a priest. Now, I know every Catholic boy wants to be a priest, and every Catholic girl wants to be a nun, but this was the real deal. I loved God. Even at that young age, I heard His voice calling me into ministry.

There was a nun at St. Benedict's who was my teacher. Her name was Sister Mary Daniel, and one day she came into class and told us that her father was very ill and dying. I could see that she was very sad. My heart reached out to help her, and with childlike faith, I believed that God wanted to heal her father.

When we went to mass that day, I said five rosaries for her father. (Any good Catholic knows that is no small feat, especially for a little boy!) Back in class, I raised my hand. Sister Mary Daniel called on me, and I told her what I had done. She was so touched that she wept, and I wept with her.

I look back at that little boy—ornery, yes, like any little boy—but with such a soft heart. I remember the childlike faith I had, the trusting, open love for God and people. The innocence. I look back at that little boy and a part of me wants to turn back time, to rush back and save him, because as I look back, I can also see what is coming.

In front of that little boy lie two paths. The path of life, of God's grace and childlike faith and love, will soon be abandoned by him. He'll get no further than those first few steps he took in first grade. In second grade he turns from it onto the bright and shining path of the world's system of knowledge and works to achieve "success," but it will be a path of death. And after he turns down that road, it will be a hard road—and a long time until he sees the path of life again.

I'd been told by my parents that I was an accident; I wasn't planned. I felt very deeply rejected, and so in second grade—I know this sounds crazy for a seven-year-old—I made the decision that I was going to be successful. I was going to get good grades, and that was the way I'd gain love and acceptance. Just like in the Garden of Eden, knowledge and works came into my life that year—as a way to make God and people like me. A way to feel good about myself. And even though I didn't realize it as a second grader, I realize now that I chose being successful over remaining in the love of God as a little child. Now please understand, I'm not saying that

I'M NOT SAYING THAT BEING EDUCATION-ORIENTED, HARD-WORKING, AND SUCCESSFUL IS A BAD THING, BUT HAVING YOUR SELF-WORTH ATTACHED TO IT IS.

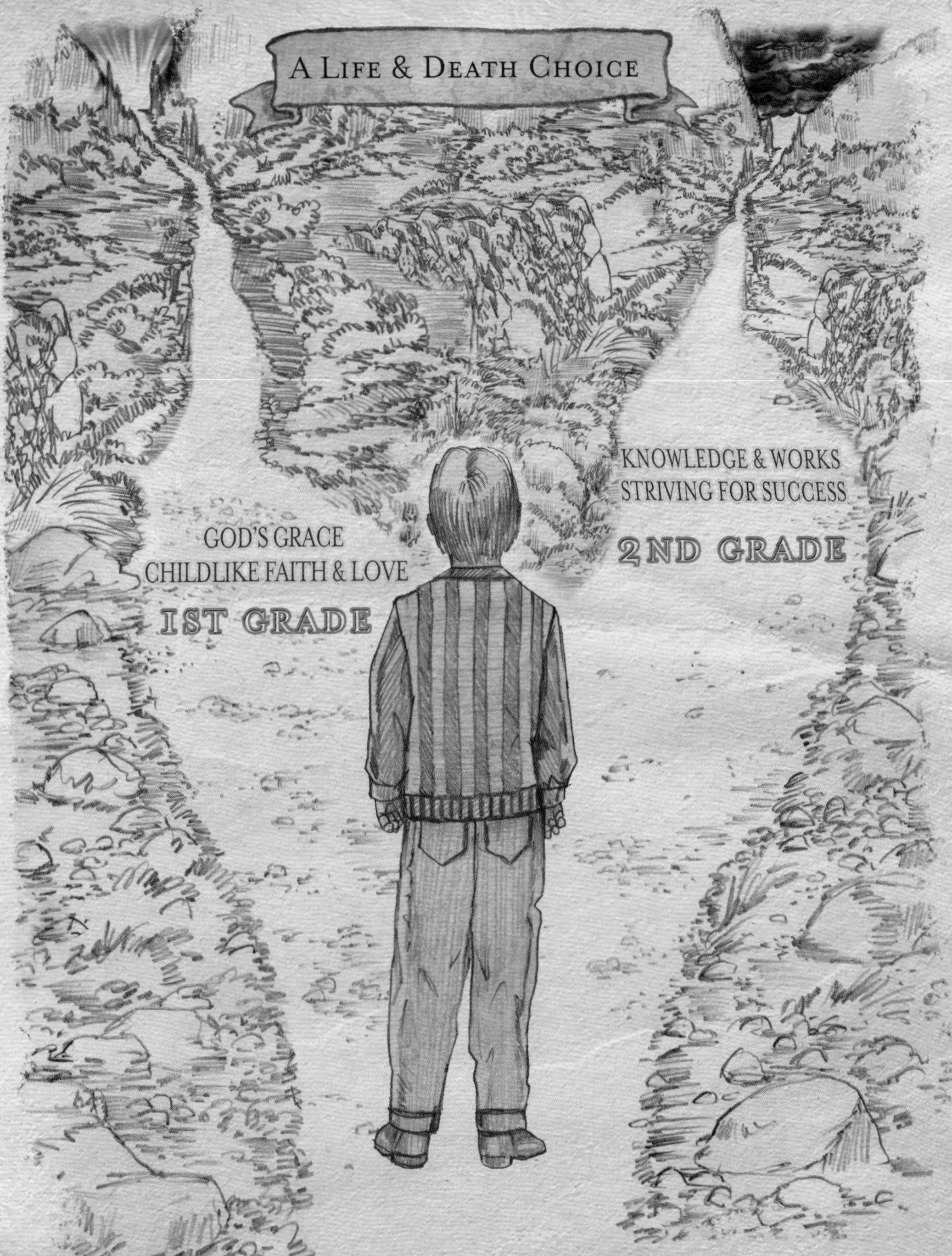
A LIFE & DEATH CHOICE
GOD'S GRACE
CHILDLIKE FAITH & LOVE
1ST GRADE
KNOWLEDGE & WORKS
STRIVING FOR SUCCESS
2ND GRADE

being education-oriented, hard-working, and successful is a bad thing, but having your self-worth attached to it is. Success does not make us sinners anymore than poverty makes us saints. The Lord doesn't look at our outward appearance, He looks at our hearts.

Throughout grade school I excelled in my grades. I still planned on becoming a priest, and so the summer before eighth grade I went to a pre-seminary entrance camp. While there I got the award for being the "best future seminarian." That fall a priest from the seminary called me and said, "Richard, it's time to get enrolled, you know. You're our number one guy, and you're going to be checking in here in September."

Instead of being excited, I flipped out! I don't know why, but I just freaked out. I lied and told him I couldn't enroll because my mom wouldn't let me. I did not go to seminary. Instead, I went to a Catholic high school from 1965 to 1969.

Those were times of great change, both in my personal life and in our country. The Vietnam War and upheaval in the United States set the tone for my early adulthood as an atheist.

First, I started asking questions about God and the church. In the beginning it was an honest search. I was a very truth-oriented guy, like I am today, very direct. I wanted to get to the bottom of some questions I had, and the brothers at my high school couldn't answer me. I started getting disillusioned with the church and God.

Second, I was a big patriot. As a youngster, I had read every World War II book in the world and wanted to join the military and become a fighter pilot. I believed in freedom, loved America, and loved what it stood for. However, with the Vietnam War I became disillusioned with my country too. I just started getting the sense that we were being sold out. I thought I was being sold a bill of goods by both my church and my country, and it's almost like I was a child who found out there was no Santa Claus. I felt betrayed and got extremely upset. I gradually came to the conclusion that my country wasn't worth anything; it was full of hypocrites and so was the church. I decided God didn't exist. So, by the time I graduated from high school and entered college, I was an atheist.

As an atheist I took on a very, very wild lifestyle. I was not a passive atheist. I was an atheist who wanted to go about and ruin everybody else's faith, like Saul in the Bible, who wanted to kill Christians. I would go around to anybody I knew who had faith and tell them how stupid they were to believe in God.

I had some very wild friends in the sixties and seventies. I'm not proud of it, but I must admit I did a lot of drugs. One time—and this has to be the epitome of stupidity, but it shows the far reaches of God's grace—some friends and I went to an amusement park. We had taken LSD, and we were tripping out. We got on a roller coaster, and I sat in the front seat. As the roller coaster was beginning to take off, I turned around and looked at everybody else on the ride. They could actually see my face. At the top of my lungs, I yelled, "There is no God! There is no God! If there is a God, I defy Him to strike me dead on this roller coaster ride!"

> I YELLED, "THERE IS NO GOD! THERE IS NO GOD! IF THERE IS A GOD, I DEFY HIM TO STRIKE ME DEAD ON THIS ROLLER COASTER RIDE!"

Those poor people turned white; their eyes were as big as fifty-cent pieces. I'm sure they were thinking, *How did we get on this ride with this nut*, and *We're all going to die!* It freaked everybody out.

When we reached the end of this wild roller-coaster ride, the other riders were all praying and making the signs of the cross. I looked back at them and defiantly said, "See, I told you, there is no God!"

That's just the way I was—a lunatic. A jerk. I lived a life of mocking God. In my room in college, I had a crucifix with the Beatle's "Sgt. Pepper's Lonely Hearts Club Band" poster behind it. I stuck a five-dollar bill between Jesus' legs, and a sign I made said "The Church of You Never Know When You're Going to Go." I was a brazen hellion of a kid who just mocked God. That was me in the wild sixties and seventies.

In 1970, when I was nineteen years old, I was at the University of Cincinnati. After four students were shot and killed by the National Guard during a Kent State war protest, they shut down all the state schools early. When I went home, my brother, brother-in-law, and I decided to go into business. We didn't have anything—our parents were blue-collar workers. Just like the classic American dream, we started in the basement of my brother's home. Our only money was wedding money from my brother-in-law, what we borrowed from my dad, and other loans my brother and I took out. Everything we tried failed. We tried thirteen different things, from a food delivery business to preprinted catalogs, and a pay-only-if-you-sell classified newspaper. You name it, we tried it, and nothing worked!

We were $100,000 in debt and about to go bankrupt when we hit on the idea of selling computerized horoscopes for three bucks. We had people send in their time and place of birth, and we used a huge IBM mainframe computer at our bank to create personal horoscopes. We talked an ad agency guy into extending us credit and ran a nationwide ad in August of 1973. It was a big winner. Here we were in this little ranch home—that's where the whole company was—and in just a few weeks, those ads pulled in $150,000 in cash sales. The mailbags came in full of money—forty-thousand envelopes full of cash and checks. We had money stacked two feet high on eight-foot Formica tables. That was more money than I had ever seen in my entire life. It was amazing.

> THE MAILBAGS CAME IN FULL OF MONEY—FORTY-THOUSAND ENVELOPES FULL OF CASH AND CHECKS. WE HAD MONEY STACKED TWO FEET HIGH ON EIGHT-FOOT FORMICA TABLES.

But there was a price to be paid for all of that success. In October 1973 my brother and I, who had always been close, split. My brother-in-law and I formed one company, and my brother formed another, separate company. Then my sister and brother-in-law got divorced. Our family was ripped apart. It was a terrible loss.

On the outside things looked good. Both businesses were wildly successful—each doing about 3.2 million dollars in sales the next year, so if we had stayed together, we would have gone from $150,000 a year in sales to $6.4 million in a single year. In those days that was huge, huge money. My company had eighty employees, and I was making three hundred thousand dollars a year in salary and bonuses. Based on my net worth, at the age of twenty-three I was a millionaire. By the world's standards, what could be more fulfilling?

But with all of that success, I still felt very empty. Through the years 1968-74, I'd suffered losses that could never be compensated for: my relationship with my brother, the deaths of my mother, my grandfather, and my godfather, and developing friction with my father. But empty or not, success to gain self-worth and love was still all I knew. It's interesting to me now, looking back, because considering the goof-ball I had been, it seems the Lord would have just let me go. Instead, my life took a different turn during that time, as the Lord with His grace and compassion began to draw me back to Him.

In the fall of 1975, I met my future wife Lu Ann. Her aunt wanted her to work at my company, so she invited me to a wedding to meet her, and I went. It was the old "love at first sight." As soon as I saw her, I said, "That's the girl I'm going to marry." And I meant it!

Very shortly thereafter we started dating, and a real weird thing happened to me. The only way I know how to describe it is that it was like becoming a born-again Christian without being born again. Her love inspired me. I told all of my friends I was finished doing drugs. I stopped chasing women, and I didn't hang around my old friends anymore. I just wanted to be with Lu Ann, and I wanted to get married. What's more, I wanted to do it right: no sex before marriage, no drugs, nothing impure.

My friends were surprised. Everyone was asking me, "What has happened to you?" And I remember telling them, "I don't know, but this is the happiest I've ever been in my entire life."

It was bizarre, considering there was no real spiritual transformation, but loving another human being—and being loved—lifted me onto a higher plane. I saw things differently. I wanted my life to be better, and I wanted to make her happy. I actually went back to the Catholic church and went to confession so I could get married in the Catholic church. I remember the priest asked me, "What do you have to confess?" And I said, "You wouldn't even want to know. All I can tell you is that I haven't killed anybody. I don't have time to tell you everything else."

Those years, from 1975 to 1978, were the happiest I could ever remember since I was a child. It was really an incredible miracle—a true outpouring of God's grace. But then my old friends decided to buy a house nearby, catty-corner from us, and I got back into the old life I had known. I started running around with my old friends, smoking pot again, and basically going down the drain. I put my wife through hell, and life wasn't happy anymore.

In the meantime my sister had remarried, and her new husband and she had become born-again Christians. They were planting seeds in our lives about accepting Jesus, and even though I thought they were crazy, I never said anything to put them down, because I loved them.

We had purchased a vacation home out in Jackson Hole, Wyoming. In February of 1979, I was still a pretty cocky guy. I went skiing with some friends, and we went "out of bounds." That's where you go up the tram, to the top of a 10,600 foot mountain, and then you don't come down the regular ski runs. Instead you go off the back of the mountain to ski out of bounds. Well, we took off and immediately got lost in the mountains, in the complete wilderness.

Any skier knows that if you lose a ski and have to sidestep up a mountain for a few yards, it's horribly hard work. When we got lost, we had to start sidestepping, with big heavy skis on, up the sides of mountains, and then when we got over one mountain, there would be another mountain, and then another and another. It was the hardest thing I ever did in my life. Here I was, this big successful millionaire, and my existence was reduced down to one thing. I would look down at my foot and say to myself, "If I can move my ski two feet, then that is a victory." And after I did that, I'd say it again and again and again, trying to make it to the top of the mountain. Each time I made it up one mountain, I thought that if there were another one on the other side, I would lay down and die because I couldn't make it up another one. It seemed like there always was another mountain to climb.

> WHILE THIS WAS HAPPENING, THERE WAS AN AMAZING OCCURRENCE DEEP IN MY SPIRIT. IT WAS LIKE THE RHYTHM OF MY HEART WAS BEATING OUT, "JESUS, JESUS, JESUS."

While this was happening, there was an amazing occurrence deep in my spirit. It was like the rhythm of my heart was beating out, "Jesus, Jesus, Jesus." I could hear it in my spirit, but at the time I had no idea where it was coming from. "Jesus. Jesus. Jesus." Up through my body and out, over and over—"Jesus."

Five or six hours later, when to my surprise I was still alive and made it back to civilization, I went home, fell down on my knees beside the bed, and said, "Jesus, I thought I was going to die today, but You let me get back home. I'm accepting You as Lord and Savior of my life. I'm sorry for what I've been doing—the pot and all of the mess I've made—and I *promise* I will stop. I want to dedicate my life to You and follow through with my calling to be a minister." That was February of 1979, and that was my salvation experience.

Two weeks later it was St. Patrick's Day, and Lu Ann was pregnant with our first child. I was back at home, and I got high again. Along with that, I drank whiskey and went over to the neighbor's house. They had teenage girls. I wanted to show off, so I took them and their friend for a ride in my 911 Porsche. We were blasting the stereo, and ironically, I remember it was the Cars' song "Let the Good Times Roll" that was playing. I was going one-hundred-twenty miles per hour on a back road when I came to a curve and the car left the road. We were completely air-borne. The car flipped end over end and landed on its side. The windshield wipers were going, the song was still playing, and miraculously no one was hurt. And I heard a voice—the closest thing ever to an audible voice of God in my life—and He said, *You broke your promise.*

I got out of the car, and my wife came and picked us up. As we examined the Porsche, a sensation came over me that something supernatural had happened. There were no trees anywhere in sight, and yet it looked as if we had hit two trees. There were two huge dents—one on each side of the rear of the car. All I can figure is that an angel grabbed hold of it in the air and set it down. I could have killed us all, but God, with His great grace and mercy, spared our lives. And He reminded me, *You broke your promise.*

After this near-death experience, I prayed again, and I said, "Okay, Lord. I am so sorry. You have spared my life again, and I'm really going to try to get this right now." For the first time in my life, I began to read the Bible. As I read the Gospel of Matthew and learned about Jesus, I wept

ALL I CAN FIGURE IS THAT AN ANGEL GRABBED HOLD OF IT IN THE AIR AND SET IT DOWN. I COULD HAVE KILLED US ALL, BUT GOD, WITH HIS GREAT GRACE AND MERCY, SPARED OUR LIVES.

for a week straight. I kept saying to myself, "I really like Jesus, everything about Him; I just never knew Him." Then the Lord spoke this to my heart: "Beware the yeast of the Pharisees." Little did I know that these two concepts, that *Jesus is the best* and *beware the yeast of the Pharisees*, would become the guardrails of my Christian walk.

Lu Ann got saved, too, and we started going to church and really walking with the Lord. As we grew and learned more about the Bible and Christianity, I began to really deal with the known sins in my life, like the drugs and cursing. I also realized that the horoscope business was not an appropriate place for a Christian businessman, but we had built up such a high standard of living that I didn't feel I could just drop out of it.

From 1979 to 1981, my plan was to develop other product lines and slowly phase out of the horoscope business. I just did not have the faith to get out without something else to replace it, so I tried to get into other products, like health and fitness. My idea was that as those new areas progressed, the horoscopes would fade out, but it didn't happen. Part of it was because I didn't want to lay people off—I had over 150 employees at the time—and part of it was that I didn't want to change my lifestyle or go bankrupt.

In 1982 I just said, "I can't handle it; I'm a hypocrite doing horoscopes." I knew this was wrong but I was afraid to stop selling them. I did not have the faith. I was ashamed, so I backslid. But just like for Jonah, when he tried to run from God, everything went wrong. I bought a stereo; it blew up. I had a boat down on the Ohio River; the engine blew up. We went back to the marina and put another motor in; it blew up. I had bought another car, an ice-green Porsche Turbo, and it stopped running whenever I drove it down the road. We'd tow it to the garage, and they'd say nothing was wrong. I'd take the car back out, and five minutes later the engine would stop.

Then I started getting sick. I went to a lot of doctors, but nobody could help me; in fact what they did only made things worse. I got back into smoking pot, and things got worse and worse and worse—I mean my life just shut down. It's as if God was saying, You can run, but you cannot hide.

So, being the brilliant guy that I was, after fifteen months of this, in the spring of 1983, I said, "Lord, that's it. I'm making a wholehearted commitment to you." And, this time, finally, I followed through on that commitment. I stopped smoking pot, after trying to quit fifteen times already. This time I really stopped, and my garbage collectors had some of the finest Hawaiian marijuana of anybody in the world, because I got rid of all of it. God gave me victory over it.

I stopped cussing, and I resolved to get out of the horoscopes and answer the call on my life to be a minister.

I thought I'd just kill two birds with one stone and sell the company so I could go into ministry. That way I wouldn't have to worry about money or my employees losing their jobs. But a funny thing happened when I put the company up for sale. For some reason, nobody wanted to buy it. And the Lord told me, *Rick, you birthed it. I don't want you to sell it because it will go on, and it is evil. I want you to kill it. You created it, and you have to be the one to end it.*

I said, "Okay." But I didn't know how. I started down the same path again with fitness, thinking that if I could get a winner with that, then I could just dissolve the horoscope business. And we did get a winner. The first fitness TV winner we did in 1985 was the Trim Track. It shot up like a rocket. But just as I was feeling comfortable that the Trim Track was my ticket out of horoscopes, the rocket came back down. There were no other winners on the horizon, and I lost faith. I started waffling again. It was scary.

Finally the Holy Spirit spoke to my heart. He showed me that my life had been like the parable of the sower. The first seed, which was stolen by the birds of the air, was when as a young person I lost my childlike faith and became an atheist. The second seed—the one that had no root and shriveled up and died—was when I met my wife and changed but then went right back into the old lifestyle. There was never any real change because I had not accepted Jesus as my Savior. The third part of the parable is that there's a plant, but it grows up and gets choked out by the cares and riches of this world. That's what kept happening to me after I was born again, because of the wealth horoscopes had generated for me.

Now, however, the Holy Spirit impressed on me that I had no more chances—there were no more parts to the parable—except to have a pure heart, which would represent good soil. It was either get out of the horoscope business and face possible bankruptcy or lose my own soul in hell. The Lord literally scared the daylights out of me. I knew He wasn't kidding, so I had to make a choice, possible bankruptcy or losing my soul.

So one day in February of 1986—seven years after I got saved—I finally sealed my wholehearted commitment to the Lord. My wife and I took our whole multi-million dollar horoscope business and stuffed it in a big trash can behind our company building. This was a business that had made us rich, and it could have made millions of dollars more in the future. We took all of the ads, all of the computer software, the mailing lists—everything to do with that business—and we poured gasoline on it and burned it. I knew that was the only way to kill it. I didn't trust myself not to go back, so I knew I had to totally destroy it.

After the big bonfire, Lu Ann and I went out to dinner. We expected to have a very spiritual time, to feel like a mighty man and woman of faith, and to celebrate. When the server set our appetizers in front of us, we looked at each other and said, "You know what? We're going to go bankrupt." We lost our appetites, our hearts were completely sick, and we went home.

An amazing thing happened next. There was an exercise product called the Stomach Streamliner sitting around in one of our warehouses. It was in our catalog, but nobody wanted to buy it. Then a TV scriptwriter came in and said, "Do you have any products you think may work on TV?"

When I told him about the Stomach Streamliner, he said, "I kind of like it. Would you give me a shot to write a two minute TV commercial for it?" I was desperate, so I said, "Sure."

He wrote a script, calling the product the "Gut-Buster." This was a play on the movie *Ghostbusters*, which had just come out. We tested it in August of 1986, and the Gut-Buster was one of the biggest mail order winners of all time. In six months we sold 2.2 million of them at $22.95, which brought in fifty million in sales. We actually made nine million dollars of profit in six months off of this one product, and it was as if God were saying, *I told you to get out of the horoscope business a long time ago*. But I had not had the faith to do it. Oh, me of little faith.

> IT WAS AS IF GOD WERE SAYING, I TOLD YOU TO GET OUT OF THE HOROSCOPE BUSINESS A LONG TIME AGO. BUT I HAD NOT HAD THE FAITH TO DO IT. OH, ME OF LITTLE FAITH.

After that we changed the name of the company to Fitness Quest. As Fitness Quest, we pioneered the industry of selling fitness products on television and then in retail stores. We had winner after winner: the Trim Track, Gut Buster, the E-Z Glider and Fit One cross country ski machines, the Abdominizer, and the Jane Fonda Step Aerobics system.

After taking that big leap of faith, burning the horoscopes, and sealing our wholehearted commitment to the Lord, Lu Ann and I were on-fire Christians. The Lord had blessed us, and we were committed to Him. The company was dedicated to the Lord; we had tracts in the lobby to witness to people; we opened up every day with prayer and had two Bible studies a week at work. We were giving thirty percent of our income into the kingdom, with plans to increase it to fifty, and were blessing a lot of people with bonuses and gifts.

Outwardly everything seemed perfect. The conventional Christian formula fit: the more we did for God, and learned about God, the better our lives got. The better we felt about ourselves. We were finally getting it right, we thought. Why had we waited so long?

A plus B equaled C, and Christianity made sense.

But then something happened in the spring of 1987. I guess you could say that's when my unconventional Christianity started. What I thought was going to happen didn't, and it all stemmed from a good intention.

I had a six-foot-four guy test the Gut Buster, and he couldn't go all the way back to do a full sit-up. So I said, "Gee, I want everybody to be able to use the Gut-Buster," and I lengthened the safety cord on it for people like him. It was a good intention, but it caused injury. Some people got hurt as they used it because the spring started breaking when it overextended with the longer safety cord. It would hit people and injure them. A very innocent mistake.

Unfortunately, this very innocent mistake got the attention of the Consumer Products Safety Commission and the Federal Trade Commission. I got into big legal trouble. This was no traffic ticket; it was the federal government, and it was a complete nightmare.

Looking back now, the years from 1987 to 1991 seem like a sort of twilight zone. On the one hand, we were making huge amounts of money. We went from twenty-five million a year to fifty million a year in sales, and then finally from 1990 to '91, the business went from fifty million to one hundred-thirteen million in sales in just one year. We were dedicated to the Lord—giving huge amounts of money to His kingdom as we felt directed.

But with the start of those legal problems in 1987, other things began to go downhill, even as the business grew. For one thing, I started getting sick. I had been a person with supernatural-like energy who never got sick. Then I got the flu—and kept getting it. That turned into Chronic Fatigue Syndrome, which means I was sick and had no energy. It was a disease that was caused by my pushing myself too hard, which resulted in a suppressed immune system. I was living on Coca-Cola, coffee, and aspirins. I still had a big company to run; still had legal problems because once the government gets on you, your problems last a long time; plus I had competitors who filed frivolous lawsuits. Conventional Christianity, the idea that I could put God in a box and A plus B would always equal C, was no longer making a lot of sense. Something was wrong with that picture.

> CONVENTIONAL CHRISTIANITY, THE IDEA THAT I COULD PUT GOD IN A BOX AND A PLUS B WOULD ALWAYS EQUAL C, WAS NO LONGER MAKING A LOT OF SENSE.

In the spring of 1992, I was on a trip, and the Holy Spirit spoke to my heart. I had all of these big plans for managing and expanding my business over the summer, and I felt Him say, *Rick, stop striving. You need to slow down, take the time to do things right, and spend more time with your family. If you don't, come October, when you move into your big mansion and open your 100,000-square-foot new addition to the company, you're going to be in big, big trouble.*

When I got back from the trip, I shared this with my board of directors and I asked for input. One of the thoughts shared at the board meeting was "We have to feed this monster. If we slow down, the business will be adversely affected." And, I made a very poor decision. I thought, "You know, the house is scheduled to be done in August; the new addition to the company is scheduled for completion in August, not October; maybe I didn't hear God right; I better not slow down." I chose to listen to a man instead of God and be influenced by fear instead of having faith.

Well, a not-so-funny thing happened after that. The house was not done in August; it was done in October. The 100,000 square-foot addition was not done in August either; it was done in October. And when October came up the company was in big trouble—just like the Holy Spirit had told me on my trip. I learned this, among other things: in human terms "big" means one thing, but when God says "big," you'd better understand that it means really *BIG*.

All of a sudden, the guy who had the Midas touch—I'd generated hundreds of millions of dollars in sales—could not make a dime. It was like the hand of God turned off a faucet. He told me, *You didn't obey Me, and I'm turning the faucet off. You can get the biggest monkey wrench, with the strongest men in the world to try to turn it back on, but it will not be back on until I say it is time.* And we could not make a dime. We went from doing 113 million in sales, with huge profits in 1991 to breaking even in 1992. We lost 10.8 million dollars in 1993 and were going bankrupt because I didn't obey the voice of the Lord. I listened to man instead of God, and operated out of fear instead of faith—and this time God turned off the faucet.

The year of 1993 was total despair. It was the darkest time of my entire life. For ten years I'd been a poster child for conventional Christianity. Even through trials I hadn't wavered in my commitment, but, in the summer of 1993 I hit a wall. I was sick as a dog, I had huge legal problems, and I was going bankrupt. You know in the Bible, when it talks about famine, plague and sword? I had all three curses at the same time. If I tried to take care of my health and rest, the legal and financial problems were not attended to, and vice-versa. I felt like I was doomed—like there was nothing I could do.

One day I sat down with Lu Ann and my assistant, who had been through everything with us, and I said, "I'm done with God. I don't want anything to do with Him anymore. That's it. I just wanted you to know."

They both acted like they were seeing a ghost. I'd been a spiritual leader for both of them, our company, and in our church—a rock during every storm—and they just couldn't believe their ears. Then a very weird thing happened. At that very moment when I thought I was giving up on God, He reached out to me. He gave me a vision of a canning jar on a shelf—that got my attention—and I said, "Lord, what is that?"

He then spoke to my heart and said, *Rick, that's your spiritual pride. You thought you were some big hotshot Christian, but you just said you were done with Me; you put Me on a shelf, because I didn't perform up to your expectations.*

I realized then, and am still coming to terms with the fact, that He is God. He is not a jar we can take on and off of some shelf. He is in charge—not us. I had begged the Lord to help me—to make my problems go away—and I was doing everything right according to conventional Christianity. But He still said no. Therefore I was ready to be done with Him. But He was not done with me. In His severe mercy, He allowed me to see that *A* plus *B* does not always equal *C*. He said, *Son, let me show you what your real problems are.*

> I REALIZED THEN, AND AM STILL COMING TO TERMS WITH THE FACT, THAT HE IS GOD. HE IS NOT A JAR WE CAN TAKE ON AND OFF OF SOME SHELF. HE IS IN CHARGE—NOT US.

In the fall of that year, the Lord showed me I needed spiritual surgery. (I will share this story in greater detail later in the book, but I will share a little bit of it here.) He wasn't willing just to put a Band-Aid over my problems. I asked Him to search me, and that's when He cut into my heart and showed me that I had drive gone mad. He showed me how I'd been striving to win approval in order to gain the love I desperately longed for. I'd been working so hard to heal my own wounds of rejection that I'd made a disease out of success—an idol. Through spiritual surgery, the Lord started to truly heal me. That's when I began to understand that I was not as big of a hotshot Christian as I thought, and an unconventional brand of Christianity began to take root. As with most physical surgeries, things got worse before they got better. The Lord had to take me to the cross.

We put everything we had—all of the money we'd made—into the company to try to save it. As a Christian I did not want to let it go bankrupt; regardless of my pride, it was against my convictions. However, nothing worked. We were totally broke. It finally got down to the point that if we didn't find a buyer for the company we were going to go bankrupt, and all of these employees whom we cared very, very much about were going to lose their jobs.

I sent my top people out to go find deals, and we ended up getting an offer from Time Warner. I won't go into all of the details, but for the readers who have gone through the pain of betrayal, I want you to know I've been there too. This process felt like a Judas experience. The Lord has healed the hurt of it, and taught me valuable things through it, but it was very difficult. I was forced against my wishes to sell the company out of a 360-145 bankruptcy—if I hadn't taken the deal, everyone would have lost their jobs.

So I took that deal. Almost everyone kept their jobs, the creditors were paid close to 100 percent and remained as vendors to the company— and I lost the company completely. We had to sell our mansion and most of our land; we lost about eighty-five percent of our net worth. I felt betrayed, violated, robbed—stripped of everything. It was all gone. The death of a dream.

After this great loss, the Lord shared something with me that really touched my heart. It was the beginning of a personal resurrection. He said, *All I ever wanted was you, not your performance, and I want you to want Me for Me, not what I can do for you.* Wow, He loves me for me, just the way I am, even if I'm not successful! What's more, the same need exists in *His* heart, to be loved just for Him, not how He can perform for me. This was an amazing and higher form of love—a love that can set a person free from fear and striving! I now understand, that apart from

> ALL I EVER WANTED WAS YOU, NOT YOUR PERFORMANCE, AND I WANT YOU TO WANT ME FOR ME, NOT WHAT I CAN DO FOR YOU.

failure and great loss, I never would have found this love, a healing love that I had been seeking my whole life. And I then remembered the very first vision I had as a Christian. I was a little boy, and Jesus took me by the hand to lead me up a mountain road. That's the opening painting of this chapter, and that's what was happening to me; he was taking that little boy who had lost his way in second grade and bringing him to a better place. The journey would not be easy, but the destination of living in a world of love, joy, peace and power would be worth it.

Since that time, the message of Philippians 3:7-11 has become the theme of my life:

But what things were gain to me, these I have counted loss for Christ. Yet indeed I also count all things loss for the excellence of the knowledge of Christ Jesus my Lord, for whom I have suffered the loss of all things, and count them as rubbish, that I may gain Christ and be found in Him, not having my own righteousness, which is from the law, but that which is through faith in Christ, the righteousness which is from God by faith; that I may know Him and the power of His resurrection, and the fellowship of His sufferings, being conformed to His death, if, by any means, I may attain to the resurrection from the dead.

My particular journey to the cross is not a path I would have ever chosen for myself, and I must admit that I didn't handle it well. Through the process I've had to face a lot of ugly things that were inside of me and ask for a lot of forgiveness. And, just as Paul goes on to say in verse thirteen and fourteen, I have not arrived. I am still reaching for the goal, still being transformed. I am still learning what it means to be loved by Him apart from my performance and to love Him back in the same way. Just me and God.

In the end, that is the prize. That is what I gained out of everything I lost: I gained more of Jesus than I ever had before—and in gaining Him I gained a much closer relationship with the Father. And I can honestly say that They are worth it! I'm going to share more of my story throughout the book—how God not only gives us love, joy, and peace *during* our trials, but also the power to change our circumstances to be blessed and be used by Him to bless others.

Here's a tip before we continue our spiritual journey. God created us all differently, and we are all at a different place in our walk with Him. He isn't asking you to be just like me or anyone else. Give God the leeway to take you on your spiritual journey the way He knows best.

My Personal One-on-One Encounter With The Lord

In what ways is my conventional Christianity not working in my life? Do I believe God may have something more—something better ahead in my journey with Him?

_____

_____

Is my identity and self-esteem attached to my personal success? What areas of my life can I now see that I am striving for success in order to gain love?

_____

_____

The Christian life is all about God's grace. Sometimes His grace comes softly, and other times it is severe—even painful. What are some ways He has demonstrated His grace in my life to this point?

_____

_____

_____

Do I understand that in God's Kingdom, sometimes loss is God's love and it actually represents gain? What examples can I think of in my own life where loss has turned into gain?

_____

_____

_____

REFLECTING ON THE ART

- What did the painting of the hand of Jesus mean to me?
- In what way does the painting that opens this chapter speak to me?
- Did the sketch have an impact on me? If so, how?

_____

_____

_____

The Wisdom of the World
Empties the Cross of Its Power

CHAPTER 2

The Wisdom of the World Empties the Cross of Its Power

I T'S THE CRIME OF THE CENTURY. No, it's the greatest crime of all time! God Himself came down from heaven to die a horrible death to save all of mankind. Jesus' crucifixion and resurrection is the single most important thing for all believers. But somehow, the most important thing in Christianity is no longer the most important thing—it's been lost.

How? The message of the cross has been stolen.

It takes a very clever crook to pull off a heist of this magnitude. Let's continue our spiritual journey by taking on the role of a detective. We'll follow five clues and find out who stole *the message of the cross, which is the first part of the lost secret.* Then, let's find out why and how it was stolen to begin the process of getting God's power back. A world of love, blessings, and fulfilled destiny awaits!

Let's read a few key scriptures to get started. First Corinthians 1:18 (NIV) reads, "For the message of the cross is foolishness to those who are perishing, but to us who are being saved it is the power of God." Paul goes on to say that the "Jews demand miraculous signs and Greeks look for wisdom, but we preach Christ crucified: a stumbling block to Jews and foolishness to Gentiles, but to those whom God has called, both Jews and Greeks, Christ the power of God and the wisdom of God"(vss. 22-24). This verse adds "wisdom" to the description of the cross. And

notice Paul's words in verse 17: "For Christ did not send me to baptize, but to preach the gospel—not with words of human wisdom, lest the cross of Christ be emptied of its power."

If we look at the key words there, *wisdom* and *power*, we see that *Jesus Christ crucified is the wisdom and power of God*. But, the wisdom of the world empties the cross of its power. That's *clue number one: the wisdom of the world*.

The word empty in that scripture is actually a pretty powerful word. It means "to nullify, to void, and reduce to nothing." The wisdom of the world brings the cross to nothing, or reduces it to nothing.

What is the wisdom of the world? I was walking down the hallway in my daughter Elisha's high school one day and I saw a big sign that summed it up perfectly: *Knowledge is power*. Sounds good, doesn't it? The same message was on CNN the other day. One of their ads said, "In today's world, information is power."

Along those same lines, what age are we living in today? "The Technology Age." And what is technology? The dictionary definition is "applied scientific knowledge." Simply put, technology is knowledge that can do work. When the computer was invented, they took the simple binary system and figured out a way to have a computer apply that scientific knowledge and make it work for people. Technology is knowledge and works.

What the world seems to be saying is that if you have knowledge and work hard, you're going to get power, right? In the natural world it makes a lot of sense. Caring parents instruct their children, "Get a good education, work hard, and you'll do well." The idea is that if you learn something and take what you learn and apply it by hard work, things will go well with you. You'll have power over your own life.

In the natural world, this can be a good formula. Remember, being an education-oriented and hard-working successful person is not bad in itself, but when my self-worth and love come from the success that it brings, that is a bad thing. As we will soon learn, though, taking a principle that works in the world and bringing it into God's kingdom is very destructive.

> AS WE WILL SOON LEARN, TAKING A PRINCIPLE THAT WORKS IN THE WORLD AND BRINGING IT INTO GOD'S KINGDOM IS VERY DESTRUCTIVE.

The wisdom of the world is *knowledge and works*. It's so good that the thief himself uses it! And that's our *second clue*. Let's use that clue to find the next one.

In the Bible, what do the words *knowledge* and *works* describe? Romans 7:7 gives this explanation of the law: "What shall we say then? Is the law sin? Certainly not! On the contrary, I would not have known sin except through the law. For I would not have known covetousness unless the law had said, 'You shall not covet.'" What that verse is saying is that the only way we can understand sin is through the law. Without it we would have no knowledge of right or wrong. The law came to show us the difference.

Galatians 3:12 says another interesting thing about the law. It says, "Yet the law is not of faith, but 'the man who does them shall live by them.'"

Those two scriptures tell us that the law is the knowledge of right and wrong, good and evil, and it involves obeying the commands—doing what is right and not doing what is wrong. Our *third clue is the law, because it's about knowledge and works*. That sounds a lot like the wisdom of the world, doesn't it?

I know we always think of the law as a Judeo-Christian thing, but guess what? The whole world has embraced the concept of the law. Every township, every city, every state, every government has laws—we can go through the entire world without finding an exception. It's not just a Judeo-Christian thing. Everybody has a system of knowledge and works.

But how could the thief—an enemy of the cross and its power—be at work anywhere near God's sacred law? Think for a moment about the Old Covenant and what we know about the Israelites under the law. What was their number one problem? Time and time again we see the same pattern throughout the Old Testament: idolatry. God gave them His love to motivate them and His laws to protect them…but they turned away from these gifts and turned to idols instead. *Idolatry is the fourth clue.*

Throughout the Old Testament (see Deuteronomy 32:21; 1 Kings 16:13,26; 2 Kings 17:12 and 21:11,21) we see how idolatry proliferated under the Old Covenant. Like a great incubator or greenhouse, the law's system was the perfect environment for idols to spring up and grow. Why do you think that was true then? Do you see how it is still true today?

Idols are our own creations. They exist by the work of our minds and hands. Our knowledge plus our work produces idols. In an environment that values works, like the world under the Old Covenant—and like the world we live in today—idolatry is going to be a big problem, and that problem creates the perfect opportunity for the thief.

To find the thief, we need only go one step further. First Corinthians 10:19-21 says, "What am I saying then? That an idol is anything, or what is offered to idols is anything? Rather, that the things which the Gentiles sacrifice they sacrifice to demons and not to God, and I do not want you to have fellowship with demons. You cannot drink the cup of the Lord and the cup of demons; you cannot partake of the Lord's table and of the table of demons." This verse says demons are associated with idols.

Now we are right on the heels of the thief. In Matthew 12:24 (NIV), Satan is called "the *prince of demons.*" If demons are attached to idols, and Satan is the prince of demons, then it follows that *where we have demons, we can find Satan.*

As we connect a few more scriptures, we will find Satan's fingerprints all over the scene of the crime.

CLUE #1: THE WISDOM OF THE WORLD. In John 12:31 (NIV), Satan is called "the prince of this world."

CLUE #2: KNOWLEDGE AND WORKS. In 1 John 4:3, Satan is described as being "the spirit of the Antichrist." If we can be saved through knowledge and works, why do we need Jesus Christ crucified? We don't.

CLUE #3: THE LAW—OLD COVENANT. If the Old Covenant could have brought us into right relationship with God, why would we need a new one? We wouldn't. (See Hebrews 8:7-13.)

CLUE #4: IDOLATRY. First Corinthians 8:1 (NIV) states, "Knowledge puffs up, but love builds up." Under the law, our knowledge puffs up our pride, and instead of resting in the love of God, we build idols out of the work of our own hands. The cause of Satan's fall was pride. He literally wanted to be a god and to become an idol.

CLUE #5: DEMONS. First Corinthians 10:19-21 says that idols have demons attached to them, and where demons are, so is their prince.

Satan, the prince of demons, is the thief who stole the message of the cross.

Why would Satan want to steal the message of the cross from believers today? Remember 1 Corinthians 1:18: "For the message of the cross is foolishness to those who are perishing, but to us who are being saved it is the power of God." *It's all about power!* Now, this is fascinating to me. In Genesis 1:26 the Bible says that as God was creating the world, He said, "Let Us make man in Our image, according to Our likeness; let them have dominion over the fish of the sea, over the birds of the air, and over the cattle, over all the earth and *over every creeping thing that creeps on the earth*" (italics mine).

We know that nothing is in the Word by accident, right? "Creeping thing" is not in there by coincidence. It states that man had dominion

Satan is the Thief

5. Demons

4. Idols

3. Law—Old Covenant

2. Knowledge & Works

1. Wisdom Of World

over everything, including every creeping thing. Guess what the word *creeping* means in Hebrew? It means "to glide swiftly" and "a reptile or any other rapidly moving animal that creepeth."

What does that describe? A snake! In Genesis 3:1, it says, "The serpent [a reptile that glides swiftly and was represented by the devil] was more cunning than any beast of the field." Guess what? In God's original plan He created us to have dominion over Satan. He gave us dominion over this entire world, including Satan, and including all of his demons. That's our God-given birthright!

Why did Satan want man to go to the tree of the knowledge of good and evil in the Garden of Eden? To steal our birthright, which gave us power and dominion over him. He deceived Adam and Eve into thinking that knowledge would make them powerful, like God, but it really took away their power. It gave him power in their lives. That's the why of it.

> IN A VERY REAL SENSE, JESUS' LAST WORDS WERE A DEATH SENTENCE FOR THE ENEMY: "IT IS FINISHED" MEANT, "SATAN, YOU ARE FINISHED!"

But Jesus bought it all back for us on the cross. His final words before He died were "It is finished." In a very real sense, Jesus' last words were a death sentence for the enemy: "It is finished" meant, "Satan, you are finished!"

What a blow! Satan hates the cross. He hates the power it made available for believers and the power it wrested from him. *Satan will do anything he can to try to get that power back.*

We now know who stole the message of the cross and why he did it. If we are to get it back, however—to claim the birthright and power that is ours through the cross of Jesus—we have to figure out what Satan is doing, on a personal level, to lure believers away from the cross. How does he accomplish it?

The Great Deception: You may have heard the old adage, "Give the devil his due." While we never want to give any glory to Satan or honor him in any way, he is still our enemy, and in this battle for power and victory it pays for us to know something about who we're fighting against. In John 8:44 (NIV) Jesus provides insight into the character of our enemy. He states, "There is no truth in him. When he lies, he speaks his native language, for he is a liar and the father of lies."

I can't, but imagine I could speak German. If I learned German, and I don't care how much I practiced, if I went to Germany, the people there would still know I'm not a native German. Why is that? I'd have an accent. But if I was raised in Germany, and German was my native tongue, I wouldn't have an accent, right?

That's the way it is with Satan. When he lies, there is no accent. He's the greatest liar in the world. Lying is his native language, so we will never hear an accent when he lies to us.

THE ULTIMATE DECEPTION FOR AN ON-FIRE CHRISTIAN IS A GOOD INTENTION.

What's the devil's best lie? The ultimate deception for an on-fire Christian is a good intention. Second Corinthians 11:14 tells us that "Satan *disguises himself as an angel of light*" (NASB). One way he does this is to take something good and misapply it and then misdirect us. This is the only thing that will work with a sincere Christian.

Think back to the time right after you were first saved. Remember the joy? Remember the excitement? Like being in love, you just can't get enough of that special person—Jesus is your first love. In fact, if you make a wholehearted commitment to Him as Lord, there's only one thing that really appeals to you, one place Satan can attack. For the sincere Christian, the most beautiful, desirable thing is our own service to God. It's the ultimate scam.

We start doing—and striving—and laboring. Satan cheers us on. "This is something good!" He says, "This is pleasing God!" But he misapplies it in our lives, we then put it in a place of preeminence where it doesn't belong, and suddenly we are misdirected. We leave our first love at the cross and go back—back to the wisdom of the world, back to knowledge and works, back to the law. Pretty soon, instead of soaring like eagles, we're caught like a rat on a treadmill: working ourselves to death but powerless, going nowhere. It's a brilliant deception. He has used the wisdom of the world to empty the cross of its power—to nullify, void, and bring to nothing.

In closing, I would like to share how I found the first part of the lost secret, or better put, how it found me. In the fall of 2000, I was sitting in an Applebee's restaurant, having lunch with my friend Steve, when the power of God unexpectedly fell. In my spirit, the Lord asked me a question: "Where is Jesus Christ crucified in the church?" The question was followed by the analogy of scoring a prizefight. The judges at ringside keep track of every blow, and in the end, give a score for each fighter. What if, just in America, every sermon in every church, every TV and radio show, every book and teaching tape, and every conversation between Christians was scored for one year on how many times the cross was mentioned? The answer resounded in my heart like a deafening blow: The cross would lose. Jesus Christ and Him crucified gets a very small percentage of conventional Christianity's time.

PRETTY SOON, INSTEAD OF SOARING LIKE EAGLES, WE'RE CAUGHT LIKE A RAT ON A TREADMILL: WORKING OURSELVES TO DEATH BUT POWERLESS, GOING NOWHERE.

Then I got a mental vision of God the Father and Jesus standing face to face, looking into each other's eyes. Their faces were full of sorrow. What They were saying was this: "Did We do this for nothing?" The impression was that after the horrible pain and agony They both went through during the crucifixion, no one was really very interested. It was the ultimate act of love on Their parts, but it has somehow lost its place of importance in the church. I was very shaken by this realization and felt moved to action. Thus the seed was planted for this book and the inspiration for the painting on the next page.

"Did We do this for nothing?"

Philip Howe

My Personal One-on-One Encounter With The Lord

ALSO FOR HOME GROUP DISCUSSION

Has Satan stolen the message of the cross from me, so that Jesus Christ and Him crucified is no longer the most important thing in my life?

_____

_____

_____

Why did Satan steal the message of the cross?

_____

_____

_____

How did Satan steal it?

_____

_____

What has God shown me about how I'm going to get my stolen birthright back and enter His world of love and power?

_____

_____

_____

REFLECTING ON THE ART

- In what way does the painting that opens this chapter speak to me?
- Did the sketches have an impact on me? If so, how?
- As I look at the painting titled "Did We Do This For Nothing?", what is it saying to me?

_____

_____

_____

Opposite: Inspired by the painting *Pain of the Cross*, by Arthur Robins.

Jesus Took the Law
Out of Our Way

CHAPTER 3

Jesus Took the Law Out of Our Way

HOW COULD SATAN TAKE SOMETHING that is good and holy, the Law of Moses, and use it against us? He uses the principle of misapplication to cause misdirection. He takes the law, which was good in the Old Covenant, and misapplies it by placing it in the New Covenant. This misdirects us, out of the new and better covenant, back into the old.

I remember the day the Lord began to change this misdirection in my life. He spoke this to my heart, "For you and the church, the Law doesn't exist anymore." I was both shocked and offended. But this was the day that I came to understand a very important principle. The biggest stumbling block on the path of my spiritual journey would be Jesus Himself! Why? Because 1 Peter 2:8 says that Jesus is "a stone of stumbling and a rock of offense." The Gospels show time and time again how Jesus offended those He was teaching. That's because Jesus had a multifaceted personality. He was compassionate, full of wisdom, and many other things, but He was also a straight-shooter when He spoke, which offended many people. I have now come to know, that if I am not being challenged on a regular basis in my Christian walk, I am not going to get all that Jesus has for me.

So back to my offense. As I studied the scriptures, I found that even though I was challenged, what He said to me was true. There are several scriptures throughout the New Testament that back this up. Perhaps the most plain and simple, however, is Romans 10:4 (NIV), which says, "Christ is the end of the law so that there may be righteousness for everyone who believes."

Jesus brought the law to an end by fulfilling it. He was the only person who ever lived on earth but was without sin, so His sinless life fulfilled the law (1 Peter 2:21-24). Then when He died on the cross, He bore every sin and curse, and defeated every demon (Galatians 3:13, Colossians 2:15). As a result, He took the law that was against us out of our way, so we could become part of His body and return to our Father in heaven (Colossians 2:14, 1 Corinthians 12:27).

The written law that involves knowledge and works has been replaced with faith in Jesus that expresses itself through love (Galatians 5:6 NIV, paraphrased). Through a new covenant, and with grace and faith, He writes the law of love in our hearts. In Romans 13:10 Paul writes, "Love does no harm to a neighbor; therefore love is the fulfillment of the law." *But it is an internal law of love.* God gives us the ability to obey it because He's given us new hearts.

THIS CHALLENGING TRUTH— THAT CHRIST IS THE END OF THE LAW FOR BELIEVERS— IS ACTUALLY ONE OF THE MOST COMFORTING TRUTHS IN SCRIPTURE.

This challenging truth—that Christ is the end of the law for believers—is actually one of the most comforting truths in Scripture. Let's look at some of the things the Bible tells us about the law to see just how scary the law can be—and how blessed we are that Jesus came and fulfilled it, to take it out of our way.

The number one truth about the law is that it can't get rid of sin; it can only expose it and increase it. Romans 5:20 says, *Moreover the law entered that the offense might abound. But where sin abounded, grace abounded much more.*

Let's take a real life situation for an example. Imagine a backcountry road with no stop signs, no traffic lights, one speed limit of fifty-five miles per hour, and there are hardly any police patrolling it. Here we see the presence of very little law. How many traffic tickets would a person get on that road? Few. However, if we take that same road and add the law—more signs, lights, different speed limits every quarter mile, and policemen all over the place—what happens? There would be more violations and more tickets. This is how the law increases sin.

Another troubling truth about the law is found in Romans 7:5, which states, *For when we were in the flesh, the sinful passions which were aroused by the law were at work in our members to bear fruit to death.* Our flesh is actually aroused by the law. This can be observed in any group of people, even toddlers.

Imagine putting a group of little children in a room with every toy imaginable. There are cookies, candy, television, videos—anything a child could want to keep him occupied for a long time. On the way out of the door, the adult in charge says, "You kids have a blast! But, now, I want to tell you one thing. See that drawer over there? Do not open that drawer. You can do anything you want in this room, but *do not* open that drawer."

What do you think would happen as soon as the adult was out of the room? There's no doubt about it—that law would arouse their passions, and they would go straight to that drawer and open it. If nothing had ever been said about the drawer, they would probably never think of it, but that's what the law does in our lives. It arouses our passion to want to sin.

It gets worse. Romans 3:10 tells us that no one can obey the law. "There is none righteous, no, not *one.*" That scripture covers everybody… there is not one person who can obey the law…nobody is good. Even a super-duper, hotshot spiritual giant who could almost obey the entire law falls short because no one is righteous. And, James 2:10 says, "For whoever shall keep the whole law, and yet stumble in one point, he is guilty of all." That's terrible, or at least it would be if we were still under the law. It's a system everyone fails under.

I believe God gives us all of these verses in order to help us—to show us just how scary life can be under the law, so that we will want to run away from the law and run to the cross.

> GOD IS TRYING TO GET THIS MESSAGE ACROSS: THE LAW IS AGAINST US, BUT THE CROSS IS FOR US.

God is trying to get this message across: The law is against us, but the cross is for us. Let's look at Galatians 3:10: "For as many as are of the works of the law are under the curse; for it is written, 'Cursed is everyone who does not continue in all things which are written in the book of the law, to do them.'" Everybody under the law is cursed, because nobody can obey the law.

One day the Holy Spirit spoke to my heart and said, *Rick, the law is not your friend.* Consider this scenario: You're driving down the highway at night, listening to some music, really enjoying yourself. Maybe you're on a date with a special person, going out to dinner, and all of a sudden you see flashing lights in your rearview mirror. Is your first thought, "Oh, what a friendly officer. He probably sees that my gas cap is off, and he's just stopping me so he can assist me"? No. For most people, the first thought that would come to mind is "Oh no! I'm in trouble!" Even though policemen are supposed to be our friends, that's not how we typically think of them when we're getting pulled over, is it?

Jesus is our friend. Colossians 2:14 says, "[He has] wiped out the handwriting of requirements that was against us, which was contrary to us. And He has taken it out of the way, having nailed it to the cross." Something contrary to us—the law—is not our friend. It is against us. But the cross is for us.

If the law is against us, why do we love it so much? Think of all of the television shows and movies about the law, not to mention media coverage of court cases and other issues with the law. As a culture we are infatuated with the law. Why? The answer is that the law is about us—what we know, what we can do. Even Christians love the law because by it we can identify and measure, "This is what I know about God…. This is what I do for God…. I'm holy because…. I'm a Godly person…." It's all about us. That's the snare of the law.

AS A CULTURE WE ARE INFATUATED BY THE LAW, BECAUSE IT'S ABOUT US—WHAT WE KNOW, WHAT WE CAN DO.

The cross is all about Jesus. Before the cross we are stripped bare. Our righteousness is as filthy rags. We are nothing. All we have at the cross is our need for a savior—and under the New Covenant, we have one. By grace we are saved through faith in Jesus, who puts the law of love in our hearts—not a set of outward rules to follow but a relationship, an inward life led by His Spirit. Jeremiah 31:33 puts it this way: "This is the covenant that I will make with the house of Israel after those days, says the

Lord: I will put My law in their minds, and write it on their hearts; and I will be their God, and they shall be My people."

There is another reason we love the law, and its source is very sinister. A seed has been planted by Satan in every human that causes us to lust after the law. To understand the huge and scary ramifications of this, we must go back to the Garden of Eden.

Based on Genesis 1:26-28, every human has a God-given birthright that says we are made in God's image and likeness to live in His presence, have dominion over the earth and Satan, and to be blessed.

> Then God said, "Let Us make man in Our image, according to Our likeness; let them have dominion over the fish of the sea, over the birds of the air, and over the cattle, over all the earth and over every creeping thing that creeps on the earth." So God created man in His own image; in the image of God He created him; male and female He created them. Then God blessed them, and God said to them, "Be fruitful and multiply; fill the earth and subdue it; have dominion over the fish of the sea, over the birds of the air, and over every living thing that moves on the earth."

When Satan tempted Adam and Eve to fall, he did it to steal our birthright. That's why from deep within our spiritual DNA comes what I call a *Divine Dissatisfaction*. We look at the state of our lives and the church and have an inner knowing that God intended for things to be much better. We cry from our hearts, "Where's the love?" and "Where's the power?" This Divine Dissatisfaction is not about grumbling; if it was, it wouldn't be divine. It's modeled by David in the Psalms, who cried out to God day and night to be delivered from his troubles, but praised God at the same time. The church seems full of two types of people: those who grumble and complain, wallowing in their troubles, and others who work at tolerating their troubles, trying to keep their spirits up by praising and thanking God. David was different. He had a Divine Dissatisfaction and praised God, both at the same time—that's one of the reasons he was the only person in the Bible described as a man after God's own heart.

So how did Satan steal our birthright? We gained some understanding in the last chapter when we discovered how he stole the message of the cross, but let's plunge in further. God told Adam and Eve not to eat of the tree of the knowledge of good and evil, and if they did they would die (Genesis 2:17). But Satan said, "You will not surely die. For God knows that in the day you eat of it your eyes will be opened, and you will be like God, knowing good and evil" (Genesis 3:4-5). Satan planted two seeds. "First, God is holding out on you; if He really loved you He would want you to be like Him—God isn't good! Second, who you are now is not good enough, you need to become something better—you are inferior!"

These seeds caused Eve to lust after the law. She looked at the tree, saw that it was good for food, pleasant to the eyes, and a tree desirable to make one wise (Genesis 3:6). She lusted for the knowledge of good and evil (the law), believing it would make her better—not inferior anymore—and give her the ability to take care of her own problems since she couldn't trust God. But guess what? It didn't work. She and Adam sinned, fell, and lost their birthright. They lost their face to face relationship with God, their rulership over the earth, and their world that was filled with blessings became infiltrated with curses. But deep inside, we remember what it was like before the Fall.

Satan's temptation produced the deadly sequence of a lie, a lust, and a loss. A lie that God is not good and I'm not good enough. A lust after knowledge and works to strive for success to gain self-esteem and take care of my own problems. The result was a loss of living in God's presence, with dominion over the earth along with abundant blessings.

I know this sequence very well. When I was told that my birth was an accident, I concluded that since I wasn't wanted, there must be something wrong with me. That was the lie that triggered my lust to strive for success. I'd show the world that I was very valuable; but eventually came the loss of my health, relationships, and my business. But as I died to self, God raised me from the ashes. He told me the truth, that I was wonderful. I replaced my striving with faith and reliance on Jesus, and I began to gain my God-given birthright back. What He did for me, He will do for you also.

Let's look at the New Testament to discover more about this sequence. Did you know there are three laws mentioned in the Bible? I didn't until it was revealed to me in the book of Romans, in chapter 7:21-25 and 8:2. It says there is the law of God (which is the law of Moses), the law of sin and death, and the law of the Spirit of life in Christ Jesus—three laws. With this in mind, let's look at Satan's deadly sequence and see how Jesus reversed it.

Romans 8:15 says we did not receive a spirit that makes us a slave again to fear. Satan's lie, that says God is not good, causes us to fear—we worry that God won't be there for us when we have problems. Along with fear, Satan also tells us we're inferior, that there's something wrong with us. That lying spirit creates a lust for the law, which is knowledge and works, to gain self-esteem and take care of our own problems. Instead of putting our faith in Jesus and entering His rest, we become toiling slaves! It gets worse. Romans 7:8-9 and 1 Corinthians 15:56 say that apart from the law, sin can't exist. The law literally powers sin and brings it to life. So the law we lust after brings sin to life. Finally, the Bible says sin causes death; in fact, it's called the law of sin and death. Just like the law of gravity causes an object to fall every time, sin brings demons, curses, and death every time.

But now for the good news. The law of the Spirit of life in Christ Jesus has set us free from the law of sin and death! This too involves a sequence. Romans 8:15-16 says we have received the Spirit of adoption by which we cry out "Abba, Father." In fact, God Himself bears witness with our spirits that we are His children. I'm not inferior, I'm the child of a good and wonderful God, made in His image and likeness. I don't have to strive to earn self-esteem, I'm content. I don't have to worry and work at taking care of my problems, He is there for me. In fact, Jesus defeated every sin, every demon, and every curse on the cross; I just need to put my faith in Him.

Romans 7:1-6 clearly states the law only has authority over me as long as I live. Once I die to self, by being baptized into Jesus' death, I get delivered from the law. No more law means no more sin. Romans 6:5-7, 14 says, *For if we have been united together in the likeness of His death, certainly we also shall be in the likeness of His resurrection, knowing this, that our old man was crucified with Him, that the body of sin might be done away with, that we should no longer be slaves of sin. For he who has died has been freed from sin…For sin shall not have dominion over you, for you are not under law but under grace.* The words *be done away with* in verse 6 mean *to be rendered inoperative.* Apart from the law, which is knowledge and works, the law of sin and death can't exist!

To really understand it, think of dandelions. If you just chop them down they'll always grow back and ruin your lawn. They must be taken out from the roots. The root of the dandelion takes up the lie from hell that says "God is not good and I'm not good enough." That lie fills the stem with a lust for the law, a desire to use our knowledge and works to gain self-esteem and solve our own problems. The law brings life to the flower, causing the law of sin and death to bloom. No root, no stem, no flower—that's the way to beat dandelions. No lie, no law, no sin—that's the way to beat the law of sin and death.

To summarize, here are the two sequences. One represents death, and the other life—here on earth and for all eternity.

SOURCE OF SIN, SATAN'S DOMINION, AND CURSES

1. A LIE that produces a judgment that God is not good and I'm inferior.

2. A LUST for the law to use my knowledge and works to achieve success to gain self-esteem and solve my own problems.

3. A LOSS of my birthright, living in His presence, dominion over the earth, and blessings—because the law of knowledge and works brings the law of sin and death into existence.

SOURCE OF RIGHTEOUSNESS, MAN'S DOMINION, AND BLESSINGS

1. THE TRUTH that God is good and wonderful. I'm made in His image and likeness, so that makes me wonderful, not inferior in any way—I'm content with who I am.

2. FAITH in the fact that Jesus died on the cross to defeat every sin, demon, and curse, so I don't have to earn my own righteousness and solve these problems.

3. I GAIN BACK my birthright, my relationship with Him, my dominion on the earth, and my blessings. The law of the Spirit of life in Christ Jesus has set me free from the law of sin and death—it has become inoperative.

The truth that God is good and we're wonderful, and faith in Jesus' work on the cross, is our access door to the wonderful world of our birthright…our passageway from death to life!

Here are two final thoughts. First, how powerful is Satan's lie, the seed he plants in every human that God isn't good and we're inferior, to get us to lust after the law? We think of our struggle against Satan living in this fallen world as we deal with our own fallen flesh. But Adam and Eve bought into the devil's lie when they were not fallen and living in paradise in the very presence of God! That's a sobering and humbling truth. We humans are very susceptible to buying that lie and then judging both God and ourselves. And we humans love the law very much, even though it doesn't like us. That's why the Lord wants to get that lie out of us and get us out of the law, so He can put us back into His wonderful world full of love and power.

Second, individuals react to the lie that God isn't good and I'm inferior differently. I wanted to achieve great success to gain self-esteem. My wife, on the other hand, gained her self-esteem through service—she would do anything for anybody, and literally took on a slave mentality. Others think that if God is not good, and they're inferior, then what's the point of trying to achieve anything. This is where many self-destructive addictions enter in like drugs and alcoholism—or simply escapism, like watching lots and lots of movies, or playing video games all of the time. The three groups all seem different, but there's one thing that they all have in common: they're all lusting after and addicted to something. But, what my wife and I lusted after never brought us self-esteem, and what the other group lusts after never gets rid of their pain.

In closing, now that we've seen through Scripture the fear—and futility—of a life under the law, we must keep things in balance. First, the law was from God, making it good and spiritual. The problem is no one is good, so no one could obey the law. So second, God used the law like a governess, to watch over children until they were of age to receive their inheritance. Think of it as a placeholder until the new and better covenant would arrive. During that wait, the law pointed out the utter sinfulness of sin, and our desperate need for a savior. A salvation based on grace and faith, and not by works. Finally, the New Covenant replaces the written law by writing the law of love in our hearts—a New Covenant, a new heart, a new creation in Christ!

We now know that even though the law was good, it was against us. But the cross is for us. In fact, Romans 8:31-32 says God chose to give us all things through His Son: "What then shall we say to these things? If God is for us, who can be against us? He who did not spare His own Son, but delivered Him up for us all, how shall He not with Him also freely give us all things?" The Bible says, "God is for us." The proof that God is for us is that He gave His only Son to die on the cross for us, through that act freely giving us all things. This is the New Covenant, the new system under which we cannot fail because Jesus has done it all for us. He came, fulfilled the law, and then died in our place so that we can live in power and victory. The law, with its system of knowledge plus works, simply doesn't exist for us anymore. Our power does not come from knowledge or works. It flows freely from the cross of Christ.

THE LAW, WITH ITS SYSTEM OF KNOWLEDGE PLUS WORKS, SIMPLY DOESN'T EXIST FOR US ANYMORE. OUR POWER DOES NOT COME FROM KNOWLEDGE OR WORKS. IT FLOWS FREELY FROM THE CROSS OF CHRIST.

knowledge or works. It flows freely from the cross of Christ. As the opening painting depicts, one greater than Moses is here! That's why our focus should not be on the old and inferior covenant, but instead, we should look to the new and superior one (Hebrews 3:1-3; 8:6-13).

Let's continue our spiritual journey and discover how to break out of the bondage that is the law, by experiencing a transformation, like a caterpillar into a butterfly.

My Personal One-on-One Encounter With The Lord

ALSO FOR HOME GROUP DISCUSSION

How do I feel about the fact that the law cannot get rid of sin—it can only expose and increase it?

_____

_____

Do I realize that not one person, in and of themselves, is able to obey the whole law?

_____

_____

Have I discovered that if I stumble at just one point of the law, I am guilty of all of it?

_____

_____

For all of the reasons above, do I now believe that the law is against me, but the cross is for me?

_____

_____

How has the lie, the lust, and the loss played out in my life?

_____

_____

REFLECTING ON THE ART

- In what way does the painting that opens this chapter speak to me?
- Did the sketch have an impact on me? If so, how?

_____

_____

_____

The Manifesto

Every human being has a God-given birthright to live in a world of relationship love and rulership power. It's a world of supernatural love, joy, and peace even in the midst of trials. And, there's supernatural power for victory over sin, Satan, and curses, to be blessed and fulfill our destiny to bless others.

A manifesto is a public declaration of intention by an important person or group. An example would be the Declaration of Independence for the United States. This is *the* manifesto, because the Lord is the most important person and group (Trinity) in the entire universe. This is His manifesto. This is the freedom we have through the cross of Jesus!

How would embracing this manifesto affect my life?

_____

_____

Do you have a Divine Dissatisfaction? Do you know deep in your heart there's got to be more to God than conventional Christianity is presenting, as you cry "Where's the love?" and "Where's the power?" Are you ready to get your God-given birthright back? If so, I strongly encourage you to read the following scriptures in sequence and ask the Holy Spirit to show you personally how Jesus took the law out of your way. Those who have done so say that it was a life-changing experience. Romans 3:10 – 8:17, Galatians 3:1 – 4:7, Colossians 2:4-23, Galatians 4:21 – 5:25, Galatians 6:12 – 16, Colossians 3:1 – 11, Romans 10:1 – 10, Hebrews 7:1 – 10:17

_____

_____

_____

_____

Am I a Caterpillar Christian?

CHAPTER 4

Am I a Caterpillar Christian?

WHAT IS A CATERPILLAR CHRISTIAN? Let's explore a concept found in Philippians 3:10-11. In these verses we hear the cry of Paul's heart: "that I may know Him and the power of His resurrection, and the fellowship of His sufferings, being conformed to His death, if, by any means, I may attain to the resurrection from the dead."

If we break this down in the Greek, the word *fellowship* means "to partner." *Sufferings* is the word "passion," just like the *Passion of the Christ* or the "passion play." The phrase *to be conformed to His death* comes from two Greek words, *sum morphos,* *sum* meaning "union" and *morphos* being the same root as our English word, *metamorphosis.* In order to truly know Jesus and experience the power of His resurrection, we must undergo a metamorphosis. And that metamorphosis is like the transformation a caterpillar makes when it changes into a butterfly.

With that in mind, let's think about this image of a butterfly and the four stages of its life. It starts out as an egg, the egg hatches into a caterpillar, the caterpillar goes into a cocoon, and then in the last stage it emerges out of the cocoon as a beautiful butterfly. Those four stages are the same four stages we have in our Christian lives, only most Christians are stuck in stage two as Caterpillar Christians.

If we compare the first stage of a butterfly's life cycle to the Christian life, the egg represents being a born-again Christian. That egg didn't do anything to be born; it was just placed on a leaf. Being born again is not about what we do or earn, it's a free gift. Ephesians 2:8-9 says, "For by grace you have been saved through faith, and that not of yourselves; it is the gift of God, not of works, lest anyone should boast."

At this stage our focus is all on Jesus Christ and Him crucified. We recognize there's nothing we can do to get to heaven. We're humble and helpless, knowing we're sinners in need of a savior. When we believe that He personally died for us and receive His free gift of salvation, there's a tremendous sense of awe and new beginning, like a tiny baby coming into the world. It's great. And then comes stage two.

At the next stage, that egg pops, and out comes a caterpillar. Caterpillars are busy, busy creatures. They have so much to do—so many leaves to eat. We see them in trees just munching away on the foliage like they can't get enough. This is similar to many born-again Christians. A whole new world has opened up, and the born-again Christian cannot get enough of it.

Imagine five majestic trees, the most beautiful oak trees ever created in the world. They are tall, with strong branches that stretch far and wide, inviting children to swing on them, build tree houses, or play underneath their shade. Their leaves are lush and green, luxuriant. A caterpillar's dream. Imagine that the first tree represents the Word of God; the second tree, prayer; the third tree is praise and worship; the fourth tree, fellowship; and the fifth tree is ministry. Like a caterpillar, a new Christian just can't get enough of these five majestic trees. We love them all, so we go from tree to tree, just munching away on all of those delicious things they have to offer.

UNLESS WE HANG FROM THE TREE, WE WILL NEVER BE RAISED FROM THE DEAD, TO LIVE IN NEW LIFE AS A BUTTERFLY.

But what does the caterpillar do after it has munched awhile? It goes on into stage three, and it spins a cocoon and hangs from the tree. It stops doing all of the activity and retreats from this big glorious world into its cocoon. As it hangs there on the tree, an observer might say it looks dead. There's no motion, no apparent life; it's brown and dead-looking. But guess what? That apparent death process was God's design for the caterpillar,

His way of transforming it into a new creation—a butterfly! Stage four means soaring on wings in the new life of a butterfly.

What do those stages represent for the born-again Christian? Well, unless we hang from the tree, sharing in His sufferings and having a transforming union with His death, we will never be raised from the dead to live in new life as a butterfly. And sadly, most Christians never become butterflies. Most of us are stuck in stage two, as Caterpillar Christians.

Stage two is necessary. God designed it for the caterpillar just like He designed it for us. The problem comes when a person stays in that stage too long. What would happen if a caterpillar just stayed in those trees feeding and never became a butterfly? What would it become? A big, ugly caterpillar. We're going to see why Satan wants to keep Christians stuck in stage two.

Let's take a look at the graph on the next page that describes the wisdom of the world. Think of sales and profits as the arrow going upward. Now, honestly and truly, if you owned a business, which one of these graphs would you choose? The one on the top or the one on the bottom? Of course, everyone would choose the one on the top. It's the way of Wall Street. It's brutal. They want it constant—every quarter, every year—increased sales, increased profits. That's all Wall Street cares about. You miss a blip and your stocks are going to go down. That's the wisdom of the world, the environment in which we live.

The church exists within this environment, and just like yeast in a lump of dough, that way of thinking has infiltrated and leavened the church. The wisdom of the world has essentially told the church, "If you continue to learn more about God and do more things for God, you will become a better Christian."

The result is that the church is full of very sincere Christians who are stuck as Caterpillar Christians, constantly wanting to learn more about God and do more things for Him. We see all of these books, teaching tapes, shows, seminars, and on and on, things that are good in and of themselves, but misdirected, they become like an addiction. Caterpillars Christians have to munch up more and more and more of this stuff because they believe the more they know, and the more they do, the better Christians they will be. It's the world's formula—knowledge and works—the wisdom of the world. Pretty soon, in all of this, the cross of Christ is forgotten.

Wisdom of the World

3. Big Ugly Caterpillar

2. Caterpillar

1. Egg

Wisdom of God

2. Caterpillar

4. Butterfly

3. Cocoon

1. Egg

World's Progress

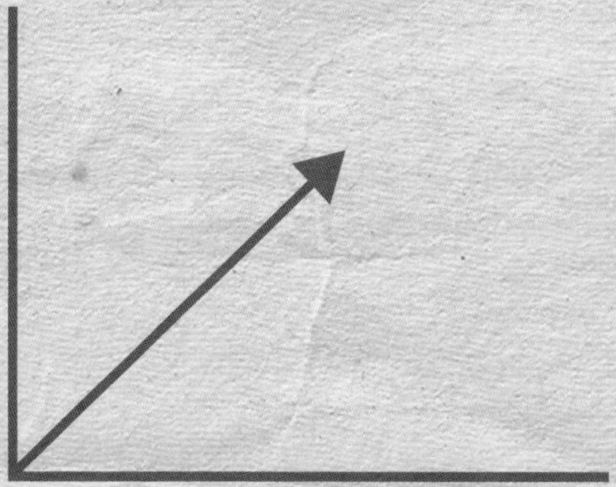

God's Progress

Look at the graph with the caterpillar, though, on the previous page. It goes from the egg, up to the caterpillar, and then down into the cocoon to be still and die. Then it goes back up into the butterfly stage. It doesn't keep on munching and moving. This is God's wisdom.

We've discovered that Satan's strategy is to take something good, misapply it, and then misdirect it. But how do you deceive a sincere Christian? You can't dangle obvious sins in front of that person and expect him to fall. It's not going to work with one who has made a whole-hearted commitment to the Lord. The way to deceive a sincere Christian is to take something good, something that looks like God, and misapply it. Play on that person's good intention. Then misdirect him. The ultimate deception for the sincere Christian is a good intention. I know this from personal experience, because that's what happened to me. I brought my business success mentality into my Christian walk. I personally was going to be the very best Christian I could be; that was my good intention. The only problem was the "I." Notwithstanding my sincerity, I forgot that it was about Jesus, and not about me.

What happens if, with all of our good intentions about serving God, we get stuck as Caterpillar Christians? I believe there are five main results.

The first thing that happens is spiritual pride. 1 Corinthians 8:1 (NIV) says, "Knowledge puffs up, but love builds up." What does all of my continuing knowledge about God produce in me? Pride. I get puffed up. I start resting and relying on what I know about God and what I do for God, as opposed to what Jesus Christ did for me, and I get puffed up. I forget about my roots as a sinner, and all of a sudden I am self-righteous, and I get very, very puffed up.

That's very prevalent in the church. If we think about it, that's why we're not very good witnesses all of the time, because we're these puffed-up, self-righteous Christians. The poor sinner out there looks at us and says, "I can never relate to these people." Stuck in stage two as Caterpillar Christians, we get full of spiritual pride, and the world can't relate to us. God wants to save the world, and that's why he hates pride. It's one of the deadly sins.

The second thing that sets in is idolatry. Remember those five majestic trees? Those beautiful places where we as Caterpillar Christians hang out? They become more important than God Himself and actually

THE FIVE MAJESTIC TREES

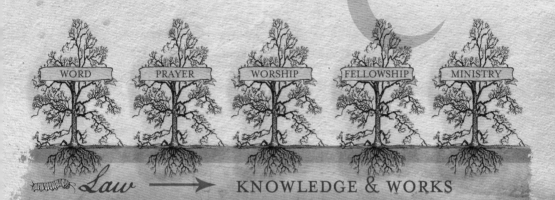

WORD · PRAYER · WORSHIP · FELLOWSHIP · MINISTRY

Law ⟶ KNOWLEDGE & WORKS

WORD · PRAYER · WORSHIP · FELLOWSHIP · MINISTRY

Gospel ⟶ GRACE, FAITH & LOVE

become idols. Even wonderful things from God (like the Bible, prayer, worship, fellowship, and ministry) can become idols if we make them more important than Jesus Christ crucified in our lives.

An example of how this can happen was told by a missionary friend of mine. He was traveling on a plane going to Africa when the Lord spoke to him and said, *You have a high place in your heart.*

He knew that a *high place* is an Old Testament term for idolatry—that the Israelites worshipped idols in the high places—and he was instantly pierced in his spirit and asked the Lord, "What is it?"

The Lord answered, *It's your ministry. Your ministry that I have called you to has now become more important than I am to you. No matter how great it is, no matter how many people get saved and no matter how many needy people get fed, never, ever, ever put ministry ahead of Me. Don't put anything ahead of Me, even if it is something from Me, because I'm God, and I'm jealous.*

Of course I am not writing against mission ministry or any of those things of God we see in the five majestic trees. I love the things of God and spend a lot of my time participating in them. But the key for me, just like for you, and just like for my missionary friend, is *priorities.* Jesus takes it a step further in Matthew 10:37-38, where He says (paraphrased), "Whether it's mothers, fathers, sisters, brothers, children, anything—don't put anything ahead of Me. Nothing is ahead of Me because I'm God."

Anything we put before the Lord is an idol. What is an idol? An idol is a false god. It's something you think is getting you to God but really isn't. In the case of the caterpillar, all of those lovely leaves we munch in the five majestic trees can become idols. As we see in the sketch, when this happens, those majestic trees shrivel up and become less effective.

THE VERY THING I BELIEVED WOULD BRING ME CLOSER TO GOD, IS ACTUALLY CARRYING ME AWAY FROM HIM.

But when Jesus is in His rightful place of preeminence above those trees, and they are firmly anchored to the gospel of Christ crucified, they then flourish and become extremely effective.

A third thing happens when we stay caterpillars too long. The more we know about God and the more we do for God, the less we need God. Isn't that strange? Why is that true? Because, if my holiness depends on my knowledge and works, then I can attain a self-righteousness apart from the cross. I come to believe that I don't need God, so the very thing I am striving to do, the very thing I believed would bring me closer to God, is actually carrying me away from Him. That's the misdirection.

Look at Luke 18:9-14, which says, *Also He spoke this parable to some who trusted in themselves that they were righteous, and despised others: "Two men went up to the temple to pray, one a Pharisee and the other a tax collector. The Pharisee stood and prayed thus with himself, 'God, I thank You that I am not like other men—extortioners, unjust, adulterers, or even as this tax collector. I fast twice a week; I give tithes of all that I possess.' And the tax collector, standing afar off, would not so much as raise his eyes to heaven, but beat his breast, saying, 'God, be merciful to me a sinner!' I tell you, this man went down to his house justified rather than the other; for everyone who exalts himself will be humbled, and he who humbles himself will be exalted."* The key phrase in this story is there in verse nine: they "trusted in themselves that they were righteous." Caterpillar Christians that are stuck in that phase become self-righteous. They begin to believe the lie that "the more I learn about God and the more things I do for God, the more it will help me become like God." Sounds familiar, doesn't it. We talked earlier about how Satan beguiled Eve in the garden. What did he say? "For God knows that in the day you eat of it your eyes will be opened, and you will be like God, knowing good and evil" (Genesis 3:5).

The knowledge of good and evil will make us like God, but here's an amazing truth the Holy Spirit shared with me: I don't want to be God. I want God to be me. There's a big difference. I don't want to be God; I want to be crucified with Christ, so that it's no longer I who live, but Christ who lives through me. I want God to be me, to flow through and work through me.

Knowledge and works is an attempt by man, no matter how sincere, to become God. The message of the cross is the opposite. It says, "I die, and God becomes me." There is a night and day difference between the two!

Remember in Applebee's restaurant, when Jesus and the Father were looking at each other, and they said, "Did We do this for nothing?" Galatians 2:20 says, "I have been crucified with Christ; it is no longer I who live, but Christ lives in me; and the life which I now live in the flesh I live by faith in the Son of God, who loved me and gave Himself for me." Look what comes next, in verse 21: "I do not set aside the grace of

God; for if righteousness comes through the law [knowledge and works], then Christ died in vain." The phrase "in vain" in the Greek means "for nothing." Without knowing it, the lifestyle of a stuck Caterpillar Christian says, "Jesus died for nothing."

If I, as a Christian, could attain self-righteousness, if I could advance my holiness by learning more about God and doing more things for God, if that's the end of my Christianity, then guess what? I head totally away from God, totally away from grace, and go completely in an opposite direction. I do not get closer to God; I get farther away from God. Unfortunately, the existing church produces a lot of Caterpillar Christians, because that's the environment we're in…but God is changing that. A well-known prophetic voice says that God spoke to him and his friends twenty years ago and said the cross is going to become popular again. I believe that's true—that it has to be true—because we're all headed in the wrong direction.

The fourth bad thing that happens to Caterpillar Christians is division. When what I know about God and what I do for God is different from what you know about God and do for God, there's an instant division. We start arguing about who is right and wrong.

A person focused on the cross doesn't do that. The message of the cross says, "Nobody is right. That's why Jesus died, because nobody is right; there is none righteous." Knowledge and works will always produce strife, but if we embrace the message of the cross, we can be in unity.

> CATERPILLAR CHRISTIANS DON'T JUST EAT THE LEAVES OFF THOSE FIVE TREES, THEY EAT EACH OTHER.

In Galatians 5:15 Paul warns, "If you bite and devour one another, beware lest you be consumed by one another!" That seems to fit perfectly with the image of the caterpillar. They are always eating leaves. Caterpillar Christians just take it one step farther. They don't just eat the leaves off those five trees, they eat each other. It's Christian cannibalism, and it happens all of the time. We bite and devour each other because all we know is eat, eat, eat, do, do, do, go, go, go, and when you get in my way, I'll eat you up. I'll trample you in the name of God, because I love God more than you love God. I'm going to eat you up and devour you. In this competitive environment, there is very little love, and sadly, that's the state of much of the church as we know it.

The fifth and final bad thing that happens to Caterpillar Christians, and thus to the church, is a lack of power. We talk a lot and do a lot, but when the trials of life hit us, we don't have much supernatural power to overcome them. Paul says in 1 Corinthians 4:20 (NIV), "The kingdom of God is not a matter of talk but of power."

At this point, if you are like me, you may be asking, "How could I have gone so long in this stage as a Caterpillar Christian? With all of my passion for God, how could this have happened?"

The first key to understanding why is that you are a target for evil. The temptation of knowledge and works is only designed for passionate Christians. A born-again Christian who has never made a wholehearted commitment to the Lord doesn't have this problem. Backslidden Christians don't have this problem because they're not on fire; they don't really care. The only people who suffer the fate of getting stuck as Caterpillar Christians are the most sincere, passionate Christians. Weird, isn't it? But, remember, the ultimate deception is a good intention.

Another key to understanding why this happens is understanding the state of the church. We are born into a church, just like we are born into a particular family. If you look at Nazi Germany as an example, most government supporters were typically not from dysfunctional families. They had fathers and mothers; many had good jobs; a lot of them believed in the Ten Commandments and were church-going people. However, if you were born into a Nazi family, what would you very likely turn into? A Nazi. Why? Because that's what you were born into. I'm not comparing the church to Nazis, it's just a way to make a point.

THIS DILUTED & POLLUTED GOSPEL—A WATERED DOWN AND WORLDLY VERSION—DOESN'T PRODUCE MUCH LOVE OR POWER!

Likewise, as the art on the next page depicts, we are all born into a leavened church. It's one that has been infiltrated by the yeast of the Pharisees (see Matthew 16:6), which produces a divided heart. Our divided heart breaks God's heart because we don't honor His great sacrifice and

OUR LEAVENED *and* **DIVIDED HEART**

SOUL

1. Wisdom Of World

↓

2. Knowledge & Works

↓

3. Law—Old Covenant

↓

4. Idols

SPIRIT

1. Wisdom Of God

↓

2. Christ Crucified

↓

3. Gospel—New Covenant

↓

4. Jesus Lord

share our affections between Him and idols. This diluted and polluted Gospel—a watered down and worldly version—doesn't produce much love or power! And sadly, that was the case with the Pharisees. They seemed to be spiritual but had little love and virtually no supernatural power.

Satan began infiltrating the church with the yeast of the Pharisees right after its inception in the first century. By the end of the fourth century, after Christianity had been legalized by the emperor Constantine, the process of taking on worldly characteristics was pretty much complete. Most of the love and power was lost, because the natural world cannot produce supernatural love and power. What happened at the fall of man was repeated: our love relationship with God and each other suffered dramatically, and our rulership power over sin, Satan, and curses was greatly diminished.

A leavened church idolizes knowledge and works, and because we were born into it, that's all we know. There seems to be no other pattern for Christians to follow, nothing else out there. But God in His mercy has given us a great example.

Let's look at the twelve apostles. Jesus went up a mountain and prayed and asked His Father before He chose them (Luke 6:12-13). He hand-picked these guys, and hung out with them twenty-four hours a day, seven days a week, for three years. You'd think that would change a person, to be in the physical presence of God for three years. But if we look at the character of the apostles before the cross, we see some interesting things.

First, they were very prideful. They said they'd never forsake Him, they'd die for Him, but in the garden they all fled. The second characteristic we see is that they were carnally minded rather than spiritually minded. They said things like, "He's come to restore Israel. He's come to throw off the Roman conquerors and restore the kingdom of David and Solomon." Their minds were on the earth and not the kingdom of heaven. The third thing we see in their lives is selfish ambition, as when the mother of Zebedee's sons James and John secretly asks Jesus for a favor: "Can my one son sit at your right hand, and my other son on your left?" (See Matthew 20:20-28.) When the other apostles heard about it, they were indignant, probably thinking, *Why didn't my mother get to Him first?* They were mad. It was a power thing. The fourth thing we see is they had little compassion. They tried to keep little children away from Jesus (Matthew 19:13) and even went so far as to ask Jesus if they should call down fire and brimstone from heaven on the Samaritans (Luke 9:54). And finally, they weren't in unity. They fought among themselves and criticized others who weren't in their group but were preaching Jesus (Mark 9:38-40). That's the character of the twelve apostles before the cross.

After the cross, though, we see a different story. Peter, the hotshot, was a broken man. Forevermore after the cross, when people tried to worship him, he told them, "Don't worship me, I'm just a man." (See Acts 3:1-16.) Second, they were heaven-minded. They became less interested in throwing off the Romans and more interested in building God's spiritual kingdom. They were beaten and battered, but they celebrated. There was nothing they wouldn't do for the cause of Christ, even when many of them were killed. They had great compassion for all of God's people, and when Paul was added, reached out to the Gentiles also. And there was no more selfish ambition; they were in unity. The Bible says "they were in one accord" (Acts 2:46). They sold things they had in order to share with those in need and met with humble hearts in their homes. Everything changed.

THE TWELVE APOSTLES WERE PREY TO THE ULTIMATE DECEPTION. EVEN THEY WERE LIKE CATERPILLAR CHRISTIANS FOR A TIME.

By giving us this example, God in His mercy is saying, *Don't feel bad.* The twelve apostles were even prey to the ultimate deception. Even they were like Caterpillar Christians for a time. *That's what you were born into, and it can happen to the sincerest of Christians.* So God in His mercy constantly reminds both you and me that Jesus is the best, but beware the yeast of the Pharisees.

Caterpillar Facts: Here are a couple of other interesting facts about caterpillars and how they differ from butterflies. First of all, caterpillars destroy where they eat. They cannot live without destroying what brings them life. Isn't that wild? Compare that to the

Caterpillar Christian. The exact place where somebody is getting fed and nurtured—that's where he or she brings destruction. Many times Caterpillar Christians destroy the body.

Butterflies, on the other hand, do not destroy what they eat. They just land on the plant, suck out the nectar, and don't bother anything. In fact, not only does the butterfly not destroy the places where it feeds, it pollinates them. The butterfly helps the flowers to reproduce because it pollinates. It multiplies where it eats.

The second thing about caterpillars is that they cannot reproduce. The original blessing and command to "be fruitful and multiply" (Genesis 1:28) is lost on Caterpillar Christians, as well as the meaning of *Pentecost*, which is "harvest, or multiplication." We've all heard non-Christian people say, "Who would want to be like those Christians? They're a bunch of judgmental, holier-than-thou, no-fun people." Caterpillars don't multiply. It's a thing of nature. Only butterflies can reproduce.

Finally, caterpillars can't fly. They are earthbound, with a lot of feet on the ground. Butterflies are free-flying, having been transformed into heavenly creations.

Take a look at the piece of art on the following page, which tells a story. See the egg, representing the born-again Christian, and then the caterpillar, which is the Christian who has made a whole-hearted commitment and dealt with his/her known sins. Then comes the cocoon stage, and that represents the Christian who is dying to self and dealing with his/her hidden sins. A Caterpillar Christian never finds out their hidden sins; he/she is so busy going and doing and learning. Caterpillar Christians never go that deep. They stay out in the world where it seems bright and open. But the world of the cocoon is dark. It's enclosed, and it is messy. When God starts showing you the junk that's inside of you, the sin you are capable of, you may be surprised how ugly it is. I know, because that's what happened to me. The Bible says in Jeremiah 17:9 that "The heart is deceitful above all things, and desperately wicked; who can know it?" And then, in verse 10, it says, "I, the Lord, search the heart." When God does His work in you, you'll be like Peter: you'll find out what's really inside and be broken.

Caterpillar Christians are not asking God to search their hearts. They're so sure that they've arrived, that they've got it right. But after we

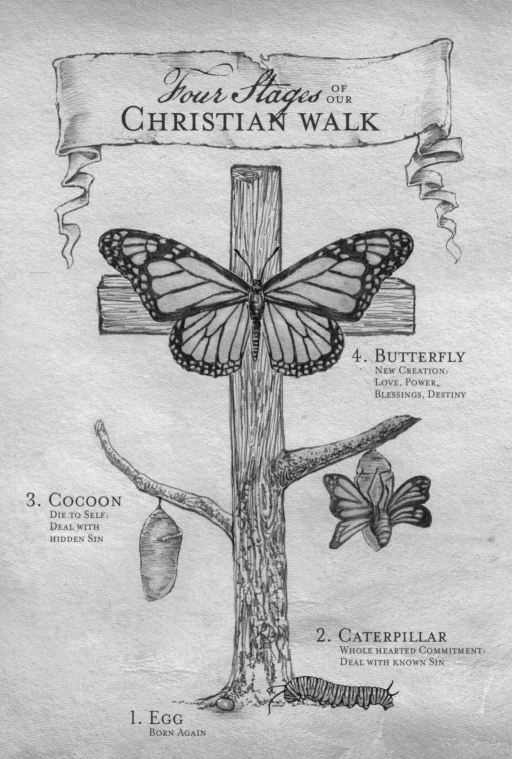

Four Stages OF OUR
CHRISTIAN WALK

4. BUTTERFLY
NEW CREATION:
LOVE, POWER,
BLESSINGS, DESTINY

3. COCOON
DIE TO SELF:
DEAL WITH
HIDDEN SIN

2. CATERPILLAR
WHOLE HEARTED COMMITMENT:
DEAL WITH KNOWN SIN

1. EGG
BORN AGAIN

go into the cocoon and die with Christ, then we emerge into a beautiful butterfly. That's the stage where we get love, power, blessings, and destiny. So this is the image. You see the tree, and it shows the butterfly on that cross. I've got to hang on that tree in the cocoon in order to emerge as a victorious and beautiful butterfly whose life is now centered in the cross!

The other thing about this piece of art is the beauty of the butterfly. Think for a minute about Jesus and His return. The Bible says He's coming back for His bride, and the bride will be without spot or blemish (Ephesians 5:27). And Jesus Christ the bridegroom—He's the Lion of Judah, the Mighty Warrior, the Lily of the Valley, the Bright and Morning Star. When you envision Him coming for His bride, can you picture Him walking down the aisle with an ugly caterpillar? We want to be soaring, beautiful, and radiant like the butterfly. He died for us. We die to self for Him—that He may transform us.

Now we have laid the whole foundation: how the devil stole the message of the cross by using the wisdom of the world to empty the cross of its power—how it creates a leavened and blended church which is watered down and weakened—how this lust for the law in the church caused its members to lose their God-given birthright—and how that church then produces Caterpillar Christians. Now that we have this foundation, the question is, what are we going to do about it? The next stages of our spiritual journey are going to show what action we can take to begin this process—going from Caterpillar Christians to Birthright Butterflies! The first step is to get out of this "Wisdom of the World System" we've been living in.

Adam and Eve were the original Birthright Butterflies. They lived in a *non-how to* world—the Garden of Eden. There, it wasn't about learning and doing…it was just about living. Jesus, who is the second Adam, has made that world available to us again, today!

My Personal One-on-One Encounter With The Lord

Am I stuck in stage two of my Christian walk as a Caterpillar Christian? What would some of the signs be that I am stuck?

_____

_____

_____

_____

Do I understand that the ultimate deception is a good intention and that's why only sincere Christians have this problem? What are some of my past good intentions that have produced a bad result? What are my good intentions now?

_____

_____

_____

_____

Has my heart been leavened by the yeast of the Pharisees and become divided? What are some things that have infiltrated my heart, causing me to have a watered down and weakened version of the Gospel that has little power?

_____

_____

_____

_____

For pastors: Am I struggling with divisions or a church split? How might dealing with Caterpillar Christianity help these situations?

_____

_____

_____

Do any of the following describe how you are feeling:

• Do you feel overwhelmed and burned out by your Christian walk? Has it become an endless stream of more things to learn and more things to do?

• Do you care deeply about the church but in your heart know that something just isn't right? When you look at the church do you ever wonder where the love and power are?

• Are you a faithful Christian who has had a relationship with the Lord for years, but your promised blessings never seem to come?

• Have you been praying for years to see and experience revival, but that too has yet to happen?

• Do you feel a call on your life for some form of ministry, to be in full-time fivefold ministry or some other form of ministry while keeping your current job, but that call is not yet a reality?

• When you do minister, is there little power?

_____

_____

_____

_____

If so, take heart, you are one of the millions of sincere Christians stuck in the caterpillar stage who is now headed to the cross to become a butterfly!

 REFLECTING ON THE ART

• In what way does the painting that opens this chapter speak to me?
• Did the sketches have an impact on me? If so, how?
• Can I now go back to the opening painting of chapter two and see myself in that picture?

_____

_____

_____

_____

Religion, That's Me!

CHAPTER 5

Religion, That's Me!

NOW THAT WE UNDERSTAND how the church and our hearts have been leavened by the wisdom of the world, producing Caterpillar Christians, we're going to look at how to get out of this system. The way to do that is to look at religion and recognize, *That's me*. We all see religion in the other person, but it's time to look in the mirror and face the truth. Just like the guy looking into the pond in the opening painting, we may be more like Pharisees than we ever imagined. It's not about someone else this time, it's about me: I've got religion in *me*.

What is religion anyway? In this chapter we're going to discover the definition of religion, the result of religion, how religion started, and what the world of religion looks like (it's a very yucky world).

I believe a simple definition of religion is this: any attempt to become holy and have a relationship with God based on man's knowledge and works instead of the cross of Christ. Imagine a balance, and on one side is man's attempt to be holy, and on the other side is the cross of Christ. It's that simple. Once we understand that definition, we see that it includes all religions of the world, as well as any cult. Any belief system not based on Jesus Christ and Him crucified falls on the side of man's attempt to be holy. That side of the balance will always come up short.

It's easy to see how this definition of religion includes religions and cults outside of Christianity, but did you know that definition can also include us? Remember what we learned about the Caterpillar Christian, how in phase one, as an egg, we're born again; then in phase two we're becoming caterpillars—learning all of these wonderful things but getting stuck there, enamored with knowledge and works. The Caterpillar Christian *attempts to become holy and have a relationship with God based on his or her knowledge and works instead of the cross of Christ.*

> WHEN MY RELATIONSHIP WITH GOD IS BASED ON WHAT I KNOW ABOUT GOD AND WHAT I DO FOR GOD, WHAT JESUS CHRIST DID ON THE CROSS IS NOT RELEVANT ANYMORE.

We've all been there, haven't we? We all have religion, and, what is the result? It's very simple: man is exalted instead of God. When it's about what I know about God and what I do for God, it's not about what Jesus Christ did for me. It's about me. I'll say that again: When my relationship with God is based on what I know about God and what I do for God, *that's about me;* what Jesus Christ did on the cross is not relevant anymore.

Why is that such a nasty thing? Because, we learn in Romans 3:10 that no one is good, not one. Even our righteousness is as "filthy rags" (Isaiah 64:6). So when our relationship with God becomes about man, it becomes a filthy thing. We have a walk and talk that looks like we're elevating God, but the reality is we're elevating man. In reality, then, religion is the elevation of *man* in the *guise* of elevating God. The word *guise* means to dress up. It's a costume, or a semblance. Religion is a mask people wear in order to look spiritual and act spiritual, but the truth is, there is nothing spiritual about it.

Instead, it produces arrogance. We boast about whatever particular thing we're into—our group, our denomination, our church—and think it's the best. What are we really doing? We're boasting about men instead of the cross.

1 Corinthians 3:19-21 says, "For the wisdom of this world is foolishness with God. For it is written, 'He catches the wise in their own craftiness'; and again, 'The Lord knows the thoughts of the wise, that they are futile.' Therefore let no one boast in men. For all things are yours [in Christ]."

A final thought on how religion elevates man. When a person was crucified during Roman times, his crime was posted at the top of his cross. What crime was posted on the top of Jesus' cross? —"This Is Jesus the King of the Jews" (Matthew 27:37). It's quite clear that the religious crowd had no interest in God being their King; to them it was a crime. Just as in the days when Israel cried out for a man to be their king instead of God and got Saul, so it was at the time of Christ, and so it is today with religion. It's really about men being kings, not Jesus.

We've defined religion, and we've examined its result, which is the elevation of man instead of God. Now we're going to look into its origin. Where did religion come from? It started in the Garden of Eden, at the Fall. God said, "You must not eat from the tree of the knowledge of good and evil" (Genesis 2:17 NIV). But the devil said, "In the day you eat of it... you will be like God" (Genesis 3:5). So man decided to eat of that tree. It all stemmed from a good intention, to be like God, but the reality is that human beings are never satisfied, so the thought of being *like* God became the desire to *be* God—to be sovereign.

The minute man fell, God said one of the curses is that you will toil. People began to have to work very hard to make a living. And what was the result of the Fall? Knowledge and works—religion. It all started in the garden.

But this is not just an Old Testament problem. In the New Testament, in 2 Corinthians 11:3, Paul writes, "But I fear, lest somehow, as the serpent deceived Eve by his craftiness, so your minds may be corrupted from the simplicity that is in Christ." Satan does the same thing today with Caterpillar Christians as he did with Adam and Eve in the Garden of Eden.

My wife always says, "God is very, very simple." Just as Paul said, there is a real simplicity, a real beauty, a real incredible attractiveness to Jesus Christ. And if you notice something about religion, it turns a lot of people off. It is not really simple or attractive. Religion repulses more people than it brings in. It stinks! But Jesus is described as the Rose of Sharon. He's beautiful. He carries the fragrance of God. People are very, very attracted to Jesus.

What is the world of religion like? It's a world that looks good but produces death. How do we know that? In Genesis 2:17 (NIV) God said, "You must not eat from the tree of the knowledge of good and evil, for when you eat of it you will surely die." But Genesis 3:6 says "So when the woman saw that the tree was good for food, that it was pleasant to the eyes, and a tree desirable to make one wise, she took of its fruit and ate. She also gave to her husband with her, and he ate." That's it. Religion looks good and seems desirable, but the only thing it can produce is death.

RELIGION LOOKS GOOD AND SEEMS DESIRABLE, BUT THE ONLY THING IT CAN PRODUCE IS DEATH.

Remember the neat thing the Lord showed us about Caterpillar Christians? We said there are two important differences between a caterpillar and a butterfly: a caterpillar destroys where he lives, and caterpillars cannot procreate. Caterpillar Christians get sucked into religion, and all religion can do is produce death; it can't produce life!

We're going to paint a picture of a world of religion, and what it seems the Lord is trying to do with this picture is to make that world so smelly and stinky that we want to hold our noses and run the other way.

Imagine a world in which everything depended on a coin toss. Everything you did—the money you made, the house you lived in, the relationships you had—totally depended on you flipping a coin, and in this world the only winning toss was heads. Suppose, however, that the only coin you possessed had tails on both sides. How would it be to live in that world? That's the world of religion.

On one side of the coin is the Law of Moses, and on the other side are man-made rules. The Law of Moses is good, but it doesn't belong in the New Covenant. Picture a lawn mower, which was made for cutting a lawn. If the mower represents the law, and the lawn is the Old Covenant, then the lawn mower works great. But if the New Covenant is a flower garden, what happens if we take the lawn mower in there? It produces death. It doesn't belong there; a lawn mower wasn't made for a flower garden. Looked at this way, we can see that the law in the New Covenant doesn't work.

A perfect example of this is found in the life of a guy named Saul—Rabbi Saul. He was one of the best children of God—the elite when it came to God's chosen people. The Bible says that when it came to the law, he was flawless. Do you know what he did? He went about killing Christians. He was so good at the law that he killed God's children and basically opposed God. So back to the coin and the side that represents the Law of Moses. What happens when we flip that up? Tails, we lose.

What's on the other side of the coin? The other side of the coin is man-made rules. Ed Gungor, in his book *Religiously Transmitted Diseases*, describes these rules as "fence laws."

Gungor writes:
To ensure that a specific law of God was obeyed, the Pharisees believed they should make up rules that "fenced" people a step back from breaking the actual command. They thought of these "fence laws" as a first line of defense against disobedience. They reasoned that if a person would have to break the man-made fence laws before breaking one of God's real laws, it would be a deterrent and a protection for people. Noble enough. [1]

---

1 Ed Gungor, *Religiously Transmitted Diseases* (Nashville: Thomas Nelson, Inc., 2006): p. 53.

However, Gungor goes on to point out:

Let's look at how fence laws are created. Parents who love their children build similar kinds of "fence laws" all the time. Take the rule "Don't get hit by a car." Good rule. If you think about this rule long enough—and you believe you must do everything possible to ensure it will be obeyed—you might be tempted to bundle another rule to it, to add a "fence" that could serve as the first line of defense so that the actual rule you are ultimately trying to obey doesn't get violated.

One logical fence law to this would be "Don't play in the street." If you don't play in the street, a car won't hit you. That's reasonable.

But pharisaic thinking goes way beyond reasonableness and gets much more restrictive. Pharisaic thinking would go something like this: The rule is, "Don't get hit by a car." We cannot allow anyone to be hit by a car...so, let's make sure that doesn't happen. Ah...let's make sure no one plays in the street—no street play will mean no one is hit by a car. Or better yet, it's probably best not to play outside at all, because then you won't happen into the street to get hit by a car.

Or even better: Don't look out the windows of the house, lest you are tempted to think about going outside, which could lead into you wandering into the street to get hit by a car.

Or perhaps best of all: Play and sleep in the closet so you aren't tempted to look outside a window at all—because you know where that can lead...

The question becomes, at what point does the person we are trying to protect lose track of what the original law was all about? When she can't look out the window, or when she is kept in the closet? And that was the problem with the fence laws. They eventually overwhelmed the actual commands of God. Jesus said to the Pharisees, "You have a fine way of setting aside the commands of God in order to observe your own traditions!" (Mark 7:9).

THAT'S JESUS' POINT ABOUT THE PHARISEES. THE FENCE LAWS BECAME WEIGHTS THAT CRIPPLED FAITH, NOT HELPED IT.

But, more than just distracting from God's law, these fence laws also became abusive. At what point does the legitimate desire to protect become a repressive system of abuse? Parents who make their kids live in closets need to go to jail. It doesn't matter if they started out loving, concerned, and protective. They end up controlling, manipulative, and repressive. That's Jesus' point about the Pharisees. The fence laws became weights that crippled faith, not helped it.[2]

Now that's a crazy story, right? We can't imagine a good-intentioned parent actually doing that to their child. But it happens all of the time in the church, across every denomination. There are tons of examples, but I'll just give three here.

THE BIBLE SAYS, "Do not get drunk" (Ephesians 5:18), so the church creates a fence law that says, "Do not drink."

THE BIBLE SAYS not to be sexually immoral, like in immoral dancing (1 Peter 4:3). The church's fence law is "Don't dance."

THE BIBLE SAYS not to look at immoral things (Ephesians 5:3; 1 John 2:16), so the church puts up a fence law that says, "Do not go to movies."

And the list goes on and on and on.

Guess what? This is news for all of us good-intentioned Christians. *God doesn't need our help.* God does not need our help to obey Him. James 5:12 says, "Let your 'Yes' be yes, and your 'No,' no," the thought being don't add anything to it. The same thought applies to fence laws. Our fence laws do nothing to help anybody obey God any better. They're all a complete illusion. They're the ultimate religious scam! They seem so good because here is my long list of do's and don'ts, and I get a star for each time I do well. But what about all of the times I don't? In a world of religion, we flip that side of the coin and it's tails. With man-made rules, we still lose.

Another aspect of this world of religion is that we don't become more holy, we become more carnal. Why is that? Religion is always an external focus; it is never, ever internal. That is the opposite of the kingdom of God. What God said when He picked out David as king was,

---

2 Gungor, pp. 54-55.

"Man looks at the outward appearance, but the Lord looks at the heart" (1 Samuel 16:7). He is not interested in how many stars we get for doing well nor in what we look like. He is interested in our hearts.

A very interesting scripture is Galatians 4:19. In this verse Paul calls the Galatians "my little children, for whom I labor in birth again until Christ is formed in you." The word *formed* as it's used here comes from the Greek *morpho* and refers to an internal reality. This speaks of a change in character, becoming conformed to the character of Christ in actuality, not merely in semblance. Religion is always the appearance of being holy, but the inside never matches up because it's all about the outside instead of the inside. Paul goes back to the subject of outward change versus inward change in Colossians 2:20-23:

> *Therefore, if you died with Christ from the basic principles of the world, why, as though living in the world, do you subject yourselves to regulations—"Do not touch, do not taste, do not handle," which all concern things which perish with the using—according to the commandments and doctrines of men? These things indeed have an appearance of wisdom in self-imposed religion, false humility, and neglect of the body, but are of no value against the indulgence of the flesh.*

The Amplified Bible states the end of verse 23 this way: *...they are of no value in checking the indulgence of the flesh (the lower nature). [Instead, they do not honor God but serve only to indulge the flesh.]*

Some leaders were telling the people "don't touch, don't handle, don't do any of these things." Paul says that these teachings are all about the external and appear to mortify or put to death the flesh, but in actuality they just indulge the flesh. Do you know why? This is a very sad thing, but when my Christian life is about what I know and what I do, then I get puffed up. In my heart I say, "Look at all of the things I know about God.... Look at all of the things I do for God. Look at all of the things I don't do: I don't go to movies; I don't dance; I don't drink. I don't do all of these things," and my flesh gets puffed up bigger and bigger and bigger. I believe that, in those times, God is saying *Who do you think you are? All righteousness comes through My Son.*

It's a very clever scam of the enemy to make us think that we're holy, that we're even mortifying our flesh, but all our being religious is really doing is puffing up our pride. Think of the Pharisees. Did all of those fence laws make them spiritual? No. They were highly religious, but the Bible says they loved money. They loved the most prominent seats. They were carnal! They were puffed up! Religion didn't bring them any closer to God, just like it won't draw us closer to Him.

IT'S A VERY CLEVER SCAM OF THE ENEMY TO MAKE US THINK THAT WE'RE HOLY, BUT ALL OUR BEING RELIGIOUS IS REALLY DOING IS INDULGING OUR FLESH.

It also didn't bring them any closer to other people. The word "Pharisee" in the Greek means "sect," or separatist. They had to "separate" from everybody else because they thought they were so holy. The saddest thing about this is that in all of their self-righteousness, they were separated from God. They missed out on Jesus. He was right in their midst, and they didn't recognize Him. And yet they thought they were the ultimate people of God. The Bible says that we are to be in the world but not of the world. We are to separate ourselves from the sins of the world but not be so aloof that we have no contact with the very people we are called to minister to. That's what Jesus did.

Let's further explore this religious world where we are not close to God, and just like the Pharisees, we also don't get closer to other Christians. We get divided. When what I know about God and what I do for God is different than what you know about God and what you do for God, there's a split. That's the reality of the church today. Everybody's group knows different things and does different things, and therefore somebody has got to be wrong. And everybody thinks they're right. So we are all divided.

It's as old as time itself. Remember what happened right after the fall of man? Cain murdered Abel. Why? Over ways of serving God. Cain thought the good thing to do for God was produce crops. Abel thought the good thing to do for God (and he happened to be right) was to produce livestock. They were different, and Cain killed Abel. That's what religion does. It does not bring people together; it drives Christians apart. And every time it's very sincere people saying, "I'm better than you...."

I'm holier than you.... That's why I can't hang out with you, because we're different." What if instead everybody was saying, "It's all about what Jesus Christ did on the cross"? We'd all be in unity, wouldn't we? We'd all have the same thing in common—Jesus—and He unifies.

What is this world of religion like?

ONE. It puts man on the throne, which is me, instead of God.

TWO. It makes me more carnal, not more spiritual.

THREE. It separates me from God.

FOUR. It brings division between people.

That's a pretty smelly picture, isn't it? God is saying, "Flee from religion." There's nothing good in it. It appears to be good; it appears to be valuable, but it isn't.

Jesus said, "You shall know the truth, and the truth shall make you free....If the Son makes you free, you shall be free indeed" (John 8:32, 36). Another scripture reads, "Where the Spirit of the Lord is, there is freedom" (2 Corinthians 3:17 NIV). Religion has nothing to do with freedom. It puts people in prison. I've done time in that prison, but the Lord in His mercy has gotten me out.

Let me share my religion prison story, when I had to admit, "Religion. That's Me." When I was an atheist and became born again, I really hated religion. I was very much against it, and I thought I was free of religion, but one day I found out otherwise. I was on my treadmill watching TV, and Marlo Thomas was being interviewed. Being a good charismatic Christian, I was a political conservative, and therefore against the liberal left. Marlo Thomas is a liberal and a feminist, and so the moment I saw her on TV, my knee-jerk reaction was, *Yuk. I don't like that Marlo Thomas.*

Well, I kept watching, and in the interview Ms. Thomas was talking about St. Jude's Hospital and how for fifty years they've been serving critically ill children. She's carrying on the legacy of her father, Danny

Thomas. And then she said, "We have never charged one dime for one child to ever be treated at St. Jude's and we have helped thousands of children that could otherwise never get help. I just want to keep this tradition going."

As I stood there on that treadmill, I could have melted and slunk underneath it. The still small voice of the Lord pierced my heart, and He said, *You hypocrite. You're over there judging her because of your religious beliefs, and she's doing something that is pleasing to me.* Like the Bible says, honor your father and mother, and in another place, help widows and orphans—which is true service to God. (See James 1:27.) The moral of this story is that *I had religion*, and I was judging another person because of our different political perspectives. For the first time, I looked in the mirror and admitted, Religion. That's me! It was painful to recognize, but it was the first step in getting free from that prison.

Another step came as I recognized my own reliance on man's knowledge and works. I've got a daughter, Mary, who was playing basketball. She was really struggling with having confidence. I would go over and over in my mind about how I was going to talk to her and help her out of the mess she was in. I just labored over it, thinking and figuring on how to best approach it. Then one day the Holy Spirit spoke to my heart and said, *Hey Rick, have you ever once, when thinking about how to help your daughter, brought up the cross of Christ?* I had to confess that I hadn't. Then He said, *That's religion.*

Ouch! Isn't that the definition of religion: any attempt by man through his knowledge and works to do something good, or do something holy apart from the cross of Christ? I was guilty. And I thought I was Mister Non-Religious. But it just isn't true. How many times, when we are concerned about a loved one, do we go over and over in our minds how to help the situation without ever bringing up the cross of Christ? This pretty much applies to everybody, so we all have religion.

Let's imagine a world without religion. What would that world be like? The original world created by God for Adam and Eve did not have

> I LOOKED IN THE MIRROR AND ADMITTED, RELIGION. THAT'S ME. IT WAS PAINFUL TO RECOGNIZE, BUT IT WAS THE FIRST STEP IN GETTING SET FREE.

religion in it. And what was that original world? The Garden of Eden. It was the polar opposite of the world of religion, and it was paradise. God was on the throne, not man. Adam and Eve were like little children—adults with childlike hearts. They were holy and without sin. What's more, they were sons and daughters of God who completely trusted in their Father for everything. They had a face-to-face relationship with God; there was no separation. On top of that, Adam and Eve were one—there was no division whatsoever between them. And as a final bonus, they had dominion over all of the earth. They even had dominion over the devil. The Bible says they had dominion over everything, including "reptiles, creeping reptiles." That included the snake, right? What a wonderful world!

But after the Fall we see a complete change. Mankind put themselves on God's throne and began to do as they pleased. They became carnal and sinful; they had fallen flesh with all of the curses that go with it. They lost their childlike relationship with their Father. They were separated from God, cast out of the garden. And there was division; the two brothers were divided, and one killed the other. And finally, who became prince of the world? Satan. He was the one behind it all—the one who introduced religion into the world. Think about it. Who needed religion to come into existence in order to gain power in the world? The devil. It's his deal, his system. It's a masquerade. It's something that appears to be God but isn't. The enemy's fingerprints are all over it.

WHO NEEDED RELIGION TO COME INTO EXISTENCE IN ORDER TO GAIN POWER IN THE WORLD? THE DEVIL. IT'S HIS DEAL, HIS SYSTEM.

We learned that the wisdom of the world empties the cross of its power, and when the cross is emptied of its power, Satan regains power. When that happens, we lose our God-given birthright of dominion. Religion appears to make man holy—to elevate us spiritually by drawing us closer to God—but in reality it elevates Satan. That's why it's so clever: religion is this whole world that seems to be Godly but isn't. It's really all about man—and really all about Satan.

I want to close with something that was very offensive to me when I heard it. It's a very radical idea, and if I did not believe with all of my heart that it was from the Holy Spirit, I would not be able to accept it myself. I was sitting in a counseling session one day, and the Lord spoke these words to my heart: *There is a world that exists that you know very little about—you and other sincere Christians in the church. This world is called the kingdom of God. In this world is a blessing, "The Blessing," and it has nothing to do with what you do right or wrong.*

> THERE IS A WORLD THAT EXISTS THAT YOU KNOW VERY LITTLE ABOUT—IN THIS WORLD IS A BLESSING THAT HAS NOTHING TO DO WITH WHAT YOU DO RIGHT OR WRONG.

This stunned me. I said, "How can this be? It sounds like heresy!" Then the Lord helped me understand by showing me that the Garden of Eden was the kingdom of God. It was a place of blessing, as the Bible describes in Genesis. He saw that His creation was good, and He blessed it...and He blessed it...and He blessed it. Did that blessing have anything to do with Adam and Eve knowing the difference between right and wrong, and doing right or wrong? No, nothing. They didn't even know they were naked. Could a world like that exist? Not only could it exist, it did.

The second thing that the Lord helped me to understand was the concept of being born again. We all know that when we are born again, we enter the kingdom of God, and it has nothing to do with what we do right or wrong. If someone came up to us and said, "I want to accept Jesus as Lord, but I need to stop cussing and getting drunk first," what would we say? We would say, "No, it has nothing to do with what you're doing wrong. Just repent and accept Jesus as you are, and He will give you the power to change." If someone else came up and said, "I read the Bible every day, go to church three times a week, and give to the poor, so I don't need to accept Jesus as Lord to go to heaven," what would we say? We would say, "No, it doesn't matter how many things you're doing right and how good you are. The only way to heaven is through Jesus Christ." Why, then, are we so surprised that a world of blessing could exist for us which has nothing to do with what we do right or wrong? The answer the Lord gave me stunned me again: *It's because you've heard a watered down version of the Gospel for so long that when you hear the real thing, you think it's heresy.* Wow, that's scary, but the Garden of Eden and being born again prove that it's true.

It's worth saying again: as Christians, we have heard a watered down version of the Gospel for so long, that when we hear the real thing, we think it's heresy! No wonder we have so little love and power in the church—to *water down* means *to dilute and weaken*—meaning less love and power.

That beautiful world really exists, and guess what? *We're not in that world.* We know very little about it, because that world is about Jesus and what He did and not about what we're doing. *But we're headed toward it, as we discover more and more about the first part of the lost secret, which is making the cross of Christ the most important thing in our lives.*

We've seen the prison religion puts us in, and now in the next chapter we're going to take a wrecking ball to the very foundation of that prison. That foundation is the law, and once we knock it down, it will never be built back up in our lives again. We're going to replace the law with the gospel of grace and discover how to apply the power of the cross for victory in our everyday lives.

My Personal One-on-One Encounter With The Lord

ALSO FOR HOME GROUP DISCUSSION

Can I now admit that I have religion? What are some examples of religion in my life?

_____

_____

When someone that I love has a problem, do I go over and over in my mind of how to help them without including the cross of Christ? What are some examples?

_____

_____

Do I have human traditions and man made rules, fence laws, as part of my Christian walk? What are some of them?

_____

_____

What do I know about a world that exists called the Kingdom Of God, that has a blessing for me, but has nothing to do with what I do right or wrong?

_____

_____

_____

REFLECTING ON THE ART

· In what way does the painting that opens this chapter speak to me?
· Did the sketch have an impact on me? If so, how?

_____

_____

_____

Judge Not

CHAPTER 6

Judge Not

AT EVERY TURN OF OUR SPIRITUAL JOURNEY, one thing always pops up: the law, which is based on knowledge and works. Whether it was me in second grade choosing knowledge and works to succeed, Satan using knowledge and works to steal the message of the cross, Jesus taking the law based on knowledge and works out of our way, Caterpillar Christians munching away on knowledge and works, or finally, religion based on what men know and do to be holy, the law has been there. Let's discover how to get rid of the law and replace it with the gospel of grace which is the cross of Christ.

1 Corinthians 15:56 says, "The sting of death is sin, and the strength of sin is the law." Phillips' translation states it this way: "It is the Law which gives sin its power." The word *power* there is from the Greek word *dunamis*, meaning "to be able or possible." And in Romans 4:15 it says—I'm paraphrasing slightly—that "apart from the law there is no sin." *So the law is the power of sin; it makes sin possible.*

Going one step further, we will now discover that judgment is what brings the law to life. Remember how Satan stole our birthright? He used a lie, so we would lust after the law, to bring sin to life. The lie that God wasn't good and we weren't good enough caused us to judge God and ourselves. A judgment set the whole sequence in motion. To understand, let's go back to the analogy of a lawnmower.

Your lawn is the world where the law belongs, and the lawnmower does a great job there; your lawn looks great. Your flower and vegetable garden represents the church, the New Covenant, where the law does not belong. Picture your garden in July or August. Your summer flowers are looking great. Your tomatoes and beans are strong and healthy and producing well. This garden is your pride and joy. Suddenly somebody comes, starts up the lawnmower, pushes it right into your garden, and begins mowing it down. What would you do? You'd be very upset, wouldn't you? Why? Because something good was misapplied, and it turned into something very bad.

Picture this lawnmower, and imagine that sin is the blade. That's what chopped all of your flowers and vegetables to pieces. What powered the blade? The engine, which is the law. But what started the engine? The pull-cord, which is judgment. Without the pull-cord, there would be no life in the engine. Judgment is the catalyst that brings the law to life, spinning the blade, and creating sin. So we must put judgment to death in our lives in order to get the law out of our life. Like everything else, it has to go to the cross. Then the law, which is the power of sin, will be gone and replaced with the power of the cross.

> SO WE MUST PUT JUDGMENT TO DEATH IN OUR LIVES IN ORDER TO GET THE LAW OUT OF OUR LIFE.

The word *judgment* in the Bible means "a decision for or against, to distinguish or decide mentally, the knowledge or the ability to distinguish good and evil or to decide what is right or wrong." The root word of *judgment* means "accusation, condemnation, damnation."

Let's take these words into Genesis three and consider how they played a part in the fall of man. The first thing the devil did was to offer a lying accusation. He told Eve, "God is holding out on you…. He doesn't really love you. The reason He doesn't want you to eat of that tree is because you're going to be like Him. And you need to be like Him because you're not good enough now—you're inferior." Satan started out with a lying accusation, which produced what in Adam and Eve? A *judgment against God and then themselves.* Going back to the analogy of the lawnmower, we see that Satan pulled the cord and produced a judgment.

Second, the Bible says that the fruit looked good for wisdom. Adam and Eve wanted to become like God, but what did they eat of? They ate from the tree of the knowledge of good and evil. To distinguish or decide mentally—the knowledge and ability to distinguish good and evil—it's judgment! They'd never even known judgment—it didn't exist in their lives—but first they judged God and themselves, and then they ate of the tree that put them into a lifestyle of judgment. *Judgment times two!* What happened after that? Damnation and condemnation and death. That's what judgment produces.

The first and only command that God gave to man in the Garden of Eden was "*Judge not.*" He created this whole universe, and He said, "There's only one thing you can't do. Don't judge. As long as you judge not, you'll have life with Me forever in paradise and have dominion over the entire world—our God-given birthright. Just don't do that one thing." It seems that if that was the only command God gave man in the beginning, it is extremely important. I believe it sums everything up: judge not.

> HE CREATED THIS WHOLE UNIVERSE, AND HE SAID, "THERE'S ONLY ONE THING YOU CAN'T DO. DON'T JUDGE."

The fall of man proves that judgment triggered the law. It powers it. And if you think about the law of the land, it proves that same point. If you break the law you will eventually stand before a judge. The judge decides whether you are good or evil, and if you are judged to be evil, then you are condemned. The legal system cannot exist without judges—no judges making judgments means no legal system and no law. Now we are on to something really big. *Judgment is really the root and source of all sin! And we know that the cross is the only source of righteousness.* If we compare the two side by side, judgment vs. the cross, they should be exactly opposite. Let's try it and see if it's true.

Let's first start with the cross. The essence of the cross, which is the essence of Christianity, is humility, faith and love. As New-Covenant Christians, we know that the first step to becoming righteous is humility. We must humble ourselves to be saved, as the Bible says in Ephesians 2:8-9: "For by grace you have been saved through faith…not of works, lest anyone should boast." Is it possible to be saved apart from humility?

I bet every born-again Christian, if he or she remembers back to their personal salvation experience—it doesn't matter how cocky we were, or where we were at the time; it doesn't matter how many people we scoffed at—at a certain point in time, we admitted, "I'm a sinner in need of a Savior." That's not cocky, is it? That's humble. "There's nothing I can do to get to heaven; I can't make it on my own. I need Jesus." That's humble, right? We first have to recognize that we are sinners in need of a Savior and then reach out in faith to receive Jesus' free gift. *It all starts with humility.*

But what is judgment? It is the opposite of humility. It is haughty. Have you ever seen the image used in some movies, in which a person is looking down his or her nose at another person? Or perhaps pointing a finger? What is that demonstrating? Judgment. *Just look at that riff-raff. I'm better than she is.* It's haughty—prideful—and we Christians do it all of the time. There is no humility in it. They are opposites.

What's the second aspect to being saved? Faith. Habakkuk 2:4 is a very famous scripture, and it says "Behold the proud, his soul is not upright in him; but the just shall live by his *faith*" (emphasis mine). And just as Christianity is associated with a humble person being saved by faith, *judgment is associated with being proud and having unbelief.* Think back to Adam and Eve. Everything was beautiful until they believed Satan's lie and judged God. They chose to stop believing that God was good *and instead believed that He was holding out on them. Their unbelief was the opposite of faith.* We now have two opposites, humility vs. pride and faith vs. unbelief. Only one more to go.

Another very famous scripture is John 3:16, which says, "For God so *loved* the world that He gave His only begotten Son, that whoever believes in Him should not perish but have everlasting life" (emphasis mine). The cross and Christianity are about love, but think about Adam and Eve. When they judged God and had unbelief, it hardened their hearts toward God, and their love for Him diminished. The same thing happens between people in relationships. The minute I judge you, I don't believe you're good anymore. Let's say we were the best buddies in the world. I thought you were great, and I talked you up to people. All of a sudden you do something I don't approve of, and I'm sitting in judgment over you. It doesn't even have to be a conscious thought, but internally I'm saying that I don't believe you're good anymore. That

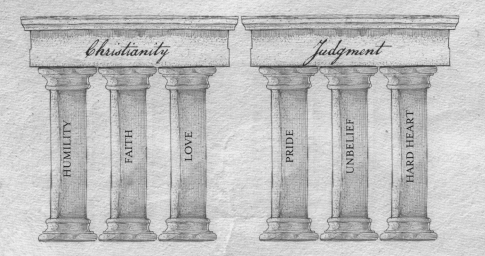

means my heart has hardened towards you and I no longer love you. *The final opposite is love vs. a hard heart.*

To put it all together, *humility, faith and love are the essence of the cross and Christianity. Pride, unbelief, and a hard heart are the essence of judgment. So Christianity and judgment are totally opposed to each other.* The sketch of the three pillars sums it all up.

If the only way to righteousness is an encounter with Jesus and His cross, based on humility, faith, and love, doesn't the opposite have to be true? The source of all sin is pride, unbelief, and hard unloving hearts, which is judgment. Replace judgment with the cross, and we are set free from sin.

Why do Christians judge so much? It's a weird thing. Judgment makes us feel holy. Think about it. Doesn't it make you feel holy and like you're serving God when you're judging everybody and everything? We think we're really arriving, but we're really taking a nosedive at nine thousand miles an hour to the pit of hell! It's a sly trick of the devil. I believe God would say of the Fall, "Little did Adam and Eve know that when they ate that fruit to supposedly become like Me, they were entering a lifestyle of judgment, which is death."

What are the fruits of a lifestyle of judgment? The first fruit of judgment is that *it separates us from God* as sons and daughters, and it turns us into slaves. Knowledge—works—toil. That's what happened to Adam and Eve.

They went from innocent children of God who had all of their needs met, into slavery after they ate of the tree of the knowledge of good and evil.

The second fruit of judgment is that *it separates us from our brothers and sisters in Christ.* When what I know about God and what I do for God, and what you know about God and do for God are different and I judge you for it, we can't have unity or fellowship. My judgment against you for being different will always produce division.

The third fruit of a lifestyle of judgment is *curses and death.* The Bible says in Galatians 3:10 that those who are under the law are under a curse. Why? *Judgment is what brings the law to life,* which then brings the law of sin and death into existence. The curses of famine, plague, and sword, that come from sin, produce death. That's what happened in Genesis chapter three, and that's what still happens today.

JUST LIKE BREATHING, IT BECOMES INVOLUNTARY, AND WE JUDGE ALL OF THE TIME.

As I've grown in the area of recognizing judgment in myself, I've seen that it's like breathing. It can become so much a part of our lives that we don't even know we're doing it. Just like breathing, it becomes involuntary, and we judge all of the time. But the good news is that *God wants to set us free,* and we can begin to be set free right now. I believe there are three things He wants to say to our hearts:

ONE. Don't judge God.

TWO. Don't judge yourself.

THREE. Don't judge anyone else.

It's very simple. Don't judge God, because He is good all the time. Don't judge yourself. We'll either be too hard on ourselves or too easy, but we'll never get it right. We need to ask God to search us, and His judgments will be right. Don't judge others, because we have no right to judge anyone; everyone stands or falls to God alone. I believe God is saying, "If you stop judging Me, stop judging yourself, and stop judging each other, then the law will not exist in your life. Your

Christianity will no longer be anchored to the foundation of the law but to the foundation of My Son, Jesus Christ, and Him crucified." His foundation is based on humility, faith, and love, and judgment has nothing to do with those three things, does it? Judgment is basically the opposite of that foundation.

IF YOU STOP JUDGING ME, STOP JUDGING YOURSELF, AND STOP JUDGING EACH OTHER, THEN THE LAW WILL NOT EXIST IN YOUR LIFE.

If we look to the person of Jesus to see what He said about judgment, we find a very, very bizarre truth. He was God, the Word become flesh, yet He did not have an opinion about anything. To paraphrase John 5:19 and John 8:28, Jesus said, "I only say what I hear My Father say, and I only do what I see My Father do. I don't have any opinions about anything." What Jesus was saying was that He didn't make judgments on His own. That's why He was also the only person who has ever been without sin. No judgment, no law, no sin. He fulfilled the law by not sinning, by not judging.

Let's consider 1 Peter 2:22-23, which reads, " '[He] committed no sin, nor was deceit found in His mouth'… when He was reviled, did not revile in return; when He suffered, He did not threaten, but committed Himself to Him who judges righteously." That passage is basically saying that Jesus didn't judge and pay somebody back. His attitude was, "You can do whatever you want to Me, but I will not judge you. I don't judge anything; I have no personal opinions about anything. That's why I don't have any sin."

It should probably be noted here that all Christians, and especially people in leadership positions, are sometimes called upon to make Godly *assessments*. Pastors, parents, all of us have to make Godly assessments or judgments. Jesus made them all of the time, but they always came through the Father. The key here is that Godly assessments don't involve pride, unbelief, or a hard heart towards a person. We're not trying to *be* God; we allow God to live His life in us, and His life is a life of humility, faith, and mercy.

Remember Adam and Eve in the garden? What were they trying to do? Become like God. That's what everyone wants to do. Like Cinderella's stepsisters, we're all pushing and shoving to fit our feet into God's shoes. Or to put it more comically, we're all scrambling to squeeze our own behinds onto God's throne of judgment. What was Adam and Eve's original sin? They said to themselves, "Let's eat this fruit to become like God." They were trying to force their two behinds onto the judgment seat of God, and now, following in their footsteps, there are six billion people on the earth striving for the same thing. We're all pushing and shoving, trying to cram ourselves onto that throne because, just like Adam and Eve, we think if we can judge between good and evil, we'll become like God. But you know what? God's watching all of this and saying, "You guys are going to all of this effort to sit in judgment over others because somehow you think that will make you like Me. But I have news for you. There is only one righteous judge—Me. And guess what? My heart is merciful." Want proof?

Psalm 136 says over and over that the Lord is good and His mercy endures forever. Look at the story of the prodigal son and the father who runs to embrace him. That father represents God the Father, who kisses and welcomes His wayward son back with great mercy. (See Luke 15:11-32.) What does James say? "Mercy triumphs over judgment" (James 2:13). If God's heart is mercy, and mercy triumphs over judgment, how could He be a God whose desire is to condemn and judge people? What did He say when He sent Jesus? John 3:17-18 out of the Amplified Bible says it best: "For God did not send the Son into the world in order to judge (to reject, to condemn, to pass sentence on) the world, but that the world might find salvation and be made safe and sound through Him. He who believes in Him [who clings to, trusts in, relies on Him] is not judged [he who trusts in Him never comes up for judgment; for him there is no rejection, no condemnation—he incurs no damnation]."

> IF GOD'S DESIRE WAS JUDGMENT, HE WOULD HAVE SAID, "SON, GO DOWN THERE AND TAKE CARE OF THOSE BAD HUMAN BEINGS THAT WE CREATED."

If God's desire was judgment, He would have said, "Son, go down there and take care of those bad human beings that we created." But He didn't say that, did He? He said, "Son, go down there and die for them and save them." If you start from the last supper and go to the crucifixion, you'll see Jesus had every opportunity to judge, starting with Judas. He could have exposed Judas and condemned him, but instead He washed his feet. In the garden, when He found the apostles sleeping, He could have said, "You're a bunch of losers. I'm done. I'm leaving before these guards come, and I'm going to find another group." But He didn't do it. The soldiers, the temple guards—Jesus could have defended Himself and even killed them for the mistake they were making. He didn't. He didn't judge the Pharisees, the chief priests and scribes, Pilate, the Roman soldiers, or the crowd that mocked and reviled Him. Instead, "[He] committed Himself to Him who judges righteously." It's simply not His desire to judge. We're all trying to become like God, and that's not what God is like.

I believe in the end—the final judgment day—our hearts and actions will judge themselves. We will choose not to be with God; it will be our decision. In the end it's going to be real obvious. I *decided* I didn't want God; *I* made the decision; *I* cut myself off from the Lord. That's how it's going to happen. As the scripture says, He's not willing that any should perish, but that all should come to Him. (See 2 Peter 3:9.) God wants everybody to be saved; His heart is mercy, not judgment.

What are we going to do? If we want to be separated from God and our brothers and sisters in Christ, lose our God-given birthright, and be cursed and die, we can choose a path of judgment. I don't want that path, do you? If we want to be united to God and become one with our brothers and sisters in Christ, regain our God-given birthright, receive power for blessings and be able to bless other people, then we will choose the gospel of Jesus Christ and Him crucified and truly draw close to God.

Is the Holy Spirit speaking to you as you read? Are you ready to remove the law as the foundation of your life by getting judgment out of your life? Are you ready to lay a better foundation for your life, made up of Christ crucified? If so, consider praying this prayer:

My Merciful Father,
I realize I have drifted away from You—from my first love. In my effort
to become holy, I have been beguiled by the enemy, and sucked into judgment.

It felt good, Lord; it felt righteous. I thought it was the way to be close to You, but now I see that it isn't.

Lord, I don't want that stain on me—the stain of judgment—and I ask You now to wash me in the blood of Jesus. Forgive me, and cleanse me of all of that ugliness—pride, unbelief, and a hard heart—the sin that comes out of judgment. Bathe me in Your love. I'm destroying the foundation of the law in my life and asking You to build a new thing in its place. Replace this evil nature with Your nature—the nature of mercy—the nature of Your Son. Transform me into His image.

As I receive Your forgiveness, I ask that You would now plant my feet on the Rock. Anchor me into the humility, faith, and love of Your Son.

I'm coming back to You, Father, by coming back to my first love—Jesus! Thank You for running to embrace me. May I never be led away again.

In Jesus' name.

My Personal One-on-One Encounter With The Lord

ALSO FOR HOME GROUP DISCUSSION

How does the law power sin, literally making it possible for sin to exist (I Corinthians 15:56)?

_____

_____

_____

_____

Do I understand how judgment brings the law to life, like a lawnmower pull-cord brings its engine to life?

_____

_____

_____

_____

Is judging like breathing for me? Do I do it all the time without thinking of it? What are some examples of how I judge?

_____

_____

_____

_____

_____

If the essence of our Christian walk is humility, faith, and love, what are the opposite fruits produced by judgment?

_____

_____

_____

_____

What did God reveal to me, personally, as I read and pondered this chapter?

_____

_____

_____

_____

_____

Have I taken judgment to the foot of the cross to put it to death, so that I can stop judging God, myself, and others?

_____

_____

_____

_____

_____

REFLECTING ON THE ART

· In what way does the painting that opens this chapter speak to me?
· Did the sketch have an impact on me? If so, how?

_____

_____

_____

Who's the Real Me?

Philip Howe

CHAPTER 7

Who's the Real Me?

SO FAR ON OUR SPIRITUAL JOURNEY, we've discovered the wisdom of the world system we were in and have replaced the law with the gospel of grace. Now we can begin an inward journey, to find out "Who's the real me?"

We each have a God-given identity that is ours alone. It is not selfish to want to grasp hold of that identity because it is a gift from God, bought with the precious blood of His Son. The world, other people in our lives, even we ourselves, may try to impose another identity on us—but what is true is what God thinks about us. That is what defines our *true* self.

Part of the journey to God's world of love, power, blessings, and fulfilled destiny is a journey to the center of ourselves. We must find out once and for all who we really are. And to find out what my true identity is, I have to ask this question: *Who am I?* Not how I see myself, not how others see me, but how *God* sees me.

Who is the real me?

There is a key scripture that speaks to this question, Proverbs 23:7. In the Amplified Bible it reads, "As [a man] thinks in his heart, so he is." In other words, how I act and what I do depends on who I think I am. And what I believe God

HOW I ACT AND WHAT I DO DEPENDS ON WHO I THINK I AM.

wants to do with us on this journey is to open the eyes of our hearts. He wants us to think a different way. When I learn to think a different way, in the heart of who I am, then how I act and what I do will never be the same again.

There's a three-part truth to who we are. The first truth about the real me—and the real you—is that we are *wonderful*. We've always been wonderful. You were wonderful from the moment you were conceived. God says so! And, the second truth about who we are, is that we are *princes and princesses*—the moment we are born again we become sons and daughters of the King of kings! We all know that in a royal family, when the king dies, his heir becomes king or queen. Since our King died on the cross, the third truth is, we have the opportunity to become kings and queens.

When we can embrace these truths about ourselves, and start thinking differently, we will do things differently. Let's allow God to open the eyes of our hearts as we study them further.

That first statement, *I am wonderful,* sounds pretty audacious, doesn't it? It *is* a rather bold truth. A counselor friend, who shared this concept with me, tells a story about going to Germany to minister. He was getting ready to speak to a crowd of Germans who had never met him before. He walked up to the microphone, looked them in the eyes, and declared, "I want you to know something. I am wonderful." I am sure they were thinking, *What kind of egomaniac is this American?* But then he went on to tell them why.

In Genesis 1:27 it says, "So God created man in His own image; in the image of God He created him; male and female He created them." Then in Genesis 2:7 the Bible says, "The Lord God formed man of the dust of the ground, and breathed into his nostrils the breath of life; and man became a living being." This is confirmed in Job 33:4, which reads, "The Spirit of God has made me, and the breath of the Almighty gives me life." In the Hebrew the word *breath* means "Spirit."

This is what happened: God took a piece of Himself, who is the great I Am, and at the moment of conception of every human being, He put that piece of Himself inside of that fertilized egg. God is great, and at that moment we became wonderful because we became a God-carrier.

Did you know that a percentage of all healthy sperm and eggs that come together do not create a human being? There is no scientific

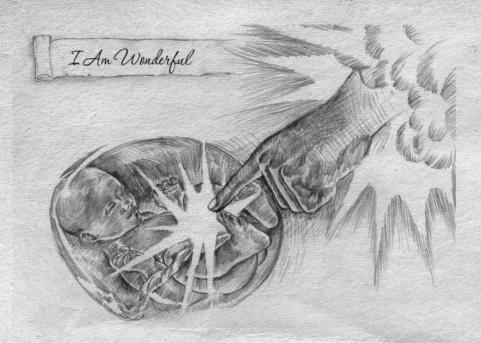

explanation for this phenomenon, but I believe the reason is that God did not decide to put a piece of Himself into that fertilized egg. Expounding on this thought, what do we call it when a woman becomes pregnant? She "conceives." The dictionary definition of *conceive* is "to become pregnant, to form an idea in the mind." Nobody is an accident— that's a lie from the pit of hell. God conceived us, thought about us in His mind, and planned for us to be here. We are "fearfully and wonderfully made" (Psalm 139:14). "His name [is] Wonderful" (Isaiah 9:6), and we are chips off the old block!

For more proof that we are all carriers of the breath of God, consider James 2:26. It says, "The body without the spirit is dead." When Jesus died on the cross, the Bible says, "He gave up His Spirit" (Matthew 27:50 NIV). We see there's a very clear spiritual truth that life begins when the Spirit

> LIFE IS CONNECTED TO THAT PIECE OF GOD THAT GOES INTO EVERY HUMAN BEING, AND THAT PIECE OF GOD IS THE PIECE OF US THAT IS WONDERFUL.

of God goes into a fertilized egg, and life ends when the Spirit of God leaves a body. This flesh is clay. Life is connected to that piece of God that goes into every human being, and that piece of God is the piece of us that is wonderful.

Let's consider the price of our redemption. We were purchased by the blood of Jesus Christ, right? That's the highest price the Father could ever pay, and He did it to save us. Would you pay a high price for something that wasn't valuable to you?

My wife Lu Ann had an experience that serves to illustrate this point. One day she lost her ring. It was a beautiful diamond ring, and it had special meaning for her because I had given it to her. When she realized it was gone, she thought she might have accidentally thrown it away with some paper. She began digging through the trash. That ring was so valuable to her that she dug through layer upon layer of stinky garbage to get to the bottom, where she found her ring. Do you know what she would have done if she hadn't found her ring in the trash can? She'd have torn through the entire house, and if she didn't find it there, she would have gone into the big garbage dumpsters head first. She would have done whatever it took to get back her ring.

> "I WILL SEND MY SON TO DIE FOR YOU TO GET YOU BACK, BECAUSE I'M NOT WHOLE WITHOUT YOU. THAT'S HOW VALUABLE YOU ARE."

If that ring was just costume jewelry, do you think Lu Ann would have gone to all of that trouble? Nobody goes to that much trouble to find something cheap or junky, and we can be sure that God would not have paid such a terrible price for us if we were not valuable to Him. When Father God took a piece of Himself, His Spirit, and put it in your mother's womb, it left a hole in Him that can never be filled again except by you. In the cross, it's as if He was saying, "I have to have you back, and I will send My Son to die for you to get you back because I'm not whole without you. That's how valuable you are."

It is hard for some of us to understand our value in God's eyes because we've always been taught that we are sinful wretches. And so we are. The song "Amazing Grace" says, "Amazing grace, how sweet the sound, that saved a wretch like me." But it is always important to remember that in Him who is the Truth, more than one truth can be in operation. While we are cringing paupers, in need of His saving grace, we are also wonderful because we have a piece of Him inside us. That's why He went to so much trouble to get us back.

Can you look in the mirror and say from your heart, "I am wonderful!"? Has He opened the eyes of your heart so that you can see yourself as He sees you? When the Lord allows you to see what He sees, you can truly look in the mirror and say that and mean it. Your life will never be the same!

It doesn't matter what opinion of yourself you had before; it doesn't matter what opinion anybody else had of you; the only opinion that matters is God's! You can look in the mirror, and you can say, "I'm wonderful." What's more, you can do that every day, because no matter what, it won't have changed. God never changes. I challenge you to start doing that today! This is the first aspect of getting your God-given birthright back—*replacing Satan's lie that you're inferior with God's truth that you are wonderful!*

Item two on the subject of identity is that *from the moment we are born again we are either a prince or a princess.* The minute I accept Jesus Christ as Lord and Savior of my life, I become a child of the Most High God, the King Immortal.

Doesn't every little girl dream about being a princess? Disney makes millions and millions of dollars perpetuating that dream. Cinderella, Snow White, the whole list of them, are all about a girl having Prince Charming come into her life and becoming a princess. To all of you little girls out there—and the ones who have grown up—God is saying, "I've got good news for you today. It's true! You are a princess! You don't have to daydream about it—you *are* a princess."

Doesn't every little boy want to be a prince? They want to ride a horse and go fight the enemy or slay the dragon. They want to grab that girl and put her on the back of the horse and ride off into the sunset. Boys want to be champions! God made us that way. And he wired us that way because *we are sons and daughters of a King.* That's the truth that makes us either a prince or a princess.

What do we have to do to earn that status? Nothing. This was illustrated to me one day as I sat in a café with my daughter. There was a little baby sitting on a table, and everybody was around the table staring at the baby. The parents, grandparents, and other relatives were cooing and smiling, focusing their complete attention on that baby. As I watched, it dawned on me that the baby was doing nothing to receive all of that love and attention. In fact, what that baby does is worse than nothing. She fills her diapers, spits up, screams—and she may do those things many times a day—but it doesn't matter. She is loved and cared for—their princess because she was born into that family.

> WHEN WE ARE BORN INTO GOD'S FAMILY, HE LOOKS AT US AND SAYS, "THERE'S MY BABY BOY! THERE'S MY BABY GIRL! MY LITTLE PRINCE! MY LITTLE PRINCESS!"

Did you know that's what happens to us when we are born into God's family? He looks at us and says, "There's my baby boy! There's my baby girl! My little prince! My little princess!" That's what He thinks about us, and I believe that's what He wants us to think about ourselves.

Challenge number two, then, is that whatever day it is, we need to look in the mirror and say, "I accepted you, Jesus, as Lord and Savior of my life. That means I'm a prince [or princess]." Believe it, and mean it, and you'll never act the same. You will never carry yourself the same way; you won't have the same posture; you won't have the same attitude; you won't have the same thoughts. We will not be the same people when we get that in our hearts. We are princes and princesses of the kingdom of heaven. This is the second aspect of getting your birthright back—*replacing being a slave under the law with being a son or daughter of God through faith in Jesus Christ.*

Now for the grand finale. Nobody can ever top God, right? We've learned that we're wonderful, and we're either a prince or a princess. But what happens to a prince or princess when the king or queen dies? What instantly happens? They become the king or queen. Our King died, so we have the opportunity to become a king or queen—but this will involve a process.

From the moment we were conceived, we have been wonderful, because we have a piece of God in us. At the moment we accept Jesus as Lord and Savior of our lives, we become a prince or princess. Becoming a king or queen involves a choice: we have to choose to die with Jesus and be raised a new creation. It's not automatic; it's a process.

Consider Romans 8:28. It says, "We know that all things work together for good to those who love God, to those who are the called according to His purpose. For whom He foreknew, He also predestined to be conformed to the image of His Son, that He might be the firstborn among many brethren."

As I shared, the word *conformed* in the Greek is actually two words, *sum morphos*, and it means, basically, a union that produces a new creation. (It's the same word behind the English word *metamorphosis* that we talked about in chapter four, describing when a caterpillar turns into a butterfly.) We have to undergo the process of transformation to be made a new creation, and the best place for that to happen is through trials.

There's a lot of debate about that, but the same word pops up in Philippians 3:10-11, where Paul says (to paraphrase), "I want to know Jesus, and I want to experience and share the power of His resurrection. I want to share in His sufferings, be conformed to Him in His death, so that some day I may attain to the resurrection from the dead, even while still in this body" (Amplified Bible). The word *conformed—sum morphos—*is there again, right after sharing in His sufferings. Guess what? There are going to be trials that involve suffering.

To become a king or a queen, let's not waste our trials. When you're going through a trial, ask the Lord to use it to transform you. When I went through my legal, financial, and health problems, I sure didn't enjoy them; but guess what, they have made me a far better minister today. Because of the pain that I went through, I can better understand the pain of people going through those same trials now. I can connect with them far better than ever before. Also, they

> TO BECOME A KING OR A QUEEN, LET'S NOT WASTE OUR TRIALS. WHEN YOU'RE GOING THROUGH A TRIAL, ASK THE LORD TO USE IT TO TRANSFORM YOU.

exposed a lot of my hidden junk, which I could then take to the cross. The Lord used the trials to build in me the character of Christ.

I didn't waste my trial, and you mustn't either. When trials come our way, we must remember that our ultimate destiny is to become kings and queens, but we must go through the cross—we need to experience *sum morphos*, a transforming union with our King—in order to be transformed into a butterfly.

Do you recognize the butterfly we've used throughout the book? It's a Monarch. According to the dictionary, a monarch is "a king, one holding preeminent position or power." It also says "a butterfly." This is where we start as an egg, are born again, and then turn into a caterpillar. What happens, as we said earlier, is that believers get stuck in the caterpillar phase; we never go into the cocoon and get transformed into a monarch—a king or a queen. But that can change today. This is the third aspect of getting your God-given birthright back—*dying to self to be transformed into a king or queen.*

It doesn't matter what building we're in, or what end of town; it doesn't matter what anybody thinks of us. God has ordained and proclaimed for every one of us to be a king or a queen—to take dominion on this earth and to be world changers. His Son, the King of kings, died so we as royal heirs could be transformed into kings and queens. He's going to bring us back to the positions we held in the Garden of Eden, where humans had rulership dominion as the king and queen of the entire earth. Satan came and deceived us, but we're going to get our dominion and birthright back. This book, *The Lost Secret*, is a part of that heavenly restoration. To get what was lost back, we need to continue our internal spiritual journey by leaving behind the life we know.

My Personal One-on-One Encounter With The Lord

ALSO FOR HOME GROUP DISCUSSION

Do I understand that how I act and what I do depends on who I think I am? What are some examples of how I'm living now that don't line up with how God sees me?

_____

_____

Do I believe that I am wonderful because God put a piece of Himself in me?

_____

_____

Do I believe that I'm a prince or princess because when I was born again I became the child of a King?

_____

_____

When a king dies, his children then become the king or queen. Do I believe that I have the opportunity to become a king or queen because my King, Jesus, died on the cross?

_____

_____

REFLECTING ON THE ART

• In what way does the painting that opens this chapter speak to me?
• Did the sketch have an impact on me? If so, how?

_____

_____

_____

Leave Behind
The Life You Know

CHAPTER 8

Leave Behind The Life You Know

IN THE LAST CHAPTER, we learned what's true and false about our identity. In Christ, the "real me" is wonderful, a prince or princess, and is destined to become a king or queen. That's the life we want—and the true life Jesus came to give us—but the "false me" still exists. That artificial person must be dealt with in order for us to embrace the new life we have in Jesus. The "false me" must be put to death on the cross in order to move on in resurrection life – a life full of love, power, and blessings – and a life of fulfilled destiny to bless others.

The way God is going to teach us how to do this is by using Abraham, a man God greatly blessed and used to greatly bless others. There was an article in *National Geographic* a while back about Abraham. In this article, the writer said, "Imagine a world saturated with ignorance and hatred, a lonely, brutish place without any hope of redemption. Now, picture a man—Abram, the Bible calls him—who hears a command from God: *Leave behind the life you know, and I will one day bless the entire world through you.* How this will happen, and why, is a mystery to this man, but he sets out."[1]

---

1 Tad Szulc, "Journey of Faith," *National Geographic* (December 2001): p. 90.

This concept, to leave behind the life you know, can be very scary. In fact, every time I teach this concept, I can tell by most people's reactions that they are scared. I'll admit it is terrifying to me! The fear of the unknown is one of the greatest human fears, but as we'll see through the example of Abraham, leaving behind the life you know can be a wonderful thing. Think about it, if we don't leave the world we're living in now, how can we ever enter God's world of love and power? Let's look at the life of Abraham within the context of the four stages of the Christian life—the four stages of the butterfly.

The Bible never describes Abram's initial encounter with God. He was living in Ur, in the land of the Chaldeans, which was full of idols. At some point, God spoke to him and said, *Guess what. See all of these idols that are here? They're nothing. I'm God.* When Abram realized that the idols of his homeland were not real and accepted the One True God, that was Abram's born-again experience. He entered the egg stage.

Then Genesis 12:1-3 (NIV) says,

> The Lord had said to Abram, "Leave your country, your people and your father's household and go to the land I will show you. I will make you into a great nation and I will bless you; I will make your name great, and you will be a blessing. I will bless those who bless you, and whoever curses you I will curse; and all peoples on earth will be blessed through you."

God spoke a birthright blessing over Abram, the one that had been lost by Adam and Eve in the Garden. The process of restoring our God-given birthright had begun—our relationship with God and our rulership over the earth—to be blessed and be a blessing. Jesus would finish the work on the cross.

The next stage, the caterpillar stage, would be when Abram went with his father from Ur to Haran. The Bible says, "Terah took his son Abram, his grandson Lot son of Haran, and his daughter-in-law Sarai, the wife of his son Abram, and together they set out from Ur of the Chaldeans to go to Canaan. But when they came to Haran, they settled there" (Genesis 11:31). They *set out* to go to Canaan, but instead of going to

Canaan, along the way they *settled*. That's much like the church today. We've settled for the Caterpillar Christian stage when God has so much more.

Abram's next step came when his father died. By obedience, he had to truly leave his father's house, people, and country and go to Canaan—Abram had to go into the cocoon stage. The next part of his life is when all of the transformation took place—and all of the scary things. Abram was transformed into Abraham. He went from being childless to becoming the father of many nations (Genesis 17:1-8). He went to Canaan, and Egypt; there was fighting and dividing land with Lot; and Sodom and Gomorrah; and then the ultimate test—Mount Moriah— where he was asked to sacrifice his one and only son Isaac. Did you know that Mt. Moriah is actually the same location as Calvary, where God's only son, Jesus, was sacrificed? And that *Moriah* means "place of clear vision"? That's what Abraham had to get to—the physical place of Calvary—the cross. That's where everything becomes clear. And when he was willing to sacrifice his only son for the sake of obedience to God, God said, *You've passed the test.* Abraham became a butterfly.

Would Abram, who was living in Ur, in the land of the Chaldeans, ever have been able to fulfill his destiny if he had remained in Ur? He would never have gone to the land of Canaan, the Promised Land, where the Lord said, "Every place on which the sole of your foot treads shall be yours" (Deuteronomy 11:24).

> FOR ABRAHAM TO RECEIVE HIS PROMISED BLESSINGS, AND FULFILL HIS DESTINY TO BLESS OTHERS, HE HAD TO LEAVE BEHIND THE LIFE HE KNEW.

Would he ever have received his promised blessings? The Bible says he was a wealthy man in Canaan. That's also where his sons were born. Finally, would he ever have been the father of many nations and had the whole world blessed through him? If he had stayed in Ur, it wouldn't have happened, right?

For Abraham to receive his God-given birthright—his promised love, power, blessings, and destiny—he had to leave behind the life he knew. Was it easy? No! Chaldea enjoyed a highly advanced civilization at the time, being in the midst of the region known as "the cradle of

civilization"—writing had been developed there fifteen centuries or more before Abraham's time—so it was a pretty good place to live. The book of Hebrews says that when he set out, *he did not know where he was going* (Hebrews 11:8). Abraham had to leave a place that was pretty good, a life that he knew, not even knowing where he was going. That was a big step, and that's what God is calling us to do. And by His grace, we will obey also. Just like Abraham, the father of our faith, we too will regain our birthright to be blessed and bless others.

I believe there's another really important point in those verses where God is telling him to leave. What did the Lord say? "I want you to leave your father's house, your people and your country." I think we can all really connect to this.

We've all been molded, influenced, and shaped by the environment we live in. The house where we grew up is our "father's house." The church we attended (or didn't) and the schools we went to—those things are our "people." And, of course, our country is our "country." I believe we are all, to some degree, prisoners of our past. We are all entangled by our past, maybe held back by it, controlled by our past in some way. We all understand who we are through the lens of our past, and I believe God is saying, *No. No more. That's not who you are; that's not the "real you." I've got better things for you.*

Let's imagine a prison and picture ourselves in that prison looking out of the bars. That person in the prison is the real you, the real me. Jesus Christ has come for a jailbreak, so we can leave behind the life we know, and enter God's world of love and power! Let's scope out this prison to figure out how the jailbreak will happen.

If we refer to the illustration, there are three windows for three rooms. The first one is our father's house—all of the things that have happened to us in the past with our family, in our home while we were growing up. The next window we look through is our religious upbringing and the schools we attended, which is our people. The third window is the United States (or whatever country we grew up in), and the culture of that room is the culture of the country.

Each room has four pieces of furniture in it that have dramatically influenced our lives and may have controlled us. The pieces of furniture are these: false teachings, wounds, good intentions, and the demons that are attached to those things, because they have become idols in our lives. I believe the Lord is saying, *I'm going to let you look inside and see those rooms—those pieces of furniture—and I'm going to let you understand what's really going on inside of you, and then I'm going to break you out.*

Let's talk about false teachings and think about a few examples. The first one is historical, and it is scary. Nazi Germany was full of "functional families," where people worked, took care of their kids, and even went to church. But in many of those families, the children were taught that they were the Aryan race and superior to others. Jews, blacks, and gypsies were compared to animals—lower than animals—and it was believed the "right thing" was to kill them. Of course this wasn't true—in fact it was grossly evil—but many children grew up not questioning it because it was a part of their family's culture. It was a false teaching that was accepted and passed down—with horrific consequences. That's the extreme of false teaching and the extreme of the damage it could cause, but how many other false teachings—none that dire, I hope—have we accepted simply because they are the beliefs of our family?

Consider this personal example. My wife, Lu Ann, had a great father, but she received a conflicting message from him. He told her something to the effect of, "Don't ever have a close relationship with anybody outside of the family. Never trust anyone outside of the family." She had a big family, a great childhood, wonderful relationships—but then she became a Christian. She was born again through the blood of Jesus into a second family, and guess what her biggest struggle was? Fellowship. Believers would try to include her and build friendships with her, but she could hardly do it. There was always some excuse as to why she couldn't enter into fellowship.

THEREFORE, TO HONOR HER FATHER WAS PLEASING TO GOD, BUT TO PLACE HIS FALSE TEACHING ABOVE THE WORD OF GOD WAS NOT.

Do you know why she had trouble with fellowship? It was because of the false teaching she received in her father's house—it was an idol in her life. Therefore, to honor her father was pleasing to God, but to place his false teaching above the word of God was not. The Bible says not to forsake "the assembling of ourselves together" (Hebrews 10:25) and to love your brothers and sisters, but Lu Ann would tell you there was an idol in her life competing with that truth, which was that false teaching. Until she got rid of that idol, fellowship was a real struggle in her life, and she was missing the blessing of other Godly relationships. We can see the dangers, both global and personal, of false teachings.

The next piece of furniture we need to examine is wounds. There was a guy in our small group one time, and I knew he had a lion's heart. He was a very gifted guy, but he never said a peep and never got involved in anything. We worked and worked and worked at drawing him out. Finally, one night he said, "I want to tell you something. When I was a kid, every time I said something, either my parents or my brothers and sisters would say, 'You're stupid; you're so stupid.' So now I don't talk."

Did God create him to be quiet? Or did his wounds make him quiet? I want to tell you something about the bondage of an idol, though. I can't count how many times we tried to set this guy free and he resisted. He would say, "You just want me to be like you," when in reality our heart was for his "real me" to be set free. That wound, the belief that he was stupid, went deep.

My daughter, Kristin, also knows something about wounds. She was a great athlete, but while playing high school basketball, she got trapped in a situation in which a coach really abused his authority. The words and actions of this coach deeply wounded Kristin and many of her friends. It was terrible. Kristin came to a point in which she said, "I will never pick up a basketball again in my life."

That's understandable, and we all do it, don't we? We set up this type of boundary to try to protect ourselves from getting hurt. But in the end, we have to consider God's will even over our own desire not to be hurt. What if God wanted Kristin to play basketball? What if he wanted her to play intramural basketball in college, to bump into a person she would witness to, who would get saved, who would then become the next Billy Graham? Without obedience none of those things would ever happen, right?

What Kristin had to decide was, who was lord of her life? Was it the coach and the wound? Or Jesus? If she bowed to the coach, vowing never to touch a basketball again because of what he did, then he was

WE CAN'T BE CONTROLLED BY OUR WOUNDS AND HAVE JESUS AS LORD OF OUR LIFE AT THE SAME TIME.

in control of her life. That wound would be controlling her, keeping her enslaved. We can't be controlled by our wounds and have Jesus as Lord of our life at the same time.

Finally, probably the most dreaded obstacle of all is good intentions. There's only one problem with a good intention—there is no such thing. They do not exist, you know why? Romans 3:10 says, "There is none righteous, no, not one." And Romans goes on to say, "I know that in me (that is, in my flesh) nothing good dwells" (7:18), and Isaiah 64:6 says that all of our righteousness is like filthy rags. So there is no such thing as a truly "good" intention.

I believe one of the most toxic things in the world is a so-called good intention, and here's my toxic story. As a kid, I was a pretty good athlete, and my dad worked all of the time. He could never be there for me. All of the other kids seemed to have dads that went with them to little league, and to make a long story short, I had a lot of bad experiences. I got cut from teams and got really wounded—terribly hurt and wounded by athletics. Because of that, I made a promise to myself. I said, "When I get married and have kids, I am going to spend time with them. I'm going to help them develop their athletic abilities, and what happened to me will never happen to my kids." That was my good intention.

And you know what? I did it. I would be at meetings, or practicing for my own tournament water skiing, and I'd have to leave because I was going to coach little league, or soccer with my son Ricky. My friends would say things like, "Rick, you are such a model father! Man, you just lay down your life for your kids!" I liked that; it fed my image as a model Christian, but do you know what happened to every one of my kids in sports? Some good things, but many disappointments as well. My good intention to form a perfect sports world never worked out.

One day the Lord revealed to me what was underneath that good intention. He said, *You have judgments against your father. You hate your father. You have never forgiven him for hurting you by not helping you with sports. And do you know what My word says? It says, "Honor your father and your mother," the first commandment with a promise, so that it might go well with you. Have sports gone well with you?*

The answer, of course, was "No." And I came to see that the Lord didn't care about my good intentions. They were all based on the wrong motives. What God cares about is the heart—and whether His Son is King of our hearts. We're not good; He is. He came down to die for us and save us because we can't do it for ourselves. We can't be good enough. We can't impress enough people. We can't create the good life or ever be our true and best selves without Him. *There is no substitution for Jesus;* nothing else works but the cross. All of our good intentions fall to the ground at the foot of the cross. That's a good thing, because my good intentions hurt me; they hurt the people around me; and they hurt God. That's just as toxic as it gets—and it's so hard to recognize, because we think of our intentions as good things.

> I CAME TO SEE THAT THE LORD DIDN'T CARE ABOUT MY GOOD INTENTIONS. THEY WERE ALL BASED ON THE WRONG MOTIVES.

Are you beginning to feel like you live in this room? Is this your furniture? Let's look at that last piece—demons. Remember (from Deuteronomy 32:16-17 and 1 Corinthians 10:20-22) that attached to every idol is a demon. What is a false teaching, a wound, a good intention? They are all idols, because they are all competing with the Lordship of Jesus Christ.

This gets very sinister. Going back to the basics, when we accept Jesus into our lives we say that He is Lord of our life; but, we have hidden idols that compete with His Lordship. We say we're led by the Holy Spirit, but we have little demons attached to those idols who compete with the counsel of the Holy Spirit. They are familiar spirits, and they tell us lies, like, "You're just a quiet guy...." "There are other activities, you're not supposed to play basketball...." "You're not supposed to be in fellowship...." and on and on. Before we know it, they are intertwined with our personalities.

We've talked about Satan being the father of lies. In John 8, Jesus said that Satan is a murderer and a liar, and when he lies, he speaks his native tongue. When the devil and demons lie, they have no accent. Their lies can become so familiar we don't even second-guess them. We just take it as part of who we are—like my friend believing he's just a quiet guy—and actually the demons' lie becomes a part of who we are. That part is the false self, though. It's not our true identity, but, thanks be to God, the Truth can set us free.

Let's pause and look at the big picture of the "real me" vs. the "false me." Jesus says in John 14:6, "I am the way, the truth and the life. No one comes to the Father except through Me." Romans 8:14 says, "As many as are led by the Spirit of God, these are sons of God." The Lordship of Jesus and the leading of the Holy Spirit are the keys to sonship and daughterhood. *As long as we still have those idols competing with Jesus as Lord, and their demons competing with the Holy Spirit as counselor, we are not fully free as sons and daughters of the Father. Instead, during the times we are controlled by idols and demons, we are slaves!* The false me, which is a slave, gets no reward for its labor or a future inheritance—no blessings and no destiny. The real me, which is a son or daughter, gets both. That's why every Christian must ask him or herself, "Who's controlling me?" "Who's the real me?" Our promised blessings and God-given destiny to bless others depends on knowing the truth!

> "WHO'S THE REAL ME?" OUR PROMISED BLESSINGS AND GOD-GIVEN DESTINY TO BLESS OTHERS DEPENDS ON KNOWING THE TRUTH!

Think of it this way. When we are Caterpillar Christians, there's a world system from man that we are in—a system of knowledge and works—and we must get out of it. As we discovered in the opening chapters, we had no idea we were in it or that it was a bad system. But there's also a world system from man *in us*—hidden idols. We had no idea it was in us or that it was a bad system, but it must be taken out. There is, however, a right and wrong way to take this system out and leave our father's house, people, and country.

I Left the Wrong Way and it Doesn't Work!

Remember Abraham and the tale of how he left his father's house, his people, and his country? Well, I did that too, but the wrong way. I was angry with my father because he wasn't the kind of dad I wanted, so one day I simply moved out of his house. Before he even knew I had moved, we bumped into each other at a Burger King. I had a big confrontation with him and just blurted out all of my anger and hatred towards him. That's how I left my father's house. Not good.

I also did a very poor job of leaving my people. I was a devout Catholic, and I asked some questions of the brothers at my high school and priests at my church. When they couldn't answer my questions, I got fed up and upset with the church. I said, "This is a bunch of malarkey. God doesn't exist, and I'm going to become an atheist." That's how I left the church.

As for my country, I loved the United States of America and considered myself a big patriot. During the 1960s and the Vietnam War, however, I got very disillusioned with the U.S., and I said, "This is a sham. This is not a good country. I don't like the United States of America anymore."

I left behind the life I knew—my father's house—my people (the church)—and my country. I did it my way, and let me tell you, it didn't work out well!

> I LEFT BEHIND THE LIFE I KNEW—I DID IT MY WAY, AND LET ME TELL YOU, IT DIDN'T WORK OUT WELL!

If we look at the genealogy of Jesus Christ in Luke chapter 3, it starts with Jesus and it goes all the way back through His ancestors to Adam. Then—and this touches my heart—after Adam, it says "Adam, the son of God." Following this example, the Lord showed me that if we want to get out of slavery and fully become sons of God, we must go back through our ancestors. We cannot reject the mother and father He chose for us nor the entry-level religious experience He chose nor our country. If we do, we'll never get back to God.

As I went through this process, He opened my eyes to see things through the lens of grace. I realized that I actually had a father with many positive traits. He had character traits from God, and I got many of those traits from him. I now have honor and respect for my father and a good relationship with him. I see now that I came from my father, and if I reject him, I'm rejecting my own self.

I also looked at the Catholic church and realized similar things. You know what? Its history goes back a long ways. There were a lot of Godly people in the Catholic church in the past, as there are now. Catholics are pro-life and have great concern for the poor and needy. If I totally reject the Catholic church, I am rejecting the fruit God has produced in that church through history and the fruit He is producing now.

And finally, as I looked at my country, I accepted that even though it has many flaws, it's a wonderful country. Real God-fearing people came to found this country, and it was founded on Christian principles. There are a lot of positive things about the U.S. It's a place of freedom, a very generous nation, and it's the country God chose for me to be born in.

I was wrong in the way I left those three things—my father's house, my people, and my country—and if you've done that too, if you've left any of those things the wrong way, I'd encourage you to reassess them. We have to humble ourselves before the mighty hand of God and say, "You chose my parents, You chose how I would come to You, and this is the country You chose for my birth. I am the clay and You are the Potter. I trust You." After all, who are we as clay to wag our fingers at those things? When we do that, we're really wagging our fingers at the Potter, who is God! In my case, the Lord said, *Guess what. When you're done with your biggest protest, Cesar Suarez is still your father. You first heard about Me in the Catholic church. You're still a U.S. citizen. You can have a tantrum all you want, but it will never change those three things.* It's amazing.

I believe He wants to tenderize our hearts. We can't walk with Him with that kind of judgment, anger, or repulsiveness. We can't live in hatred of the sources of our life. It may feel like a high spiritual plain, but it's Death Valley. It's nowhere. That's what He taught me. Though this chapter is not primarily on forgiveness, we are to forgive our parents, our churches and schools, and our country. For all of the false teachings, wounds, and good intentions that came out of those things, we are to forgive them and say, "I forgive you just as I have been forgiven. I forgive you because you didn't know what you were doing." I release you. You don't owe me anything; your account is clear. My Source is God, and I'm going to put the ax to any bitter root that's been growing in me. At the foot of the cross, we forgive, we release, and the slate is clean. We have honor and respect and we have love for them.

Then guess what happens: now we can leave behind the life we know. My wife can leave behind the false teaching of her father and have fellowship with others. She can say, "I'm leaving that false teaching, but I'm not leaving my father." That's the difference. We can leave a false teaching or a wound without leaving the source of that false teaching or the source of that wound.

In leaving, we embrace. It's a mind-boggling concept, but remember, the Kingdom of God is about opposites: give to receive, be humble to be exalted. We leave by embracing. So we need to ask the Lord to search our hearts. Whatever's between us and our father's house, people, and country, let's deal with it. I would encourage everybody to do that. No matter how old we are, we can all still have issues. Time does not heal all wounds. I know an eighty-eight-year-old woman who, to this day, talks about her parents' deaths and being in an orphanage. That wound is as real to her today as it was then, but with Jesus it doesn't have to be. Look what Isaiah 53:3-4 says:

> He is despised and rejected by men,
> A Man of sorrows and acquainted with grief.
> And we hid, as it were, our faces from Him;
> He was despised, and we did not esteem Him.
> Surely He has borne our griefs
> And carried our sorrows;
> Yet we esteemed Him stricken,
> Smitten by God, and afflicted.

He bore the sorrows and pains of our wounds so we wouldn't have to. But how do we give them to Him? The key is the phrase *remission of our sins*. We need to both forgive the person who wounded us and remit their sin also—that is, give the pain, sorrow, and any damage caused by that sin to Jesus on the cross. Then not only are they released, but we are released also, so that wound does not affect and control us for the rest of our lives.

Getting rid of idols—and I can say this from experience—is very humbling, even breaking. We'll get into it a lot deeper in the next chapter, but I want to plant a little seed here. A humility seed. It's in Jeremiah 17:9-10, and it's God's way of helping us to see how badly we need Him. If we have any delusions that we can figure this out on our own—what our hidden idols are and what's really going on inside of us—we need this scripture. It says, "The heart is deceitful above all things, and desperately wicked; who can know it? I, the Lord, search the heart, I test the mind, even to give every man according to his ways, according to the fruit of his doings." If my heart is deceitful above all things, how in the world could I ever rely on my own heart, my own soul and mind, to figure out the truth? It's not going to happen. I will be deceived, and I will deceive myself.

I'll plant another seed. It says in Proverbs 28:26 (NIV) that "He who trusts in himself is a fool." And, Proverbs 3:5 says to trust in the Lord with all of our hearts and lean not on our own understanding. Why does the Lord tell us this? Because our minds and emotions can be tricked very easily.

Want proof? Consider how television works. I was in the television business, and I can tell you, everything in it is staged. It's all fake. But really, it's doubly fake. They take a fake staged scene, and then they have electrons that either fly through the air or through cables, and then they reconfigure them and they put them on a screen. That means what we see is really twice fake. Nevertheless, it can make us laugh and cry. It can make us angry or hate. It can make us scared. It can make us feel every emotion known to man—and it's all fake! Scary, isn't it?

The enemy's method is the same for the sincere Christian. His version of TV is our hidden idols with demons attached. He tricks us into feeling that what we're doing is a good thing—good ministry, good works, good parenting, good stewardship, good intentions. Yet all the while it's fake. We're operating with false motives, out of our false selves. Remember, an idol is a false god, something that appears to be good and God but isn't. So, as we say to the Lord, "Search me, and bring the *false me* into Your light," we must again apply the principle of embracing our past in order to leave it.

Embracing My Sins To Leave The Right Way

We've discussed that there is a right and wrong way to leave our father's house, people, and country. We must forgive, embrace, and respect them in order to leave the lifestyle of our *false me*. After we ask the Lord to search us, we will discover a second thing: our *false me* sinned and hurt the people around us who we love the most. What do we do about that?

When He shows us the sin and junk that was inside us that we were not aware of, and how it hurt Him, us, and the family and friends we love, we can't run and hide like Adam and Eve did. When they sinned, they covered themselves with fig leaves and hid behind the trees (Genesis 3:7-8). Spiritually speaking, we must stand naked and not try to defend ourselves. We must admit our sins to God and those people we have hurt. As we repent and ask for forgiveness, we confess that we desperately need God's grace that was poured out for us on the cross. What we are doing is fully embracing our past in order to leave it.

How can anyone of us do such a difficult thing? We can, when we come to know that we are wonderful—we're made in God's image and likeness because a piece of Him is in us—that we're a prince or a princess, because when we were born again we became the son or daughter of a King. We know who the *real me* is. We also know that the *false* me is forgiven by God. Romans 8:1 says there is no condemnation towards me because I am in Christ. In fact, all my sins have been remitted, meaning all of the judgment and punishment that I deserve has been taken by Jesus on the cross. In God's sight, which is the only view that matters, all of my sins have been removed. In fact, He says this: *For I shall be merciful to their unrighteousness, and their sins and their lawless deeds I will remember no more* (Hebrews 8:12 NIV).

Even though I understood who the *real me* was, and the *false me* was forgiven, for me, this was not an easy concept to carry out. For example, my *false me* was overly driven. I pushed myself and those around me very hard, and at times tried to control them, and this wounded them. But, I had also done many things with a pure heart that had blessed them. For some, all they remembered were the wounds, not the blessings. In their woundedness, they falsely accused me of things that went beyond my actual sins. This was very painful for me.

THE OPINIONS OF PEOPLE DIDN'T MATTER TO JESUS BECAUSE HE KNEW WHO HE WAS AND THAT THE FATHER LOVED HIM.

Here's how the Lord got me through. He spoke this question to my heart, "If it takes you being falsely accused of some things in order for those people you wounded to be set free by Me, will you do it?" When He asked this question, I realized that it was what Jesus did to save me! But His pain was far worse, because He was without sin. Not a single thing that He was accused of was true! That certainly put my little pity party in a whole new perspective. Philippians 2:7 says Jesus made Himself of no reputation; the opinions of people didn't matter to Him because He knew who He was and that the Father loved Him. Because of that, His only desire was to obey His Father and help people. When I fully embraced my past sins in front of these people, repented, and chose not to defend myself even against their false accusations, a funny thing happened—it actually improved my self-esteem! Through this toughest of tests, I came to the place where how I felt about myself was not connected to how others felt about me—whether they were right or wrong. It's a wonderful place of freedom!

This two-part big picture that we must embrace in order to leave behind the *life we know*, can be understood through the verses of this song:

AT THE CROSS
I know a place, a wonderful place
Where accused and condemned
Find mercy and grace
Where the wrongs we have done
And the wrongs done to us
Were nailed there with Him
There on the cross.[2]

First, no matter how many bad things happened to me from my father's house, people, and country I can now forgive, embrace, and respect them because it's all been taken care of at the cross. I leave the lifestyle of the *false me*, but I don't leave them. Second, I do the same with my *false me* sins that have hurt God, myself, and those around me. I can admit them, fully embrace my past, without defending myself, repent, and ask for forgiveness—because at the cross they're all gone. That's how to leave behind what's been done to us, and what we've done to others, the right way.

---

2 Randy Butler, Terry Butler. Copyright © 1997 by Mercy/Vineyard Publishing. All rights reserved.

So we say to the life we knew, "Good riddance!" We're leaving that life behind—our father's house, our people, our country—and all of the associated baggage, which is the false teachings, the wounds, the good intentions, and the demons. We're going to the cross and dying to self. I know that sounds scary, but the good news is that, while the false self is being put to death, the real self—the real person—is being set free. We got brainwashed into thinking it's a bad thing to leave the old life behind, but it's a *good* thing. We will never enter the promised land to receive our inheritance, and fulfill our purpose and destiny, until we leave behind our false identity.

So let's go! Let's move out and claim our purpose, our destiny, our power, our peace—through the blood of Jesus. Remember, there's a right way (and a wrong way) to do it, so let's leave behind the life we know by first embracing it and then moving on in victory to a new life.

My Personal One-on-One Encounter With The Lord

ALSO FOR HOME GROUP DISCUSSION

Do I understand how much control my past has over me, that literally a false me was created by my father's house, people, and country? What are some examples of this in my own life?

_____

_____

_____

_____

Do I realize that these hidden idols in me, in the form of false teachings, wounds, and good intentions, compete with the Lordship of Jesus? As I say "Search me, O Lord", what hidden idols are beginning to surface?

_____

_____

_____

_____

Do I understand that the demons attached to these idols compete with the leading of the Holy Spirit? As these hidden idols began to surface, what lying familiar spirits were attached to them that were affecting my personality? (Example, a demon saying, "You're just a quiet guy.")

_____

_____

_____

_____

Do I truly believe that the wrongs I have done, and the wrongs done to me, were totally taken care of at the cross? If so, can I fully embrace both these things by bringing the _false me_ to the cross, to leave that lifestyle behind? What is the Lord asking me to bring to the cross now?

_____

_____

_____

_____

Am I tired of being a prisoner of my past, and am I ready to be set free by leaving behind the life I know, so that I can receive my promised blessings and fulfill my God-given destiny?

_____

_____

_____

_____

❧ REFLECTING ON THE ART ❧

- In what way does the painting that opens this chapter speak to me?
- Did the sketch have an impact on me? If so, how?

_____

_____

_____

_____

Vertical Beam of the Cross

REMOVING HIDDEN IDOLS

CHAPTER 9

Vertical Beam of the Cross
REMOVING HIDDEN IDOLS

Search me, O God, and know my heart;
Try me, and know my anxieties;
And see if there is any wicked way in me,
And lead me in the way everlasting.
Psalm 139:23-24

NOW THAT WE ARE LEAVING THE OLD LIFE BEHIND, we are ready to go to the cross—the first part of the lost secret. It's time to embrace the cross, and to do that, we're going to focus first on the vertical beam, the one that points upward and connects us to God. It's just between us and Him. Let's ask God to shine His searchlight on our hearts. Let's authorize Him to search us deeply, completely, to see if there are any hidden things we need to deal with and put behind us. We've talked about how to leave, and now we're going to talk about the things we're leaving, which are idols.

You know those verses above, from Psalm 139? It's a very interesting thing, but in Hebrew, the word *wicked* in that passage actually means "idols that cause pain." As we make those verses our prayer, let's allow the Lord to reveal to us any idols that are causing pain—to us, God, and the people around us—so we can remove them from our lives forever.

In Joshua 24, there are two kinds of idols that are identified, and they come from two different places. Joshua 24:14-15 says,

> *"Now therefore, fear the Lord, serve Him in sincerity and in truth, and put away the gods which your fathers served on the other side of the River and in Egypt. Serve the Lord! And if it seems evil to you to serve the Lord, choose for yourselves this day whom you will serve, whether the gods which your fathers served that were on the other side of the River, or the gods of the Amorites, in whose land you dwell. But as for me and my house, we will serve the Lord."*

There were two kinds of idols: idols from across the river and idols in the Promised Land.

We've discussed the idols of our father's house, our people, and our country—idols like those Abraham had to leave across the river. I think we all understand those. But what about the idols we've picked up in the Promised Land—the Caterpillar Christian idols?

THERE IS A BIG DIFFERENCE BETWEEN THE THINGS OF GOD AND GOD HIMSELF.

You know, God says, "I am a jealous God; don't put anything ahead of Me" (Exodus 20:3-5, paraphrased)... This is what He taught me about Promised Land idols: There is a big difference between the things of God and God Himself. The things of God are the five majestic trees we caterpillars like to live in—the Word, prayer, praise and worship, fellowship in church meetings, and ministry. Those are all wonderful things from God, but they are not God. If we ever put one or more of those things ahead of God, guess what that is? Idolatry. An idol is a false god, because it is not God Himself.

I believe God is saying, "Let's keep first things first. The most important thing is not how much you learn about Me or do for Me. It's about Me and you." If there's one thing God wants us to get out of this, it's that *He doesn't want anything between us and Him.* Again, I'm not saying that the five majestic trees are bad. They are wonderful, but we can never place them above Him.

This can shake a lot of people up, but if we look at the different cultures in the church, we'll find lots of idols. In some places it's prayer. Prayer is the big thing—they are cutting-edge with prayer. Or worship. It's all about worship. They say, "You're going to be worshipping in heaven all of the time, so worship is the most important thing." Worship is big. Then there's fellowship and ministry—same thing. Many of the movements that have gone amuck, many of the churches we see out there today—they would swear on a polygraph machine that they don't have any idols in their culture. But they do. And God is a jealous God.

There is no more lucid example of this than the life of Abraham. Isaac, his son, was a gift that came from God. He was not God, but He was God's promised blessing—God's idea. Yet, in Abraham's final test on Mount Moriah, God was saying, "Here is the gift from Me, My promise that is totally Me. He is the most important thing in your life. Kill him, because I want to find out if you love Me more than anything."

The closest thing to God in Abraham's life was Isaac. He was the manifestation of God's promise. And yet, God wanted to see if Abraham was willing to give him up—even put him to death—to prove that God was first. That's a perfect picture of what we all must do at the cross. God is saying to each one of us, "What idols have you picked up, strange as this may sound, from Me?" What are the things you've picked up in the Promised Land, once you were born again?

WE'RE LOOKING AT EVERY ONE OF OUR IDOLS…ALL OF THEM.

That's why this is a real shake-up message—because we're looking at every one of our idols. All of them, every one. Even the ones that look good. Maybe especially those! Remember, Satan takes something good, misapplies it, and then causes bad things to happen.

How good is the Word of God? Since my ministry call is being a teacher, I don't think the Bible is good, I believe it's great! What happens, though, when Satan tempts me or you to make the Word of God more important than God Himself or Jesus Christ crucified? He takes something good and misapplies it, puts it in a place that it doesn't belong—on the throne—and turns it into an idol.

You may be like me. When the Bible came up as a possible idol, my thought was: John 1:14 says that Jesus was the Word that became flesh, so my love for the Word is the same as loving Jesus Himself. But a thought came to me. When I go to heaven and meet Jesus, I won't be hugging a Bible with arms, legs, and a head attached, I'll be embracing a person! God who became man in a risen and glorified body! A living being with thoughts, feelings, and emotions. The person of Jesus is different than the Bible. Those of us who love the Word need to understand that. Then, the Word will be much more effective in our lives.

Think of a cannonball being the Word, and a cannon being Jesus. If we try and lift that cannonball and throw it, there won't be much effect. But if we shoot it from a cannon, we put a lot of force behind it. Jesus, who is the power of God, is the cannon force behind the Word. That's why Jesus said in Revelation 2:3-4, you "have labored for My name's sake and have not become weary. Nevertheless I have this against you, that you have left your first love." The message is this. We can put a lot of effort into the Word, but if we want it to be powerful and effective, we must keep Jesus as our first love.

Back to Abraham and Isaac. God never really wanted Abraham to get rid of Isaac, something from the Lord. He wanted Abraham to have both Him and Isaac, but to keep his priorities straight. So it is with us and the five majestic trees, including the Word. He wants us to have both, but with Him first! Then the Word, prayer, worship, fellowship, and ministry will be backed with much more power!

A closing thought on how much we love God Himself versus things from God. 1 Peter 2:6, says, "Behold, I lay in Zion a chief cornerstone, elect, precious, and he who believes on Him will by no means be put to shame."

What's my favorite thing? Is it Jesus?

The chief cornerstone is Jesus, and the word *elect* in the Greek means "favorite thing." If we were really honest with ourselves, would we say that one or more of the five majestic trees is our favorite thing in our Christian walk, or is it Jesus Christ and Him crucified? That's certainly something to pause, pray about, and consider.

If you're still struggling with the concept of God Himself vs. the things of God, remember, Jesus is a rock of offense. The biggest stumbling block on our spiritual journey will be Jesus Himself! Ask the Holy Spirit to show you whether this concept is wrong or if it's Jesus offending you—He will.

Moving on, let's take a closer look at idolatry. I know the Bible teaches that sin is sin, but we Christians are famous (or infamous) for harshly judging what we believe to be the "worst" sins, like homosexuality, but when it comes to gossip or gluttony—well, those go on at most any church potluck. We shrug them off as not really important. God says we're not supposed to do that. It's like a "white lie;" to Him there's no such thing. A lie's a lie, and sin is sin.

With that said, however, I do believe two seemingly conflicting truths can exist side by side in Him who is the Truth. The second truth I believe about sin is that *idolatry is the biggest and baddest sin*. Let's prove it by looking at three things in Scripture.

Number one is that idolatry was the first sin. Have you ever heard the saying, "You only have one chance to make a good first impression?" There's only one chance for something to be first, and guess what happened to be the very first sin? Idolatry. In Genesis 3:5, Satan told Eve, "For God knows that in the day you eat of it your eyes will be opened, and you will be like God." It was not enough to be God's child, she wanted to *be* God.

God said to Eve and He says to us, "I want you to be my child."

We say, "No, I want to be You." And He says, "No, you don't understand. I AM God."

Wanting to be God—judging right and wrong, being in control, being lord over our own lives—is idolatry. It was the first sin.

The second thing we will look at in the Scriptures is the Ten Commandments. Exodus 20:1-5 says,

And God spoke all these words, saying: "I am the Lord your God, who brought you out of the land of Egypt, out of the house of bondage. You shall have no other gods before Me. You shall not make for yourselves a carved image—any likeness of anything that is in heaven above, or that

Finding My Hidden Idols

My Kids
My Mate
Being Good
Working Hard
Ministry
The Word
Being Liked
Control
Sports

is in the earth beneath, or that is in the water under the earth; you shall not bow down to them nor serve them. For I, the Lord your God, am a jealous God."

Idolatry is the first commandment, though we tend to focus more on the other nine. *Gosh, I don't lie; I don't steal; I don't covet my neighbor's wife; I don't cheat; I don't kill. Look how good I am doing, Lord.*

And He says, *You've got big problems. You're full of idols, and that's the number one commandment. Don't put anything above Me. Not anything.*

> **IDOLATRY IS THE FIRST COMMANDMENT, THOUGH WE TEND TO FOCUS MORE ON THE OTHER NINE.**

Let's go on a hunt for idols. They can be in the strangest places! I'm going to tell you some of the idols we've seen in the church. One is the Godly spouse. We have husbands who say, "My wife is just so much more spiritual than me. She's the spiritual head of the house. If I want to check things out with God, I just go to my wife, because she's close to God."

That sounds great—sounds honoring. And many of these women *are* intensely Godly women. But when their husbands put them on a pedestal, they become idols. And God is saying, *I appreciate the fact that you have a spiritual wife. I'm crazy about her, too. But, guess what, I'm God. And I have called you to be the spiritual head of the house.*

What about work? I work. I'm a hard worker—have worked hard all my life. We're not to be lazy. It's a good thing to work hard, but work can get misapplied and misdirected, and then that good thing becomes an idol. It happens all the time.

Another one is kids. Parents love their kids so much they'll do anything for them. We're supposed to love our kids as gifts from God; we're supposed to bring them up to know Him and love Him. But they're not to be in *His* place. They need to learn from us that even they don't come before God.

These three things are all things we would never think could be idols, but they are, and the people that are in the bondage of idolatry have totally rationalized it. They are deceived, and they don't even know it. They're clueless. I know because I've been there!

Here's a little anecdote—a classic example of kids becoming idols. My wife and I were church hunting, and we said, "We're going to find a church for our kids. We're going to do research and find the church that has the best youth group for our kids, because we love our kids." Sounds pretty holy, huh!

We started out. We went from church to church to church, and our kids never got connected anywhere. We lived in a desert for seven years because it never worked! And, at the end of the complete folly of our good intention, do you know what the Lord said to us? *Can I ask you a question? Why didn't you ask Me where to go to church? I'm God. Don't you think maybe I know what the best place for your kids and your whole family is, better than you do? You never asked Me.*

So much for being parents of the year in the local newspaper. It's all a bunch of bunk. It was idolatry—that's all it was—and it never worked. Through our good intention to help our kids, we became lord of our own lives. This goes for every area of our lives: God is saying, *Why don't you ask Me? Am I Lord of your life? Or are you lord of your life?* Who is Lord?

For the slam dunk of why idolatry is our biggest and baddest sin, we'll go to Mark 12:28 (NIV). It's a straightforward question to Jesus: "Of all the commandments, which is the most important?" We've found out that idolatry was the first sin in the garden; it's the subject of the first commandment in the Ten Commandments; and now an expert in the Law asks Jesus, "Which is the most important commandment?"

Jesus didn't quote the first commandment. He quoted Deuteronomy 6:4-5: "'The most important one,' answered Jesus, 'is this: *Hear, O Israel, the Lord our God, the Lord is one. Love the Lord your God with all your heart and with all your soul and with all your mind and with all your strength'*" (Mark 12:29-30).

IF SOMEONE WE LOVE DEEPLY HURTS US, IT CRUSHES OUR HEART. THAT'S A ROMANTIC TERM.

Can I love God with all my heart, soul, and strength if I have idols in my life? Or is there shared affection? Is there a *divided* heart, a shared heart, or a whole heart? All is *all*, isn't it? God said, "Don't have anything—no gods—none—besides Me. Love Me with *all* that you are." If I've got idols, that isn't loving Him with all of my heart, soul, and strength, is it? Part of my heart is bound to those idols. So here we have it three times in the Scripture. The biggest and baddest sin is idolatry.

We talked earlier about how in Psalm 139 the word *wicked* means "idols that cause pain?" How do idols cause pain? The first thing is that they hurt God very, very deeply. Ezekiel 6:9 says, "I was crushed by their adulterous heart which has departed from Me, and by their eyes which play the harlot after their idols." Isn't that a romantic term, that if someone we love deeply hurts us, it crushes our heart?

Think about if your mate was cheating on you. How would you feel? What if your mate said, "I love you ninety percent of the time, I really do, but ten percent of the time I've got to have something else going on the side. I've got this other relationship that I have to keep going." Husbands, could you handle that? Wives?

What if I told my wife, "Honey, I know you'll understand, because I do the lawn for you, I've provided for you, and I'm a good father. Here is my list of good things that I do for you, and I know you're going to understand when I keep a mistress on the side. It's only once every ten days that I go to her. You understand that, right?" Lu Ann would knock my block off, and rightly so. More than that, though, she'd be deeply wounded.

Why do we think the Lord feels any different? It bothers Him a lot. He didn't hold anything back from us; He gave His one and only Son for us. That's how much He loved us. He has nothing left—nothing better He could give. And yet we play the harlot. What did He do to deserve that? It's agonizingly painful to Him. Just as much as it would break our hearts, it breaks His.

The other pain that is caused by idolatry is the pain it causes us. Let's go to Psalm 115:3-7 to see how *we* get hurt. It says,

> *But our God is in heaven;*
> *He does whatever He pleases.*
> *Their idols are silver and gold,*
> *The work of men's hands.*
> *They have mouths, but they do not speak;*
> *Eyes they have, but they do not see;*
> *They have ears, but they do not hear;*
> *Noses they have, but they do not smell;*
> *They have hands, but they do not handle;*
> *Feet they have, but they do not walk;*
> *Nor do they mutter through their throat.*

This next part (vs. 8) astounds me:

> *Those who make them are like them;*
> *So is everyone who trusts in them.*

Those who have idols become like them.

Let's go to Matthew 13:14-15 and see if there's a connection between Psalm 115 and this other, very famous scripture. It says,

> *And in them the prophecy of Isaiah is fulfilled, which says:*
> *"Hearing you will hear and shall not understand,*
> *And seeing you will see and not perceive;*
> *For the hearts of this people have grown dull.*

Their ears are hard of hearing,
And their eyes they have closed,
Lest they should see with their eyes and hear with their ears,
Lest they should understand with their hearts and turn,
So that I should heal them."

I believe that verse is describing Caterpillar Christians. We hear a lot of preaching and teaching. We see a lot when we read the Bible and Christian books. But we have become like our idols; our eyes have been closed, our ears are hard of hearing, and our hearts have become dull, so we never really change on the inside and turn and go in a different direction. In all of our doing, Caterpillar Christians never truly get transformed into new creations in Christ. It's called going through the motions.

How do idols cause us pain? They make us dumb and numb, just like them, and block our access to God's healing power. Combining Psalm 115:3-7 and Matthew 13:14-15 helps answer our question *"Where's the power?"*

> HOW DO IDOLS CAUSE US PAIN? THEY MAKE US DUMB AND NUMB, JUST LIKE THEM, AND BLOCK OUR ACCESS TO GOD'S POWER.

What can we do about these idols that cause God and us pain? Everybody is ready to do something about it, right? But what? Thanks be to God the answer is simple. Not easy, but simple. We must go to the cross. The first thing is humility. We admit to God that we don't even know what our idols are. It's impossible. Jeremiah 17:9-10 says,

The heart is deceitful above all things,
And desperately wicked;
Who can know it?
I, the Lord, search the heart,
I test the mind,
Even to give every man according to his ways,
According to the fruit of his doings.

We understand that when we're born again, our spirit is brand new, but the heart—which also includes our soul (our mind, will, and emotions) has to be transformed through a longer process. We can't rely on it to find out what's really going on inside our lives.

That's why Proverbs 28:26 says, "He who trusts in his own heart is a fool." I'm a fool. You're a fool. Whenever we, as Christians have our little knee-jerk reactions about what is right and wrong in situations, we're fools. Something happens and we react: *I think that's good.... I think that's bad.... I think right now I'm being good.... I think right now I'm being bad.... That worship is out of order.... This is correct worship.... This is where I'm supposed to go to church.... This is where I'm not supposed to go....* The list goes on and on and on. How do I know? How do you know? Our hearts are deceitful above all and desperately wicked. Shall we then trust ourselves? No! The number one thing is to be humble. Say, "I don't know."

I'll use myself as an example on how we really don't know what's inside of us or what's causing our problems. I shared how I was at the end of my rope in 1993—in the pit of all pits. I had major health problems, family problems, legal problems, and I was going bankrupt. I was a Christian, serving God with all of my heart, but a Caterpillar Christian, and I cried out to the Lord. I said, "God! In one second You could heal me; You could solve all of my legal problems; You could solve my family problems; and you could give me a winning product for Fitness Quest. You could get me out of this! *Why won't You do it, God?* Why won't You do it?"

And (I'll never forget it) Father God spoke to my heart and said, *Son, let me show you your real problems. You have a hole in your heart. You have a cold spot in your heart. It's like the black holes in outer space, and no matter how much success you achieve, it gets all sucked in there. And it's never enough.*

He showed me that I had drive gone mad. You know how drive in our body causes our cells to reproduce—that's a healthy thing. But when it's out of control, it's called cancer. That's what I had. And that out-of-control drive was the source of all my problems. It made me sick, because I ran so hard and so fast that my body finally broke down. My drive to do good and my good intention with the Gut Buster safety cord started my legal problems. My attempt to do so many projects at the same time caused me to go broke. I was trying to do so many things at once that I wasn't doing anything justice, so none of the products became the next winner.

The Lord spoke to my heart and told me, *If I answered your request, in a very short period of time you'd be back in the same mess that you are in now. Your drive gone mad would make you sick again, bring other legal problems, and cause you to not have winning products.* Later on I came to realize the real reward of Him not answering my request. If he would have cut my trials short, I never would have been transformed and brought out of conventional Christianity. I never would have suffered loss in order to gain the greatest thing of all, Him!

During the course of these events, I was talking to a friend on the phone, and the Lord spoke these words to me: *You need spiritual surgery.* He gave me the scripture that says, "Create in me a clean heart, O God" (Psalm 51:10). You know what that word *create* means? It means "to cut." The Lord needed to cut my heart—to perform spiritual surgery in order to take out the junk that wasn't supposed to be there and put in what should be—to deal with my real problems. But I had to authorize Him to do it. It wasn't fun, and it got pretty ugly.

You know the story of David and Bathsheba? (See 2 Samuel 11:1–12:25.) When David walked out on his balcony and saw Bathsheba bathing, do you think in that moment he had any idea of what was in his own heart? Here's a man who loved God and whom God called to perform great and mighty deeds in Israel. He was called "a man after [God's] own heart" (1 Samuel 13:14; Acts 13:22). Do you think he knew his own heart? When he first saw Bathsheba, I don't think he had any idea there was adultery and murder in his heart, but they were there. Down deep, they were there all of the time.

I can tell you what, before my spiritual surgery, I could have passed any polygraph test. If anyone had asked me whether I had hidden idols in my heart—the nasty, filthy, stinking things that God had to remove—I'd have said flatly, "No."

"Do you have this?"
"No!"
"This?"
"No!"
"What about this?"
"No, no, no, no, *no*!"

I was totally unaware that any of the junk was in me, but guess what? It was there. God knew it, but I didn't.

This is very bizarre, but it's one of the most profound moments of my life, and of my spiritual surgery. I was at church, and I was down at the altar. I was worshipping God under the anointing of the Holy Spirit, and all of a sudden, from inside me, came every foul, vulgar word you could possibly imagine. They just came spewing out! It was so strange and shocking.

Later on, however, through Christian counseling, the Lord showed me that I was full of lies, pain and rejection. I was full of anger, hate and jealousy. I was full of every vile thing in the world, and I had no clue till that day at the altar when God revealed it to me. I had no idea. But the Father had put His hand on my shoulder and said, *Son, let Me show you what your real problems are.*

SON, LET ME SHOW YOU WHAT YOUR REAL PROBLEMS ARE.

Was it fun? No. Did it make me feel good about myself to find out all of that ugly stuff was in me? No. But you know the old saying, "Better out than in!" It's true for other things, but it's definitely true in spiritual surgery. *Better out than in.*

This is worth noting. All of us to some degree suffered rejection and lack of perfect nurturing as children. Since we're all different, we reacted in different ways. I strived for success. My wife, on the other hand, got into the slavery of service. Her striving was to be the perfect daughter, mother, and homemaker. Others see themselves in less than favorable light. They actually underachieve and live below the level of their God-given gifts and calling. No matter how we react, we all need spiritual surgery.

At the end of the chapter I'm going to include a prayer—and it's an individual decision whether a person wants to pray it—to authorize God to give us spiritual surgery. First, though, I want to share what I believe is wisdom: do not do it alone. Ask the Holy Spirit if you need to get a counselor, and I'll just say this about a Christian counselor: he or she has to be cross-based, and repentance and forgiveness-based. If they're not into that, then don't go to that counselor. Or do it with a small group of people. (I will share principles on how to form a home support group in chapter fifteen.)

In closing let's talk about those demons that are attached to idols. Remember, idols are man-made gods—gods of this world—and Satan is prince of this world. The devil's demons have a legal right to be attached to them. In fact, picture these idols as a beautiful beach. The demons set up lounge chairs, umbrellas, take out their drinks, and are really enjoying themselves.

The Lord showed me this about spiritual warfare, and how to break up their little beach party. He said, *If you want to write a one hundred page book on spiritual warfare, write ninety-nine pages about going to the cross and dying to self, and making Jesus totally Lord of your life and being led by the Holy Spirit. Then you can spend the last page on whatever else you want.* Why? Because if a person dies to self, gets rid of their idols, makes Jesus Lord of all his or her life, and is led by the Spirit, then the party's over for Satan. "*It is no longer I who live, but Christ lives in me*" (Galatians 2:20).

Picture yourself walking up to this beach; however, it's no longer you, but Jesus in you. Do you think those demons will just sit there casually sipping their drinks? The "warfare" happens like this: The demons see Jesus, and they're gone. There's no discussion, nothing to talk about, it's over. Jesus is the mighty King of glory. He's a mighty warrior, and demons can't live in His presence. They have to get out of there. *The devil will wrestle with us in our flesh, but he can't touch Jesus.* James 4:7 summarizes spiritual warfare: "Therefore submit to God. Resist the devil and he will flee from you."

This process of embracing the vertical beam of the cross and saying, "Search me, O Lord, and show me my hidden idols," all happens in the cocoon. The cocoon is a messy place, but it's worth it! It's worth it so the real me can emerge, a wonderful prince or princess becoming a king or queen—a Birthright Butterfly. It's worth it to stop causing God, myself, and the people around me pain. It's worth it to have the power of the cross released to receive my promised blessings. It's worth it to receive the power I need to fulfill my destiny to bless others.

The false me, controlled by idols and demons, can never experience these things. Just like in the art at the beginning of the chapter, these idols must be exposed by the bright light of the cross of Jesus Christ. No matter how hard it seems, God says it will be worth it!

We've embraced the vertical beam of the cross...now it's time to explore the horizontal beam.

My Personal One-on-One Encounter With The Lord

ALSO FOR HOME GROUP DISCUSSION

Do I understand that idols are false gods, something that appears to be good and God but isn't? What might some of my idols be?

_____

_____

Have I discovered that idols come from two places: across the river which is my father's house, people, and country, but also from the Promised Land, which are the five majestic trees?

_____

_____

When I ask myself, "What's my favorite thing?" am I honest enough to admit that one or more of the five majestic trees have taken the place of Jesus Christ and Him crucified? If the answer is yes, which of these five trees have become idols in my life?

_____

_____

Why is idolatry the #1 sin?

_____

_____

When I choose idols, what am I actually doing to God's heart? What painful experience, in human relations, does the Bible compare idolatry to?

_____

_____

Does the prayer on the next page express the deepest desire of your heart? If so, use it as a guide as you ask the Lord to search you.

_____

_____

Spiritual Surgery Prayer

Search me, O God, and know my heart; try me, and know my anxieties; see if there is any wicked way in me (idols that cause pain); and lead me in the way of everlasting. Create in me a pure heart and put a new, steadfast spirit within me. I trust You, Lord, like I would a surgeon, to open me up and expose my hidden idols so I can take them to the cross. I do not want shared lordship any longer between You, Jesus, and idols. I choose this day to make You Lord over every area of my life. I invite You now to be Lord of my entire heart, which is both my emotions and thinking, Lord of my body and my behavior, Lord of my tongue and the things that I say, Lord of my will and all of my decisions, Lord of my sexuality, Lord of my time, my home, my family, my work, my money and my possessions, and all of my relationships with others. I also ask You to expose any demons attached to those idols that are competing with the Holy Spirit as counselor. I will then command them to flee in the name of Jesus and through the power of His blood. From this day forward, I only want to receive counsel from Your Holy Spirit. Thank You, Jesus, that Your blood was shed that I might be free.

Amen

 ## Reflecting on the Art

· In what way does the painting that opens this chapter speak to me?
· Did the sketches have an impact on me? If so, how?

_____

_____

_____

_____

_____

Horizontal Beam of the Cross

DEALING WITH OFFENSES

Horizontal Beam of the Cross
DEALING WITH OFFENSES

IF WE'RE HONEST, the lost secret of the cross is not an easy one to embrace. It's a scary thing to do. But I believe at this point in the book the Lord is reaching out to calm your fears. He sees the big picture, and He wants to instill in your heart—once and for all—that the cross is *for* you, not against you.

You can stand before that cross, and no matter what you're going through, you can reach out and take hold of it. You can grab hold of that cross and hang on for dear life. When the going gets tough, if you are grabbing onto the cross you will never be blown away; you will never be destroyed.

I've been there. I know. Now the cross is my anchor. It's my lifeline in an unpredictable sea. No longer am I tossed about like a person without any hope. The winds may come, and lightening may strike all around me. Worldly success may blow in and out. But with my head resting on the chest of Jesus—just like the apostle John at the last supper —I'm secure. I know that Jesus Christ in me cannot be overcome.

What does Jesus promise when we grab hold of that cross? First and foremost, He transforms us into His image and likeness; we become new creations in Christ. He then reconciles us as sons and daughters to His Father, who becomes *our* Father. Next, He reconciles us to ourselves—no more false me versus real me—we see ourselves as wonderful princes and princesses becoming kings and queens. Finally,

He reconciles us to each other as brothers and sisters in Christ, and we will never be alone—*never*. We won't have to fight battles alone; we will always have fellowship. Whatever separation there was between us and God, us and ourselves, and our brothers and sisters in Christ, that separation is gone. In this supernatural world of love we also have joy and peace, even in the midst of our battles.

After that, He promises to release power. Victory over sin, victory over demons, victory over the curses in our lives—complete victory is ours in the cross, because Jesus won the victory for us there. He bore every sin and curse, and He stripped the principalities of their power and made an open display of them all on the cross (Colossians 2:15).

We don't have to walk slumped down as failures. We're going to have power to walk in victory, the power to receive our promised blessings, and fulfill our destiny to carry out our call to bless others. What is more, I believe we will do it with signs and wonders following. God is not playing games; this is the real deal. But we have to use the cross as our handholds.

What are we holding onto when we grab the cross? We're holding onto the horizontal beam of the cross. We've talked about the vertical beam, right? It symbolizes our relationship directly between us and the Lord.

But guess what? A cross is not a cross without a horizontal beam. It's just a big "I." That's all it is. It has to be crossed! What is the horizontal beam? It's *people*. And what the Lord is showing us is that if we want to find out where our hearts truly are toward Him—vertically—then we need to check out where we are horizontally. That's the part we leave out in the church, and that's the *second part of the lost secret...real Christian community!* In chapter fifteen we will discuss how being in home group relationships, connected by the cross, releases God's love and

TO REALLY KNOW HOW WELL OUR VERTICAL RELATIONSHIP WITH GOD IS GOING, WE MUST CHECK OUT OUR HORIZONTAL RELATIONSHIPS WITH PEOPLE.

power. But for now, let's focus on how our relationships with each other are an indicator of the health of our relationship with God.

What's the very first thing we do to check out a person's physical heart? We go to the doctor's office and take their pulse, right? If we want to find out what's going on with our hearts, with regards to the Lord, the pulse is this: How are we loving one another? Simply stated, to really know how well our vertical relationship with God is going, we must check out our horizontal relationships with people.

In Scripture, Jesus was very clear about how we are to love. He says in John 13:34-35, "A new commandment I give to you, that you love one another; as I have loved you, that you also love one another. By this all will know that you are My disciples, if you have love for one another."

The old commandment was, "Love your neighbor as yourself" (Leviticus 19:18). That's not good enough. Do you know why? Because apart from Christ, we don't really love ourselves. The new command is to love one another *as He* loves. That's the new standard—the gold standard.

Jesus puts it all together in John 14:15 when He says, "If you love Me, keep My commandments." What He is saying is, if you truly love Me vertically, you will keep My commands. And My horizontal command is to love one another as I have loved you. That's a pretty tall order, but by God's grace we can do it.

Let's explore this horizontal beam a little bit. A lot of Christians (and I was one of them, and to what degree I still am I don't know, but my prayer is to daily put the old man to death at the cross) say that they really love God, and their proof—their résumé—is what they do with the big five. Remember the five majestic trees? We say, "My proof that I love God is that I am into the Word all of the time, I pray a lot, and I praise a lot (lots of thanksgiving, praise and worship); I go to church services on Sunday morning and Sunday night and Wednesday; I go to conferences, seminars, and camp meetings; and I do a lot of ministry projects. That proves that I love God, right?"

Admit it. We've all been there, haven't we? We've measured ourselves and other people—at least to some degree, some of the time—by looking at how we did on the big five. But there's one hitch. There was another group of people when Jesus walked the earth called the Pharisees. They *said* they loved God more than anyone else. They knew more *about God* than anybody else, and they did more things *for God* than anybody else, but it's interesting. This all worked as long as God was invisible.

1 John 4:20-21 says this: "If someone"—and that someone could be me, or you, or the Pharisees we're talking about—"says, 'I love God,'

and hates his brother, he is a liar; for he who does not love his brother whom he has seen, how can he love God whom he has not seen? And this commandment we have from Him [Jesus]: that he who loves God must love his brother also."

It all worked in the fake little world the Pharisees were living in. They were able to deceive themselves and others into believing they were holy; it worked great as long as God was invisible. But when Emmanuel came—"God with us" (Matthew 1:23)—they killed Him. *They killed Him!*

Now fast forward two thousand years. Is God with us as Emmanuel today, visibly? Yes He is. You know why? Because the Bible says everyone is made in God's image and likeness—all human beings have a piece of the Father in them. And those human beings who have accepted Jesus as Lord and Savior of their lives take another step. We have Jesus Christ and the Holy Spirit living inside of us—we're the temple of the living God.

GOD IS VISIBLY HERE FOR ALL OF US, AND HERE'S THE QUESTION: HOW ARE WE TREATING HIM?

Therefore we aren't in any different boat than the Pharisees are. God is visibly here for all of us, and here's the question: How are we treating Him?

He's right here, as you read this book. He's in our marriages and with our children. He's in the church and all around us, in the people we know. He's right here in visible form. And I believe He is saying, "Don't tell Me how much you love Me just based on your vertical relationship. Show Me how much you love Me based on your horizontal relationship, and then you will get *all* of the cross." That takes it to a little different dimension— to a little different place. It brings much more reality to our relationship with God, and it separates the fakers and actors from the real deal.

Do you think it's an accident that He warned, "Be on your guard against the yeast of the Pharisees" (Matthew 16:6 NIV)? His meaning was to beware of hypocrisy. You know what the meaning of the Greek word for hypocrisy (*hypokrisis*) is? "To act or be an actor." Some of us are great actors—we're acting a good part. But, as a TV host during my childhood, Captain Penny, said, "You can fool some of the people all of the time, and all of the people some of the time, but you can't fool Mom." We can't fool God! He sees through the act every time. The church may go through the motions, but we can't act with God. His standard is, "How are you loving one another?" And He sees our *hearts*.

Remember when we talked about the leavened and blended church, and how when you blend something, you water it down or dilute it? It becomes weakened. And that's what Caterpillar Christians are living in—a leavened and blended church, watered down by the wisdom of the world. To connect that concept with what we're addressing here, what kind of Christians would a weakened church produce? Weakened church = weak Christians = weak relationships. And when the going gets tough, relationships fall apart because they are weak. Just like a tree without strong roots, a storm can blow it down. We need to change our weak relationships into strong, deep ones.

One way we do that is to be each other's mirror. Did you ever try putting on make-up or shaving without a mirror? Try it sometime. I can't see my own face without a mirror, so I will never see all of my blind spots without you as my mirror. This is a very important concept when it comes to the horizontal beam of the cross. We will never deal with all of the junk inside of us just by vertically saying, "Search me, Lord." We need each other. We need to bump into each other and interact with each other for all of our blind spots to be exposed. John Donne said, "No man is an island," and no woman is either. We need each other desperately in order to deal with our blind spots. That's why the second part of the lost secret of Christian community is so important.

WE NEED EACH OTHER DESPERATELY IN ORDER TO DEAL WITH OUR BLIND SPOTS.

But I don't just need you for my blind spots. I also need you when I'm down. We're on this journey together, and I need your help along the way. We've got to be vitally linked to each other to be linked to Him. Like sap flowing through the branches that are attached to the vine, we can't function without each other. And cutting off ourselves from one another eventually cuts us off from life—from Him who *is* our Life. There are a million reasons to get unlinked—a whole bunch of reasons, like wounds and distasteful experiences—but God is saying, "No. Hold on. Hold on to that horizontal beam."

Let's go back to being mirrors for each other. There is a whole list of scriptures that say this in one way or another. Proverbs 27 (NIV) contains just a few: "Better is open rebuke than hidden love" (verse 5); "Wounds from a friend can be trusted, but an enemy multiplies kisses" (verse 6); "Perfume and incense bring joy to the heart, and the pleasantness of one's friend springs from his earnest counsel" (verse 9); and "As iron sharpens iron, so one man sharpens another" (verse 17). God is saying, "You have friends there for a reason, to rebuke you when you need rebuked, to give you a blow when you need a blow." Right? We just can't make it without our friends.

That leads us to the concept of accountability. I know there has been a ton of abuse in this area, and people are scared to death of it because they don't understand it. But we have a choice to make whether or not we're going to be connected to—and accountable to—other Christians. It's a choice. If I make that choice, I'm coming to you to say, "This is my destiny; this is what God called me to do or change; this is what God told me to work on. I am asking you to hold me accountable for that. I'm asking you to cover my back, where my blind spots are. I'm asking you to be there, to discipline me and rebuke me when I need it."

You're not butting into my life or trying to manipulate or control me. You're not telling me what to do. I'm asking you to do this. As it says in Ephesians 5:21 (NIV), "Submit to one another," I am choosing to submit myself to you. To be vulnerable to you. You can't help me unless I open up myself to you, so for the sake of safety, I'm choosing to be accountable.

It's really this simple. I come to you and say "Here are the areas of my flesh that I'm working on to put to death on the cross. And here's my God-given purpose and destiny that I'm walking out. If there's anything that you see that I don't, please let me know."

Do you know why God wants us to enter into these accountability relationships? Because He loves us. There's an aspect of God's love that never flows directly, or vertically, from God to us, because He chooses to use a vessel. Those vessels are people. We will never be totally transformed or fully fulfill our destiny without the help of other believers. A cross is not a cross without the horizontal beam.

A CROSS IS NOT A CROSS WITHOUT THE HORIZONTAL BEAM.

We see that we need each other for accountability, for support, for blind spots. Another big reason we need each other—and this one is not quite so obvious or pleasant—is for hurts. Sometimes there are hurts that greatly help us.

Remember the movie *Snow White and the Seven Dwarfs*? Remember all of those little guys, how they would go to work down in the mines? And what was down there? Cartload after cartload of precious gems. There were diamonds, rubies, emeralds—every little kid watching the movie wanted to get into one of those carts and go down to dig.

Did you know that place exists outside of Disney's fantasy world? It is the most precious mine that could ever be tapped for our spiritual growth. Do you know what it is? Rejection. The times we've been hurt. That's where the diamonds are.

In Isaiah 53:3 the Bible says that He was "despised and rejected by men." If we apply the kingdom principle of loss turning into gain, we can see why our hurts greatly help us. Rejection takes us into the cocoon of loss, but what we gain through the experience is identification with Jesus. It's a cross experience. By partaking of His sufferings, and being conformed to His death—our *sum morphos* transforming union into Birthright Butterflies—*we gain God Himself*. And I'll say this again: We only get so much of the jewels with the vertical beam of the cross. We will never hit the mother load until we visit our rejections—the offenses in our lives—and put them under the Lordship of Jesus Christ. When that happens to you personally, you'll be blown away at the riches. I have been.

Why do we run from it? The reason is flat out proof of how shallow and carnal we are as Caterpillar Christians: fight or flight. When an offense occurs, we handle it like we live in the animal kingdom. When there is a confrontation, animals either have fight or flight. There is no middle ground; they never try to reconcile. And in all honesty, that's the same as the church much of the time. We say we're different, and we say that we're spiritual and not carnal. But most of the time, I'm either going to get together with you to straighten you out, and we're going to get into a fight, or we're done. I don't care how long I've known you. I don't care about the depth of my relationship with you. I don't care about anything else. I'll never talk to you again in my life—and we're super-spiritual Christians?

Are we? We're not. We're more like members of the animal kingdom. They do that. And the last time I checked, there's not one animal that is born again; they don't exist. But there are lots of born-again Christians who fight like cats and dogs because we're not quite as spiritual as we think we are. We're on a big high horse.

That's a sobering segue into the Lordship of Jesus over our offenses. What did Jesus say? "Not everyone who says to Me, 'Lord, Lord,' shall enter the kingdom of heaven." There will be people who plead with Him, "But, Lord, we did mighty things in your name...we've cast out demons..." And He will say, "That's all great, but are you doing the will of My Father?" (Matthew 7:21-23, paraphrased).

Let's look at offenses and see what Jesus said about them. He said four basic things about how to deal with an offense with a brother or sister. This means that we each have a decision to make...will Jesus be Lord over the offenses in our life? The first is, "Be humble." In Matthew 7:3-5 Jesus asks "Why do you look at the speck in your brother's eye, but do not consider the plank in your own eye? Or how can you say to your brother, 'Let me remove the speck from your eye'; and look, a plank is in your own eye? Hypocrite! First remove the plank from your own eye, and then you will see clearly to remove the speck from your brother's eye."

We've learned that Jesus is the wisdom of God, so let's explore the wisdom of His words. First, Jeremiah 17:9 says, "The heart is deceitful above all things, and desperately wicked; who can know it?" Second, the Bible says that Satan is the accuser of the brethren (Revelation 12:10). Jesus is warning us that when we get offended we may be dealing with a double deception. The problem may be with me, but the devil is saying it's the other person's fault. The plank is in my eye, and the little speck is in theirs. Radical concept, huh?

What Jesus is saying is that when I'm offended the first thing that I should think is that it is probably my fault. Jonathan Edwards, the great revivalist, understood this when he said: "I am most suspicious of my own heart."

I've observed first hand in my Christian walk that Jesus' words are true. First, many times when a person gets offended, it is not because someone did something wrong to him or her, it's because someone told that person the truth and, in so doing, bumped into a hidden idol—a false teaching, a wound, or a good intention. When this happens, watch out; usually the relationship is over.

The second thing Jesus said is that when the truth is told, a choice is made. Do I focus on myself, or blame the other person? Satan, the accuser, always jumps in and says, "You're innocent. It's the other person's fault."

The fact that our heart is deceitful and Satan is a lying accuser of the brethren says that many times—not always—it's about us, not the other person. Therefore when we are offended, humility cries out, "Stop. Search me, O Lord. Is the problem with me? Is the voice I'm hearing from You, Lord, or is it Satan the accuser?"

In this process it might be good to stop right here and consider all of the people who have offended us. Say, "Lord, I'm going to back track and I want to know what part of the offense was me?" This revelation is more precious than gold or silver. We will find out more about ourselves, learn more about the character of Jesus, and become more like Him through this activity than you could ever imagine. "Show me, Lord; search me. Where is my fault?" After you do this, you should seek the Lord about going back to the person to reconcile with them. That's number one—humility.

The second thing Jesus said is that He wants us to love unconditionally. "A new command I give you, to love one another as I have loved you." If I start with the assumption that it's probably my fault—which it may be, at least to some degree—and God says no, it's totally the other person's fault—I'm still to love that person. Jesus says, "You have heard that it was said, 'You shall love your neighbor and hate your enemy.' But I say to you, love your enemies" (Matthew 5:43-44). Even if it's totally the other person's fault, it's still about me! He wants *us* to love *them* unconditionally, like the Father does.

EVEN IF IT'S TOTALLY THE OTHER PERSON'S FAULT, IT'S STILL ABOUT ME!

This is a reality I never understood until the Lord showed me the truth of how He loves. In fact, it so impacted me that I made it the Dedication of this book. (Since this is the "unbook", it appears at the end.) It says, "This book is dedicated to Jesus Christ and Him crucified, who allowed us to torture and murder Him in order to save us."

He allowed me to torture and kill Him, in order to save me. And He commands me to love that way. What on earth does that mean? Here's the question He put in my heart: *If you were across from a person at a table, and you had a gun, a .44 Magnum, and you knew that person was going to burn in hell for the rest of eternity unless he killed you, would you give him the gun? If it was the only way for him to be saved, would you do it? Would you give him the gun and say, "Go ahead, point it at my head, and shoot me"?*

That's what Jesus did. The Bible says no man took His life from Him; He laid it down. Would we allow somebody to kill us in order to save them? That's what it means to lay down your life for a friend. That's what it means, according to Jesus, to love.

Therefore, in an offense, even if it's totally not my fault, I must choose to love you unconditionally. Maybe, for a period of time, He will even require me to let you hurt me in order to save you. (However, if you are in a truly verbal or physically abusive situation, and it's not getting better, you should go to your pastor or a counselor to seek advice; they may tell you to leave that situation for a time.) An offense is always about *me* in the sense that He requires *me* to be humble, and *me* to love. I am responsible for my sins, and guess what? If I don't love others the way Jesus loved me, then that's a sin.

He said, "A new commandment I give to you, that you love one another; as I have loved you" (John 13:34), and, "Greater love has no one than this, than to lay down one's life for his friends" (John 15:13). If I do not obey His commands, I am sinning. It's always about me. Either I was the one in the wrong in the first place, or partly wrong, or I am totally innocent and still obligated by my Lord and Savior to love you as He loves you. Wild, isn't it?

The question is, how many Christians—born again, Spirit-filled, Green Beret Christians—are Christ-like? We all say we do, but who among us can keep His commands? Who could ever love as He loves—enough to allow someone to kill us in order to save them? And yet that is exactly what He commands us to do. He says, "If you love Me, you will keep My commandments" (John 14:15 NASB).

I've got bad news for everybody, including myself: it ain't happening! It is totally impossible to love others as Jesus loves. Do you think I'm going to hand you a .44 Magnum and have you kill me in order to save your hide? Not in a million years. I'd shoot you before I'd let myself be shot. Who's kidding whom? I could be a Bible school graduate and go to one thousand camp meetings, but when it comes to the moment of truth, I won't let you shoot me. I can't love as Jesus loves. It's totally impossible!

So the Holy Spirit has used the whole .44 Magnum story to make a point: living a Christian life is impossible! That's the message of the cross in a nutshell. Jesus is saying, "Give up! You have to die, and I've got to live through you in order for you to love as I love, because you can't do it." Anything else is a joke; it's just a big rouse. It's a bunch of people play acting; it's not Christianity. Why? Because we can't do it. *Without the cross and death to self, the Christian life is impossible.* That's it in a nutshell.

> WITHOUT THE CROSS AND DEATH TO SELF, THE CHRISTIAN LIFE IS IMPOSSIBLE. THAT'S IT IN A NUTSHELL.

The words of Jesus on dealing with offenses are, first, *Be humble,* and second, *Love like I love,* which is impossible without going to the cross. What is third? *Have faith, and pray for the person who offends you.*

Matthew 5:44–45 says, "Pray for those who spitefully use you and persecute you, that you may be sons of your Father in heaven." Don't try to change the person, but pray for him or her. Leave the work up to God. By faith, view the situation as part of a process in which God wants to change you and bless you, and through which He is also working in that person's life. You may never see the result you desire, but it is still a privilege and an act of obedience to pray. And you may see a miracle! Stay open. Leave the results to God and be at peace.

Love them unconditionally, pray for them, and then you know what I would add? We need to pray also for ourselves. I have to say, "Lord, help me to die, because I don't have the ability to do that. I'm going to rely on You to help both me and the other person."

There does come a time—and this is item four—when we need to *share the truth in love.* Only after numbers one through three have been done, and only after the Holy Spirit has released us, should we go to the person one-on-one with the purpose of gaining them back.

Matthew 18:15 (NIV) says, "If your brother sins against you, go and show him his fault, just between the two of you. If he listens to you, you have won your brother over." It goes on to say what we should do if he doesn't listen, which is to take two or three witnesses, and then finally to bring him before the church.

Have you ever seen this done effectively? If so, you're very lucky. Matthew 18 contains the red words of Jesus. He's the Lord of everybody, and church members all say they've accepted Jesus as Lord and Savior of their lives, yet I have never, ever, even once seen this entire process in a church confrontation. It's one of those deleted sections of the Bible. It is treated as though it doesn't exist, and we wonder why the church isn't working so hot. We're not following the words of Jesus!

Did you ever hear the saying "Making a mountain out of a molehill?" If you're ever asked to mediate an offense between two believers, here's a way to shrink the "offense mountain" down to size. Have each one of them write out this four part list:

ONE. What was my role in the offense; where was I at fault?

TWO. What are the Godly character traits of the other person?

THREE. How has God used the other person to bless me?

FOUR. What was their sin—offense—against me?

You will be amazed that after they read 1 through 3, the offense listed in 4 won't look so big anymore—the mountain will have shrunk to a molehill. You can also choose to do this on your own if someone's offended you.

We've seen how we all need each other for fellowship and addressing our blind spots. We've also seen how our hurts can be used by God to greatly benefit us and actually move us along from the Caterpillar Christian stage into that of the Birthright Butterfly. Offenses are valuable because of the jewels that can come out of them—the humility, the love, and the faith. Such deep treasures cannot be mined from any other place or situation. The horizontal beam forms the whole cross. We're going to die, and it's going to hurt, but we're going to be raised as new creations, with Jesus living His life in us. It's the whole enchilada!

In closing, I would like to share another time at lunch with my friend Steve, a time when the Lord taught us a profound truth. Steve

Forgiveness Forms the Cross In Me

A TRULY WHOLE PERSON

had been a full-time pastor who was happily married. Suddenly, he experienced a divorce, and shortly thereafter, he left the ministry. He went through a dark time in his life, when, as he put it, he was dancing with the devil on Saturday night. He repented of his sinful lifestyle and knew that the Lord had forgiven him.

However, one day he was led by the Holy Spirit to look in the mirror and say, "I forgive you Steve." He then realized God had forgiven him but he had never forgiven himself. He then felt an internal release to forgive others. Before that lunch, I had never thought about forgiving myself. My focus had just been on the Lord forgiving me.

The Lord gave us an image at the lunch table which was put in a sketch on the previous page. It was God handing an olive branch to me and forgiving me, then me handing the olive branch to myself and forgiving myself, and finally me in turn handing the olive branch to someone else, to forgive them. This complete three-part process of forgiveness forms the cross in me. Me forgiving myself is the centerpiece, the missing link between God forgiving me and me forgiving you. Only then can I become a whole and complete person.

The Lord went on to explain how forgiveness was the taproot of the cross. The taproot of a tree is the deepest, most important root for the life of a tree. Forgiveness is the taproot of the cross because it has a voice that says it's not about me, it's about what Jesus does for me when I sin and for others when they sin against me. So don't just accept forgiveness from the Lord. Go the whole way, and don't beat yourself up for your sins, because it's not about you. After you've forgiven yourself, do the same to others. Don't beat them up—let them off the hook—because it's not about them either! When we truly understand that it's not about me, or you, the process of dying to self and being transformed can flourish. Reconciliation as sons and daughters of the Father, and brothers and sisters in Christ, will follow. The power of the cross will then emerge out of this oneness, like a mighty oak shooting skyward!

We are now well into our spiritual journey, and have discovered both parts of the lost secret—making Christ crucified the most important thing in our lives and experiencing real Christian community. We're on our way to getting our God-given birthright back and entering a

Forgiveness is the Taproot of the Cross

POWER

RECONCILIATION

TRANSFORMATION

FORGIVENESS

wonderful, two-dimensional world. It's a place of supernatural love, joy, and peace even in the midst of trials, and access to God's power to be blessed and fulfill our destiny to bless others. We've discovered that we were Caterpillar Christians in a wisdom of the world system of knowledge and works, and the way to get out was admitting "Religion, That's Me" and living by "Judge Not." We also discovered who the real me is, a wonderful prince or princess becoming a king or a queen—a Birthright Butterfly. Unfortunately, though, the real me was a prisoner of my past because of the worldly system of hidden idols that was inside me. That's why we had to leave behind the life we knew by embracing the cross. As we read the next chapter, we will understand why it is so important to do so.

My Personal One-on-One Encounter With The Lord

ALSO FOR HOME GROUP DISCUSSION

Do I now understand that the cross is for me and not against me? How does this now make me feel?

_____

_____

_____

_____

What is the proof of how much I love the Lord? Hint: This is the horizontal beam of the cross.

_____

_____

_____

_____

The other aspect of the horizontal beam is that no one can do it alone, which is the second part of the lost secret. We all need support and have blind spots that only others can see. Do I reach out to other Christians for help? Am I an input-oriented Christian, and do I choose to make myself accountable to other trusted Christians?

_____

_____

_____

_____

How do I deal with offenses? What offenses in my life might God use to take me into the cocoon where He can transform me, and teach me more about how Jesus loves?

_____

_____

_____

_____

The New Covenant standard is to love one another as Jesus loved us. Who does Jesus want to love through me right now?

_____

_____

_____

Am I now putting offenses, when they come, under the following four-part Lordship of Jesus Christ?

HUMILITY—Ask the Lord to show me what my role was in the offense, and what involvement Satan may have had in falsely accusing the other person?

LOVE—Forgive the person the way that Jesus forgives me, and love the person the way that Jesus loves me.

FAITH—Pray for the person that God will show them their problem and help them to change.

SHARE THE TRUTH IN LOVE—After you have done the above, and are released by the Holy Spirit, go to the person one-on-one to gain them back. If that doesn't work, bring two witnesses. And, if that still doesn't bring reconciliation, bring it to the church.

REFLECTING ON THE ART

- In what way does the painting that opens this chapter speak to me?
- Did the sketches have an impact on me? If so, how?

_____

_____

The Great Custody Battle

FATHER GOD VS. SATAN

CHAPTER 11

The Great Custody Battle

FATHER GOD VS. SATAN

W**E'VE SEEN THAT EVEN THOUGH EMBRACING** the vertical and horizontal beams of the cross is not easy, both are necessary to our growth and development as children of God. In this chapter, we're going to explore another reason for embracing the cross. It is absolutely essential because there is a joint custody battle going on, and the stakes are very high.

Picture for a moment a court proceeding involving a divorce, and a judge is deciding the fate of a little girl. One side of the courtroom is light and life, and the other side is darkness and death. It's a long, drawn-out process, and everyone is waiting on pins and needles to find out what will happen. Finally the judge is finished deliberating, and he sits down in his seat. He delivers this ruling: "I'm going to award joint custody. The child will go with one parent one week and the other for the next, and we will alternate every week."

He slams the gavel down, and that's the order of the court. As the people begin to leave, you see a dark figure approach the child and take her by the hand. Wrapping his sharp, ugly claws around her, Satan whispers in a sinister voice, "You're mine for this week."

That's a pretty chilling image, isn't it? Is that possible? Could it be possible for a child of God?

Let's consider John 8:42-44. "Jesus said to them, 'If God were your Father, you would love Me, for I proceeded forth and came from

God; nor have I come of Myself, but He sent Me...[but] you are of your father the devil, and the desires of your father you want to do.'"

If Jesus had been speaking to the Pharisees, or other Jews who didn't believe in Him, this passage would not pose a custody problem. However, if we go back up to verse thirty-one, we find out whom Jesus was addressing. "Then Jesus said to those Jews who believed in Him." *Who believed in Him.* This speech wasn't addressed to the people who didn't believe in Jesus; it was addressed to those who did! All of a sudden that creates a problem, doesn't it?

Let's look at another scripture, 1 John 3:10—which, incidentally, is an epistle written to born-again believers. "In this the children of God and the children of the devil are manifest: Whoever does not practice righteousness is not of God, nor is he who does not love his brother."

What John is saying is that when we choose to sin and not love our brother, *in those times the devil is our father.* That's to us Christians. Ouch.

Remember earlier in the book where I referred to Jesus as a stumbling block along this journey? Well, here is another place where that happens. This is a very offensive scripture, isn't it? It's offensive because we tend to believe that as born-again Christians the devil could never be in a custody battle over us. We're God's children. The truth is, however, that even though Satan can never have full custody, he still fights for partial custody. There is a great custody battle going on.

WHAT JESUS DID ON THE CROSS ISSUES A DIFFERENT VERDICT, AND THAT VERDICT GUARANTEES THAT THERE IS NO JOINT CUSTODY.

Now the *good* news is this: Jesus won the battle on the cross. What Jesus did on the cross issues a different verdict, and that verdict guarantees that there is no joint custody. We are in our Father's house for all the days of our life, and we sit at our Father's table. Satan has no custody whatsoever.

Why is that incredibly important? Because the Scripture says, in Numbers 26:55, that "the land shall be divided by lot; they shall inherit according to the names of the tribes of their fathers." What this is saying is that our inheritance depends entirely on who our father is. That shouldn't surprise anyone—it's the same for earthly fathers.

Another reason the verdict won on the cross is very important has to do with destiny. Many psychologists agree by saying that when it comes to kids, we get nurture from our mother but our destiny is from our father. What have we said over and over again in this book? The power of the cross is going to get us two things: our promised blessings and fulfillment of our God-given destiny, with signs and wonders following, right?

What we're learning is that *our promised blessings, our inheritance, and our destiny are connected to who our father is.* And, *if our father some of the time is Satan, we're not going to receive all of our promised blessings, nor will we totally fulfill our destiny.* It's really just a simple concept.

So how could a sincere Christian ever have Satan as a part-time father? One word: *deception.* It's deception, because no child of God would ever voluntarily choose to have Satan as their father.

On the subject of deception, we're going to keep reading in John 8, where Jesus was talking to the Jews who were believers in Him. He said, "If you abide in My Word, you are My disciples indeed. And you shall know the truth, and the truth shall make you free." Their reply to this was, "We are Abraham's descendants, and have never been in bondage to anyone. How can you say, 'You will be made free'?" (John 8:31-33).

Can you imagine such a silly statement on the part of those believing Jews? First, Abraham's descendants were in Egypt as slaves to Pharaoh for hundreds of years. They were brought out of slavery. (That's why they celebrate Passover every year, to remember being brought out.) After being delivered from slavery in Egypt, they didn't obey God's laws and were taken captive to Babylon under Nebuchadnezzar, and they were slaves again for seventy years.

And what was the case during Jesus' time? Israel was occupied by Rome. They were slaves right then, at the moment of their conversation with Jesus. They sat there bold-faced, and said, "We've never been in bondage to anyone. We're not slaves to anyone." Why? They were under the delusion that because they were seeds of Abraham, God's chosen people—because they were good—they weren't slaves. They just couldn't imagine it being true.

Could that happen to us? Could we say, "I'm a born-again Christian; I go to church; I have Bible studies; I watch Christian TV and listen to Christian radio; and there is no way I could ever, ever be a slave.

There is no way I could be under joint custody in Satan's house." It's the same thing—deception.

They were God's chosen people who believed in Jesus. But Jesus said, "Satan is your father." Are we God's chosen people, seeds of Abraham? Galatians 3:29 says, "If you are Christ's, then you are Abraham's seed, and heirs according to the promise." Romans 11:17-24 says, to paraphrase, "The Jews are the olive tree, but you Gentiles have been grafted in through Christ."

Are we God's chosen people? Yes. Do we believe in Jesus? Yes. Then could Jesus' words apply to us? Yes. How could a sincere Christian be deceived by Satan and allow him to become his father?

Let's keep going in John 8:34-36. "Jesus answered them, 'Most assuredly, I say to you, whoever commits sin is a slave of sin. And a slave does not abide in the house forever, but a son abides forever. Therefore if the Son makes you free, you shall be free indeed.'" Simply put, *sin produces slavery*. Slaves were not in the father's house, but they lived in quarters outside the house. The Bible says that if you sin as a child of God, as one of God's chosen people, then that puts you under joint custody of the devil. How could that happen to us?

Well, the ultimate deception is a good intention. Hidden sin. When born-again Christians have good intentions—things that seem good but aren't—that's how the devil gets us. We learned that in the earlier chapters. He is never going to boldly come up to us, like a kidnapper, and grab hold of us and drag us away. He's never going to get us to go to his house that way, because we'd recognize him. We'd tell him to scram in the name of Jesus. No, he's much more subtle. He's going to *deceive us with good intentions*.

What did we learn earlier? There are two systems of good intentions. There's the good intention system that we're in, which is knowledge and works. In this system we believe that somehow, if we learn more about God and do more things for God, we'll get closer to God. That's the law, which happens to be the wisdom of the world. Satan uses the lie that God isn't good and we're inferior to make us lust after the law, to take care of our own problems and earn self-esteem. In so doing, he sucks us into the world's system.

The other system of good intentions is the system that is in us. We get this system from the hidden idols of our father's house, our people and country, wounds, false teachings, and the good intentions those things produce. These man-made idols are the world's system in us. We are in a world system, and a world system is in us. Satan is prince of this world, so is joint custody possible?

Proverbs 6:27 (NIV) says, "Can a man scoop fire into his lap without his clothes being burned?" In our minds we're saying, *Well, because I am a born-again Christian, I'm able to have the world's system in me and operate in the world's system.* But it doesn't work that way. Satan is prince of the world. The whole world is under his control, so if by our good intentions we get duped into having these world systems as part of our lives, that gives him access to our lives. We give him the right to mess with us when we get deceived with good intentions.

Let's refer to the heart diagram on the next page to understand that this really is a fatherhood issue. Do you see Jesus as Lord versus idols? The Bible says no one comes to the Father except through the Son (John 14:6). If Jesus brings us to the Father, who would idols bring us to? Satan!

In an earlier chapter, we learned very specifically from Deuteronomy and also from the New Testament that demons are attached to idols. Romans 8:14 says, "As many as are led by the Spirit of God, these are the sons of God." If those who are led by the Spirit of God are the children of God, doesn't the opposite have to be true? If we're led by demons, doesn't that make us children of the devil? If one is true, then the other has to be.

> IF THOSE WHO ARE LED BY THE SPIRIT OF GOD ARE THE CHILDREN OF GOD, DOESN'T THE OPPOSITE HAVE TO BE TRUE?

Please hear what I am saying. First, a Christian cannot be possessed by demons, but we can be influenced by them. Second, a born-again Christian is a child of God, but we can get duped into joint custody. We can be deceived and sucked into living in Satan's house for whole seasons. God is saying, "I want you in My house all of the time!"

The last scripture we're going to look at on this subject is Romans 8:7: "The carnal mind is enmity against God; for it is not subject to the law of God, nor indeed can be." The word *carnal* here is *sarx* in the Greek. *Sarx* stands for animal *and* human—the flesh world. Our carnal and

This is a Fatherhood Issue

SOUL

1. Wisdom Of World

↓

2. Knowledge & Works

↓

3. Law—Old Covenant

↓

4. Idols

↓

5. Demonic Counselor

↓

6. Satan as Father

SPIRIT

1. Wisdom Of God

↓

2. Christ Crucified

↓

3. Gospel—New Covenant

↓

4. Jesus Lord

↓

5. Holy Spirit Counselor

↓

6. God the Father

A Divided Heart Leads to Joint Custody

worldly mind is under the authority of the prince of this world. Again, our carnal mind can be duped into joint custody.

We talked about this earlier, but it's worth visiting again. When animals have a confrontation, there are only two things that ever happen, right? Fight or flight. If a raccoon gets into your garbage can and your dog comes out, they're not going to have a heart-to-heart conversation about it, are they? There's not one recorded instance in history where a dog and raccoon have sat down and said, "You know, why don't we just talk about this?" The dog says, "You're hungry, and I like to eat garbage too, and I'm sure that you were very, very tempted, but this is my master's garbage can, so could you just put the lid back on and kind of head out of here and just not let it happen again?" Has that ever happened? Ever?

There's only one of two things that happen one thousand percent of the time in the animal world. They either get into a fight, or there is flight. Why? Because they're animals. They're carnal—*sarx* in the Greek. They're of this world, where Satan is prince.

What about when there are offenses in the church? The vast majority of the time, what happens between Christians when there is an offense? Fight or flight—it's true. Normally it starts out with a fight, and then after the fight, there's flight. There's division.

The children of the heavenly Father who live in God's house don't do that, though. They reconcile. They go to the foot of the cross and say, "Hey, whatever you did, Jesus took care of it, so let's go to the foot of the cross and have forgiveness, and let's reconcile with each other."

> WHAT IS SCARIER? LEAVING BEHIND THE LIFE WE KNOW OR HAVING SATAN AS A JOINT-CUSTODY PARENT?

Does this give us a little inkling that maybe there are times in Christians' lives that they're doing a little joint custody time in Satan's house? Because guess what—Satan does not reconcile, ever. That's just not his cup of tea. So like it or not, when we don't make Jesus Lord over our offenses, we're victims of joint custody. We are that little child being led away by Satan.

This brings us back to the concept of leaving behind the life we know. Remember that *National Geographic* article with Abraham? Remember how scary it seemed to think about leaving behind all we are used to, all that is familiar? What is scarier? Leaving behind the life we know to follow Jesus and go to the cross, or having Satan as a joint-custody parent? The Lord is giving us a choice.

The key is the heart. *The human heart is a very scary place. It takes a lot of courage to go in.* It does, doesn't it? Our hearts, our own hearts, are very scary places, especially if we've been reading our own press clippings about what good Christians we are. To really go in and say, "Holy Spirit, show me what's inside of me"—well, it's a scary thing. It's a messy thing. *It's a cocoon thing.*

Did you know a cocoon is a very messy place? So is the cross. It's very, very scary, but I believe what God is saying is, "The fear of the Lord is the beginning of wisdom" (Psalm 111:10). He scared me with the fear of the Lord by letting me imagine being that little child whom Satan takes by the hand. I had to bow before God and pray, *Oh, my God, if I have a choice, I will go to this fearful place of the cross, because at least there I know that I have a High Priest who understands my infirmities. I've got a God that's sensitive. At the cross I've got Somebody who loves me.*

I WILL GO TO THIS FEARFUL PLACE OF THE CROSS BECAUSE AT THE CROSS I'VE GOT SOMEBODY WHO LOVES ME.

King David, the man the Bible describes as the man after God's own heart, cried out to the Lord in a similar way. When he really messed things up, God gave him the choice of who would punish him, the hand of God or the hand of men. Do you know what David said? "God, You punish me. I trust Your mercies, and I'll put my life in Your hands, but don't put me in the hands of men" (2 Samuel 24:14, paraphrased).

Do you know what God is saying to us right now? "Trust *Me*. Don't keep holding on to your own life; don't trust yourself more than you trust Me. Truly give your heart to Me."

Let's make this our prayer: *Lord, it's scary, but search me. I know that no matter what You find You're still going to tell me that You love me. No matter what You find—it's all been taken care of by Jesus Christ on the cross. There is nothing that can separate me from Your love and from the love of Christ, so I would much rather choose to fall into Your hands and for You to put my false person to death than for the devil to have joint custody over me.*

He's motivating us to get out of Satan's house and get into His house—the heavenly Father's house. And I'll say this again, as offensive as it sounds, *this is for born-again Christians.* This is not about the unsaved. This is saying that born-again Christians can be deceived. *The ultimate deception is a good intention, and we can be deceived into joint custody.*

We're going to close now with an interesting story. There's a high school near where I live called Massillon Washington High. It's very famous for football. In fact, there was a national documentary done about it, and *Sports Illustrated* had a big article when Massillon and their rival, McKinley High School, played their one-hundredth anniversary football game. Their weight room has a quote on the wall that caught my attention. It was by Chris Spielman, who had played

TRAIN AT A LEVEL WHERE YOUR OPPONENTS ARE UNABLE OR UNWILLING TO GO.

football at Massillon and went on to become an All-American in college and an All Pro in the NFL. The quote says, "Train at a level where your opponents are unable or unwilling to go." The clear message is, do this and you will win.

Who is our opponent? Did you know that Satan's name means accuser, but it also means "adversary"? So, Satan is our opponent. Where is he unwilling to go versus where is he able and willing to go? If we can find that out and go there ourselves, we can win, right?

Satan is comfortable with *the wisdom of the world.* In the wisdom of the world's system of knowledge and works...he loves it there. We start out great as a born-again Christian. Then we become a Caterpillar Christian, and we're learning and growing. But we get stuck. We get totally enamored with the system of knowledge and works—doing more for God, and judging good and evil—we get into that.

Is Satan willing and able to go there? You bet. Guess what? He's the one who tempted people to go there in the first place. Remember, the Bible says Eve was beguiled by the serpent in the garden to eat of the tree of the knowledge of good and evil. He's all for it, he's very willing and able, and he encourages many millions of Christians to go there. Applying the quote from the weight room, the system of knowledge and works is like lifting little five-pound dumbbells. We may think we can really beat Satan by constantly learning and doing more, but he's already got us beat.

The second place is *hidden idols*. They are man-made gods in us—gods from our earthly father's house, our people, and our country—gods that came from the world we grew up in. Guess what? Satan says, "I'm prince of this world. I am legally prince. The entire world is under my dominion. I am glad to go there!" He is more than willing and able. He runs this system, so he's very happy to compete on that playing field.

Now fasten your seat belts. This is the third place, and it was very offensive to me, and could be to you also. Where else is Satan willing and able to go? *The five majestic trees*—those five things of God—the Word, prayer, worship, fellowship, and ministry. Do we need proof?

Think about when Jesus was tempted in the desert. Was the Word off-limits for Satan? No, he quoted it. What about prayer? Prayer is talking to God, isn't it? Check out Job 1:6-12. It says Satan presented himself to God and talked to Him. So prayer isn't off limits for Satan either. How about praise and worship? He was in charge of it before he fell from heaven (Isaiah 14:11-15). He knows a lot about it. And we all know he gets right in the middle of fellowship and ministry. How many times have you heard pastors and believers share how they sensed spiritual warfare going on during a church service or a time of ministry? *Satan is more than able, and more than willing, to compete within the arena of the five majestic trees.*

Does that mean we can't use those against him? No. Jesus spoke the Word back to Satan; He prayed; He worshipped; He sought fellowship; He cast out demons during His ministry. Please don't over-react to what I'm saying, but we mustn't under-react either. Don't ever think Satan is unable or unwilling to go to the five things of God in order to deceive us, because he can. That doesn't mean we abandon them or that we quit using them against him. Understand, though, that we

> ARE YOU READY FOR THE GOOD NEWS? YOU WILL NEVER FIND SATAN AT THE CROSS.

don't *honor* the enemy but we *respect* our enemy. There's a big difference. We'd better understand how he operates if we want to beat him.

Are you ready for the good news? Where is the devil unable and unwilling to go? Where can you be guaranteed not to find him? *You will never find Satan at the cross.* He's unable and unwilling to go there. He doesn't want any part of it!

First, *Satan can't embrace the vertical beam of the cross.* He cannot stand in the light; he's a liar and the father of lies, and he will never, ever, *ever* go and stand in the light of the Holy Spirit and ask to be searched. He cannot go there. He's a creature of darkness. It's completely impossible.

Second, *Satan also can never embrace the horizontal beam of the cross.* He cannot deal with offenses. He can never say that, never do that, because he's a murderer. He can never forgive, and he can never love.

The third place *Satan cannot go is the place of humility.* He can never go to the foot of the cross and lay down his pride. Satan cannot go there, you know why? Because he's arrogant. He can never, ever humble himself, because he is the most arrogant creature in the entire universe. He wanted to be God, remember?

Finally, *he can never go to the cross because he was totally defeated there.* When Jesus said, "It is finished," it meant "Satan you are finished." He'd rather forget it ever happened.

God has given us a secret. We do lots of spiritual exercises that don't do us much good when it comes to real spiritual training, but if we will go to the cross we are going where our opponent is unable and unwilling to go. We die, Jesus takes our place, and then *Jesus fights Satan for us, and that's where the victory is.*

Now we're at a place he can't go! Sayonara, joint custody. I'm not living in Satan's house anymore, and there is no way he can keep me there because I'm at a place he can never go. Jesus has taken us to His Father's house through the power of the cross.

My Personal One-on-One Encounter With The Lord

ALSO FOR HOME GROUP DISCUSSION

Do I now understand that it is possible for a sincere Christian to spend time in Satan's house with joint custody? How much time am I spending there?

_____
_____
_____
_____
_____

The ultimate deception is a good intention. Is it clear to me now that Satan lures sincere Christians to his house through the deception of good intentions? Are more of my good intentions being revealed to me?

_____
_____
_____
_____
_____

Has the very scary thought of living in Satan's house part-time helped me to overcome my fear of "Leaving Behind the Life I Know"?

_____
_____
_____
_____
_____

What does it mean for me, personally, to train at a level my opponent is unwilling and unable to go?

_____
_____
_____
_____
_____

Am I ready to get my God-given birthright back, to live in a world of love, joy, peace, and power in my Father's house?

_____

_____

_____

_____

REFLECTING ON THE ART

• In what way does the painting that opens this chapter speak to me?
• Did the sketch have an impact on me? If so, how?

_____

_____

_____

The Author's Journey

CROSS ENCOUNTERS

CHAPTER 12

The Author's Journey

CROSS ENCOUNTERS

I RECENTLY BUMPED INTO an old high school friend of mine who reminded me of an encounter we had back in 1972. We'd both been drafted for the Vietnam War and were on a bus ride to get our physical examinations.

"You know, I will never forget that bus ride," he told me. "I've told tons of people about it, especially after all of the success that you achieved."

I'd totally forgotten about that ride until he reminded me of it, and the story he told shook me to my core.

He said, "I got on the bus and sat down next to you. You were reading Adolf Hitler's autobiography, *Mein Kampf*. As you read it, you turned to me and told me you were going to be a millionaire."

I had forgotten all about that darkest side of my depraved past when I was an atheist, when I had actually admired Adolf Hitler! Back then my highest aspiration was to be president of the United States. I had read everything I could find about Hitler and how he rose to power. My plan was to become a multi-millionaire through marketing and get the money to finance a campaign. I wanted to follow in Hitler's footsteps, using marketing propaganda to get into office, and become a very, very powerful man. I believe now that there were many layers to that ambition, rooted in the lie that I was inferior, with an overwhelming drive to prove myself worthy to the world. Regardless of all of the reasons, however, admiring Adolf Hitler was evil. I was truly depraved, with no boundaries, and no way to fence evil in.

After my friend reminded me of that story, I was very emotional for two days. (By the way, neither of us went to Vietnam; his number 96 never got called, and I had a 4F classification for bad vision.) I thought about what Jesus did on the cross—how far he went to save a person as far gone as I was. During those two days, the Holy Spirit spoke to my heart, and He said, *Rick, there were millions and millions of other people that also admired Adolf Hitler in the nineteen-thirties and forties...God-fearing, church-going Germans. They were very regular people.*

Strangely enough, if you read and talk to the GIs, they say that out of every country they entered in Europe, whether it was England, France, Belgium, the one most like the United States was Germany. The highways, the houses—everything reminded them of home. These people were no different than you or me, but, they idolized Adolf Hitler, and as a result, six million Jews—God's chosen people—were murdered. What's more, millions and millions of other people were killed by church-going, God-fearing people who followed Adolf Hitler.

So what was the purpose of the bus ride story my friend reminded me of? It helped me to understand how depraved human beings can be, and how depraved I was. The Lord then connected that truth to a series of visions and experiences He had given me about the cross. And anytime the Lord shares something with us, it's so we can eventually share what we've learned with others. There were lessons and teachings in these visions, which I'm now sharing with others.

I realize there may be readers who are unfamiliar with or even skeptical of visions. Clearly, people had visions all throughout the Bible, and I believe the God who is the same yesterday, today,

> I BELIEVE THE GOD WHO IS THE SAME YESTERDAY, TODAY, AND FOREVER STILL GIVES HIS PEOPLE PROPHETIC VISIONS.

and forever still gives His people prophetic visions. Peter, in his great sermon in Acts 2, preached that dreams and visions are signs of the last days and the out-pouring of the Holy Spirit. Because I believe we are in the last days and experiencing a fresh out-pouring of the Holy Spirit, I believe these visions are becoming more and more common. They are a part of God's plan to accomplish His will among us today. There are two kinds of Biblical visions: open visions and mental images. Mine were mental images but with the feeling of actually being there.

Before I share some of my "Cross Encounters" through the visions He gave me, I want to say that I don't claim to have experienced even one-millionth of what Jesus went through on the cross. I could never comprehend all of His agony. But He has given me a little sliver—just a tiny glimpse—and I believe He wants me to share it. I'm certainly not up on any pedestal. I'm simply a messenger of the cross, who is on a spiritual journey like everyone else. As I share these visions, you will see that I too was a Caterpillar Christian who had to go into the cocoon of the cross. I might add that my transformation into a Birthright Butterfly is still a work in progress.

The first vision was given in the spring of 1993. My pastor's wife was very ill; she had shingles, which in middle age is a very painful condition. That was when I was in a deep pit in my own life, but I went over to lay hands on her and pray. As I did, I got a vision of the feet of Jesus. There were spikes through His feet, and the blood was running down the cross. It was actually following the grain of the wood, which was very distinct. The blood would flow down the grain of the wood and then drop to the ground. After I prayed, she quickly thereafter was healed.

A second vision connected with the first one. In it I saw the cross firmly planted in a mound of dirt here on the earth. In a third vision I was at the foot of the cross and looking up. There was a very distinct sign over Jesus' head, and I know it was in Latin and Greek and Aramaic, but for some reason I was able to read it. It said, "Jesus, the King of the Jews." As I stood at the foot of the cross looking up at that sign, the Holy Spirit said, *I want you to look up the word* king *in the Greek and Hebrew.*

I obeyed, and do you know what the most basic derivative for the word *king* is? *Foot.* The idea of *king* is that His foot rules. He puts it on the neck of His enemies; all things are at His feet. The concept of a foot indicates a king, and the lesson is that there's victory at the foot of the cross. When we're at the foot of the cross, we are at the foot of the King of all Kings. He's the Lord of all Lords, and there is victory and power under His rule. And His kingship flows from the foot of the cross.

I believe the lesson of these three visions is this: Jesus truly came down from heaven to the earth; His cross was firmly planted in this earth; His blood flowed down and touched the ground; then total victory over every sin, demon, and curse was won. At the foot of the cross, the King of all Kings and the Lord of all Lords has total dominion and rule. As the painting opening this chapter depicts, it may not be easy to get there, but if by God's grace I can get to the foot of the cross, the devil can't get me! At the foot of the cross, all the wrongs that we have done, and all the wrongs done to us, are totally taken care of. At the foot of the cross, we have trained at a level where our opponent was unable and unwilling to go. We are seated with Christ high above all principalities and powers. Our God-given birthright of power and dominion over Satan is restored.

AT THE FOOT OF THE CROSS, THE KING OF ALL KINGS AND THE LORD OF ALL LORDS HAS TOTAL DOMINION AND RULE.

With this lesson in mind, how important is the cross? In the spring of 1994, when I was in the midst of losing my company, Fitness Quest, I had another vision of the cross, which I believe answers this question. I was in my office, and I was totally alone. I went to the window and was looking out at the warehouse, the new one-hundred-thousand-square-foot facility, and I had a totally supernatural experience. There was a speck of dust on the window, and like a special effect in a movie, my eyes zoomed into it. It was as if everything else surrounding me disappeared. All of the focus was on that one speck of dust. Then the Holy Spirit said, *I want you to understand something. Everything that has ever happened in the entire universe and everything that ever will happen can be totally distilled down to one thing: Jesus Christ on the cross. All things were created by Him, for Him, and through Him—God is reconciling everything back to Himself. It can all be understood by Him on the cross. His resurrection was never the question; the Father would have never left Him in the grave. The question was, would He endure and stay on the cross? Jesus had to make a choice.*

The obvious lesson there is the preeminence of the crucifixion and resurrection of Jesus—that one thing is the most important thing. It is absolutely preeminent over everything in the entire universe, which is stated clearly in Colossians 1:15 – 20. There is a second lesson, however, and it is this: Jesus had a free will; He had to make a choice and say, "Not my will, but your will be done Father." I had never really understood that before. *So just as He made a choice based on His love for His Father and us, we have to do the same.* We also have a free will. Will we choose to make the cross preeminent in our lives and embrace it, to die to self because of our love for God and the hurting and dying world He wants us to minister to?

Many years later, after this experience in my office, I read two separate articles in National Geographic magazine. On the cover of the one issue were these words, "Search For The God Particle." The article was about this mystery: According to the "Big Bang Theory" for the start of the universe, the equal amounts of matter and antimatter created should have annihilated each other, leaving a largely empty universe. But the universe if full of millions of galaxies, it's not empty. Scientists think the reason is this: They know about particles called atoms—made up of electrons, protons, neutrons, quarks, and gluons. But they believe there has to be an invisible particle that brought mass and matter into existence—it's called the *God particle*.[1]

The second article was on the Hubble telescope, and it revealed another mystery. The movement of distant galaxies and supernovas suggest that there must be an invisible force in space. In fact, when scientists tried to mathematically calculate it, they came up with a number that was infinitely bigger than all the known matter and energy in the entire universe. This calculation really had them scratching their heads.[2]

These two articles posed two questions: "Why is there anything?" and "What force fills the emptiness of space?" The answer to both questions is Jesus. John 1:3 says, "All things were made through Him, and without Him nothing was made that was made." Colossians 1:17 in the Amplified Bible says, "And He Himself existed before all things, and

> SO JUST AS HE MADE A CHOICE BASED ON HIS LOVE FOR HIS FATHER AND US, WE HAVE TO DO THE SAME.

1 Joel Achenbach, "The God Particle," *National Geographic* (March 2008): pp. 90-105.

2 Timothy Ferris, "Raising Heaven: Hubble Telescope," *National Geographic* (November 2007): pp. 140-153.

in Him all things consist (cohere, and are held together)." Jesus is the invisible God particle the scientists are looking for, the One who brought all matter into existence. And, He is the infinitely powerful invisible force that fills the universe and holds it all together.

After reading these articles and meditating on these scriptures, I now better understand the "speck of dust on my window" experience. Everything in the entire universe really can be distilled down into one thing—Jesus Christ on the cross. This thought then came to me:

Grasping The Power Of The Cross

When you take the preeminent being of the entire universe—Jesus— the one and only entity that contains the fullness of the Godhead—through whom all things that exist were made and are held together—and that being volunteers to step down from His place of preeminence to be beaten and destroyed—only to be raised from the dead—then there is nothing left to do—it's all been taken care of—for everybody—for everything—for all time. It is finished.

When He who is all and all, lays it all down, all is taken care of. That's how powerful and complete the work of the cross was. Did Paul understand something that we don't, when he said, "But what things were gain to me, these I have counted loss for Christ. Yet indeed I also count all things loss for the excellence of the knowledge of Christ Jesus my Lord, for whom I have suffered the loss of all things, and count them as rubbish, that I may gain Christ" (Philippians 3:7-8)? Do we truly understand that when we get Jesus, we gain everything?

Another vision, one that was quite disturbing, correlates with Isaiah 50:6. I never even knew that this scripture existed before I had this vision, but it says, "I gave My back to those who struck Me, and My cheeks to those who plucked out the beard; I did not hide My face from shame and spitting."

In this vision there was a crowd of people who absolutely hated Jesus' guts. In most instances the Bible says that He passed through the crowds who wanted to kill Him or stone Him, but during His time of the cross, He went towards the crowd. He gave Himself to the crowd, and it was real. He gave His back to be flogged, and He gave His cheek. In the

vision I saw, the people actually took their fingers and pulled His beard out of His face, and Jesus gave Himself to that. I wept.

As I was in this vision, the Holy Spirit showed me that humans react with fight or flight when we are hated. We either beat up the person who hates us, or we run away from them. But Jesus actually went toward the hatred in order to once and for all dissolve it. He went into it in order to get victory over it—that's what the scripture in Isaiah means. *Only this kind of love can bring victory over offenses and hate in the church and the world — and this love can only come from one place—Jesus! He allowed people to torture and murder Him in order to save them from their hatred.*

I'm going to share three other experiences from the Lord in a sequence, and there's a lesson here. One day before my trials started, I was just a happy-go-lucky Caterpillar Christian. I was standing in my study, and I picked up a book called *Jesus is for Jews.* I had received it from the ministry *Jews For Jesus.* When I opened the book, the scripture I saw was from Jeremiah 29, and it said, "You will seek Me and find Me, when you search for Me with all your heart" (vs. 13).

It's never happened to me before or since, but that scripture literally knocked me down into a chair. It physically knocked me down. And I heard the Holy Spirit say, *I am God. I am the Most High God who is the possessor of heaven and earth—that's who I Am. And if you seek Me with all your heart, you can have Me as your personal possession.*

To help me understand, the Holy Spirit explained it to me in very human terms. You've seen how ladies sometimes collect Lladros—those figurines that are very valuable—and they put them in a cabinet to display. Or what about men and their prized guns? A man with a very expensive Remington shotgun might put it in a case with a lock. Those are possessions that are very valuable too. The Lord showed me that we as Christians can have Him literally as our personal possession in the same way. I had always known our bodies were His temple, but to take it to the next level, to say that I as a mere human could have God Himself as my personal possession, was amazing and exciting to me! Little did I know what He was actually talking about, and how He would make His point later in my life.

THAT I, AS A MERE HUMAN, COULD HAVE GOD HIMSELF AS MY PERSONAL POSSESSION, WAS AMAZING AND EXCITING TO ME!

Fast forward, then, into the desperation years—to the midst of my big trials. It was 1997 or 1998. We were at a prayer meeting, and a friend of mine came up to me and said, "God told me to come and pray for you."

I said it was okay, and then he said, "The Lord has a love for you that is unbelievable. He told me to pray for you, and you're going to get this love."

I'll be honest with you; I was thinking he was a little off, but I was desperate for God's love. What did I have to lose?

As my friend laid hands on me, I immediately fell on the floor—and this sounds stupid, but it happened. I started swimming like a salmon. I felt like I was a salmon going upstream, back to the place where I was conceived, back to where I came from. I had the sensation that I had to get to God. I just had to get back to God, and as I was swimming, the Holy Spirit spoke to me: *I'm going to give you a love that doesn't care. I'm going to give you a death love. I'm going to give you a martyr's love.* I had never heard of love described that way before, "a love that doesn't care."

When I got up, my friend said, "It isn't over yet. In the weeks to come, you're going to have other encounters with the Lord God. God is not finished."

A couple of weeks later, I was in bed with my wife in our big mansion. Our bedroom had a twenty-four foot ceiling, and our bed looked like something out of a Cleopatra movie.

I HAD NEVER HEARD OF LOVE DESCRIBED THAT WAY BEFORE, "A LOVE THAT DOESN'T CARE."

It was a fifteen-foot-tall poster bed with curtains draped all around it. Lu Ann got out of bed and went downstairs, and I was just lying there, not thinking about anything or doing anything spiritual. I looked up and sensed the power of God was coming through the ceiling. It literally came down through the ceiling, and like a half-moon stainless steel knife, it went straight through my body.

The Holy Spirit said, *I want you to go listen to Celine Dion's love theme song from the movie* Titanic, *"My Heart Will Go On."* It made no sense to me; it wasn't praise or worship music, but I obeyed.

I got up, went down into the weight room, and I put that song on the huge Infinity speakers we had in there. I sat down on a weight machine and listened. For what seemed like hours, I played that song over and over again, hearing the lyrics,

> *Near, far, wherever you are*
> *I believe that the heart does go on*
> *Once more you open the door*
> *And you're here in my heart*
> *And my heart will go on and on.*
> *Love can touch us one time*
> *And last for a lifetime*
> *And never let go till we're one.*[3]

---

3 Celine Dion, "My Heart Will Go On," from album *Let's Talk About Love* by James Horner, Will Jennings. Famous Music Corporation (ASCAP)/ Blue Sky Rider Songs (administered by Irving Music, Inc.), 1997.

As I listened to that song, it was like there was an insane love coming at me. God's insane love would come toward me, as if He was saying, *I have to have you.* And then an insane love would come out of me, back towards Him saying, *I have to have You.* Back and forth, back and forth, as I kept pushing the replay button for I don't know how long. I was beginning to better understand "a love that doesn't care."

Two weeks later I felt led to do it again. I went back down to the weight room, and this time it was different. I put the song on, and I don't know for how long it was, maybe ten seconds, He brought me back to the Father's bosom. In that brief encounter, I was back in His bosom, my true home before I was in my mother's womb. Then He brought me back here. As soon as I got back, I was so lonely; I missed my true home with the Father so much. It was the loneliest feeling I had ever experienced in my entire life! I was in China one time on business where I was away from my family and really missed them, but this was a thousand times more intense.

I was so lonely I thought I was losing my mind. I knew if I sat there any longer, I would, so I tried to watch TV, but the minute my mind would stray from what was on TV, this unspeakable loneliness would come over me again. Finally I got through it, and there was a voice inside that said, *I've got to get back, no matter what. I've got to get back. That is my home—it's where the salmon was trying to swim back to—it's where I originated. I have to get back to that place. No matter what it takes, even if it means that half-moon-shaped stainless steel knife going through my body.* I now understood "a love that doesn't care," a death love—a martyr's love.

I'VE GOT TO GET BACK, NO MATTER WHAT. THAT'S MY HOME.

So how do I get God as my personal possession now and make sure I get back to Him for all eternity? I didn't know yet, but I was about to find out—by learning what it meant to choose to die—to die to self.

I was at a Christian counseling session, and I was going through a lot of trouble; there was a lot of junk coming to the surface in my life. These counselors decided to pray for me. When they did, there was the third supernatural event. I instantly entered a scene, just as real as real can be, and I was in front of a firing squad. The soldiers were in a line, with their rifles pointed at me, and a big executioner was getting ready to put a black hood over my head.

I had the sense that God was going to give the command to shoot me. I was terrified. I felt it was really going to happen, that I was going to die. I was waiting for a big, booming voice from heaven to say, "Fire!" and I started screaming out—literally screaming at the top of my lungs in front of these counselors—"I don't want to die! I don't want to die! I don't want to die!"

I was in a cold sweat. It was very real, and as I was screaming, I was waiting at any point for His voice to say "Fire!" And then there was this silence, and out of that silence came a sweet, soft voice, and I knew it was Jesus. He said, *I died for you.* That's all He said, with no pressure whatsoever. The sense was, an all-powerful God wasn't in heaven commanding me to die for Him, but an all-powerful God did choose to die for me. Based on that truth, He wasn't commanding that I die; He was giving me a choice and gently encouraging me by reminding me that He made that same choice for me first. He was helping me to understand that holding on to my life wasn't as important as I was making it out to be. He was helping me to understand "a love that doesn't care."

If we connect those three encounters, I believe the Lord is saying, *You know what? You genuinely have the chance to possess Me for real as your personal possession. I made the decision to have a love that doesn't care when I died for you on the cross. Will you make the decision to have a love that doesn't care and embrace the cross to die to self for Me? Because when that happens, you will get Me now and get back to Me for all eternity.*

Jesus said to me, *Rick, I have a love that doesn't care. I did not care about My own self; I died for you.*

And now I can say, *Jesus, I have a love that doesn't care. I don't care about my own self. I will die to self for You.*

The Lord showed me that when this duet is sung, nobody can interfere. There's not a person on the face of the earth, and there's not a demon in hell, including Satan himself, that can ever mess with that kind of love. When we have this kind of love between God, us, and each other, the Lord will fill us with power.

In a nutshell, that's what I'm trying to explain as best as I can in this book. *This is what Christianity is about, and it's not conventional. It's not the norm. It's the lost secret.*

What lessons have I learned on my spiritual journey? The very first thing that I learned, as I was weeping and reading the Bible right after I got saved, was this: I really liked everything about Jesus; He was truly the best thing that ever happened in my life. I also learned: Beware the yeast of the Pharisees, and how getting infatuated with knowledge and works as a Caterpillar Christian could rob me of my relationship with my best

JESUS IS THE BEST, BUT BEWARE THE YEAST OF THE PHARISEES.

friend. Little did I know, that these two concepts I received as a baby Christian would turn into the two towering pillars of my faith.

The next thing that I discovered is that very sincere Caterpillar Christians like I was do not have God figured out. If I didn't even know what was inside of me, how could I ever presume to have God all figured out? So the whole idea that I was a super-spiritual, Green Beret Christian and had it all figured out was a joke. The idea that anyone attains that is just not true. I learned that. The good news is that He has me figured out. He knows what I need, and that's good enough for me.

Early in this book, I showed these two graphs, representing the world's progress and God's progress. I learned those graphs are true. I was convinced that in order to grow spiritually, my life needed to look like the first graph. But in reality, I was just growing into a big ugly caterpillar. I am genuinely convinced now, that God has a plan for on-fire Christians to fail, just like the original twelve apostles. That place was their encounter with the cross, their failure replaced by Jesus' success! I believe that the only way we ever really "get it"—meaning, get Him, and understand what Christianity is about—is to fail. I am convinced of that.

World's Progress

God's Progress

Further, I am convinced that the reason for this planned failure is love. God wants us to know that love truly is what matters—a supernatural three-dimensional love. First, we can never understand how much God loves us until we find out how rotten we are on the inside. Why is that? Because of what Jesus said: "If you only love people who are nice to you, what credit is that to you? Even tax collectors and sinners do that" (Matthew 5:46, paraphrased).

If how much God loves me is based on how good I am—how I perform—then that's not really love. *Anybody can love like that.* But when you find out the junk that's inside, and God says, *I still love you, no matter what,* then you begin to understand the deep unconditional love of the Lord. I would argue that conventional Christianity never goes there. Caterpillar Christians only understand performance-oriented love, not failure love.

The second dimension of this love is that we can never truly love ourselves unless we fail. Do you know why? Well, as a very success-oriented person, I loved myself and valued myself as long as I was successful. But when I failed at everything and was a worm in my own eyes, the love of Jesus freed me to love myself regardless of performance. He showed me that He loves me, I'm wonderful, I'm a prince because I'm born again, and I'm on my way to becoming a king. Those things don't change with my performance. They are eternal truths, and if I choose to embrace those eternal truths, I am free to love myself. No strings of performance attached.

The third dimension is that we can never really love God or others unless we fail. Remember the sinful woman that burst into the Pharisee's house and anointed Jesus' feet with expensive oil? (See Luke 7:36-50.) She washed His feet with her hair. It caused a huge scandal among the Pharisees. They said, "If He was a prophet, He'd know what manner of woman was doing that." Do you know what Jesus said? "The one who is forgiven much loves much. The one who is forgiven little loves little. You will never have the capacity to love Me big, or love others big, until you have failed and been forgiven." To sum up my love lessons, *I learned that failure was worth it to better*

YOU WILL NEVER HAVE THE CAPACITY TO LOVE ME BIG, OR LOVE OTHERS BIG, UNTIL YOU HAVE FAILED AND BEEN FORGIVEN.

understand how much God loves me, to finally love myself apart from success, and to gain a greater capacity to love God and others. Oh yes—it was all worth it—because great loss can produce great gain.

I also want to share that God is faithful. Once the trial has produced the needed transformation, the Lord then blesses. My chronic fatigue syndrome is gone and my health is getting better and better. The legal problems were all resolved. Miraculously, I did not lose all of our finances, and my family still maintained a wonderful lifestyle. The riches I did lose were replaced with something far more valuable—rich relationships. My relationship with God, myself, my wife and children, Christians and friends, far exceeds what I had before. And I believe more supernatural love, joy, and peace is coming, along with more power to receive my promised blessings and fulfill my destiny to bless others.

If somebody asked me what my perspective is twenty-one years into my unconventional Christianity journey, I'd have to honestly say that the cross has been the worst thing and the best thing that has ever happened to me, both at the same time. It was everything I feared—like Job—and everything I needed. God's lavish grace, which I didn't deserve, His severe mercy when I needed disciplined, and this multidimensional love—these are the treasures I found at the foot of the cross. Jesus is all. And that is all that matters.

My summary of all my *Cross Encounters* is this: It's not about learning more about God and doing more things for God—it's about Jesus. And because of what He did for me on the cross, I can get God as my personal possession. When I get Him, I get everything—love, power, and my promised blessings. I can then fulfill my destiny to bless others by giving Him away. When my mission here on earth is accomplished, I'll go back to Him. Get God, give God, get back to God—pretty simple, huh?

My Personal One-on-One Encounter With The Lord

ALSO FOR HOME GROUP DISCUSSION

What specific vision or insights in this chapter has the Lord used to help me understand the cross of Jesus better?

_____

_____

_____

_____

Based on the depth of the depravity humans are capable of, do I appreciate everything Jesus had to go through to rescue and save us?

_____

_____

_____

_____

Do I truly believe that when His cross was planted in the earth and His blood touched the ground, that victory over every sin, demon, and curse on this earth was won?

_____

_____

_____

_____

We were all in the Father's bosom before we were placed in our mother's womb. Is the cry of my heart now, *I've got to get back*?

_____

_____

_____

_____

Do I now realize how failure helps us understand how much God loves us apart from performance, to love ourselves apart from performance, and greatly increase our capacity to love the Lord and one another?

_____

_____

_____

CONVERSATION STARTER

We have now discovered that the fullness of the Trinity is in Jesus, everything was created through Him, and He fills and holds the whole universe together. He volunteered to be beaten and destroyed, only to be raised again. Is this truth that He who was all, laid it all down, to take care of all things, worth focusing on and understanding? What would happen if this would become a big topic of conversation for many Christians?

_____

_____

_____

REFLECTING ON THE ART

· In what way does the painting that opens this chapter speak to me?
· Did the sketches have an impact on me? If so, how?

_____

_____

_____

_____

Satan's Field of Slaughter

GOOD INTENTIONS

OFFENSES

Philip Howe

CHAPTER 13

Satan's Field of Slaughter

PICTURE IN YOUR MIND a supernatural battlefield. Strangely, to our natural eye, this battlefield looks like a very prim and proper place. It's full of very good people who seem to be doing all the right things. In fact, the focus of all these people is God, because the battlefield is the church!

But let's put on a pair of supernatural goggles like the night vision goggles worn by soldiers. Instantly a whole different scene comes into view. It's Satan's field of slaughter, the painting that opens this chapter. The carnage is horrible—the devil is wreaking great havoc in the church. His weapons of choice are good intentions and offenses, and they are really working. The fallen Christians in the scene have no idea they are being slaughtered. They never had a chance.

So it is today in the church. Jesus won the battle on the cross, but Satan is winning the battle now, because he is deceiving well-intentioned Christians. But help is on the way. Jesus, who is the Lion of the Tribe of Judah, is coming on the scene in the painting. What's the first thing Jesus must bring to this field of slaughter to change the tide of the battle? *Truth*, to dispel the deception. Jesus is the light of the world, and He is the way, the truth, and the life. So let's shed the light and truth of Jesus on Satan's swords.

The two swords are "Good Intentions" and "Offenses." Interestingly, two of the devil's names are, Lucifer and Satan—umm, could there be a connection? Lucifer means light, so literally Satan is an angel of light. His most effective tactic is to dress something up that is evil and make it look good—a masquerade! Let's break down his good intentions and see how this works.

We've learned that Caterpillar Christians get sucked into the wisdom of the world system of knowledge and works, which is the law. Learning more and more about God and doing lots of works for Him appears good, doesn't it? But let's penetrate the masquerade and go to the source of this system—the fall of man in the Garden of Eden. Eating of the tree of the knowledge of good and evil to become like God was not good. It was a sin. It was based on the lie that God wasn't good and we weren't good enough. It was man's attempt to take care of our own problems and gain self-esteem. In addition, the law and the Old Covenant have no place in the New Covenant. So much for being good. Remember, there is no such thing as a good intention, and the ultimate deception is a good intention.

One last thought on good intentions: Can something that caused a problem in the first place ever be used to get rid of that problem? The knowledge of good and evil caused man to start sinning, so how could it ever be used to stop sin? The truth is this: using the law to stop sin is like pouring gasoline on a fire. Remember Romans 5:20 (NIV): "The law was added so that the trespass might increase."

How about the good intention system in us of hidden idols? Idols are false gods—things that appear to be good and God, but aren't. No matter how Godly these idols from our father's house, people, and country seem, we must remember that they are from man. Man's system is a fallen world system, under Satan's control. There is no good thing in our flesh, and even our righteousness is as filthy rags (Isaiah 64:6). Also, whose idea was idolatry in the first place—someone or something trying to take the place of God? It was Satan's idea to try and overthrow God and become a false god. Are we starting to get the idea that all these good intentions we get sucked into have their source in Satan? It's true! Lucifer, the angel of light, is the master at deceiving sincere Christians. My wife and I have come up with this saying to guard against being deceived with good intentions: "Is this a good idea or a God idea?"

How about the devil's second sword, "offenses"? A world full of good intentions based on knowledge and works is the perfect breeding ground for offenses. Why? When what I know about God and do for Him is different than what you know and do, there's going to be an offense. But it doesn't stop there, because the devil's second name is "Satan." The name *Satan* means accuser of the brethren, and boy, does he! He's really good at it; Jesus said he is the father of lies, and when he lies, he speaks his native tongue and has no accent. When he lies to me about you, making all kinds of accusations against you, most of the time I buy it hook, line, and sinker and get offended. I'm reeled in like some unsuspecting fish.

Where there are offenses and accusations, relationships end, sometimes in a very dramatic fashion. Let's look at the story of Cain and Abel. Cain got offended, never dealt with it as God suggested, and he murdered his own innocent brother. So Satan was there from the very beginning. He swung his sword of good intentions by tempting Adam and Eve to eat from the tree of the knowledge of good and evil. He swung his sword of offenses when Cain murdered Abel. One...two. The swords were swung in the book of Genesis, and Satan's been swinging them ever since on poor, unsuspecting human beings.

ONE...TWO. THE SWORDS WERE SWUNG IN THE BOOK OF GENESIS, AND SATAN'S BEEN SWINGING THEM EVER SINCE.

As believers we need to wake up! We must realize there is a real war going on, a power struggle. To help us understand, think of this principle of physics: nature abhors a vacuum. For example, if a jet is flying at 40,000 ft. and a window breaks, all the air will rush out of the cabin to fill the "thin-air vacuum" outside of the plane. There is a similar principle in the spiritual realm: power abhors a vacuum. When there are areas of our life that are not under the Lordship of Jesus, idols rush in to fill the vacuum. Where the Holy Spirit is not our counselor, demons rush in to fill the vacuum. When we are not in our Father's house, Satan rushes in to grab our hand and take us to his house for joint custody. It's as real as an airplane window blowing out, but we are just not aware of it.

What we have just described is a heart that has been leavened and divided by the yeast of the Pharisees, which is knowledge and works. A heart with a watered down and weakened version of the Gospel. Weakened and war make for a bad combination. With this in mind, what I'm about to share, I say with great sorrow. I have known sincere believers, who were very passionate with the five majestic trees. They were full of God's word, prayed continually, praised and thanked God even during trials, went to church twice on Sunday and Wednesday night, and ministered to those in need. This is what the church taught, and was all they knew. This system worked well as long as there were no major problems. But when a serious health, financial, or marriage problem arose, the power for victory wasn't there. In fact, some of these dear believers died, went broke, and got divorced.

I'm not saying believers won't experience problems, that loss can't turn into great gain, or that sometimes the Lord calls those who love Him home at an early age. My business went broke and I lost it, but that turned into great gain for me. Isaiah 57:1 says, "The righteous perishes, and no man takes it to heart; merciful men are taken away, while no one considers that the righteous is taken away from evil." But what I do believe is this, when Jesus died on the cross and was raised from the dead, He defeated every demon and curse. In fact, here are His direct words to us: "I saw Satan fall like lightening from heaven. Behold, I give you the authority to trample on serpents and scorpions, and over all the power of the enemy, and nothing shall by any means hurt you" (Luke 10:18-19). Deep within our spiritual DNA, we know that this was the way it was meant to be. We are to have power and dominion over Satan, not vice versa. So when we see a believer who is standing on the Word, praising God, and seeking prayer during their trial die, go broke, or get divorced, a Divine Dissatisfaction arises in us. This is why millions of Christians are asking God, "Where's the power?"

I believe there is a simple answer. When Jesus Christ crucified is in His rightful place of preeminence above the five majestic trees and those trees are firmly anchored in the Gospel, we will have power. When that's not the case, we won't. And that is not the case today in most western churches. That's why finding the lost secret of the cross and community is so important. To illustrate, let's show the contrast between two different worlds, that of a Caterpillar Christian without the lost secret, and a Birthright Butterfly with the lost secret.

A Caterpillar Christian's World

1. **KNOWLEDGE**: Learn more and more about God. (Genesis 2:17; Romans 5:20)

2. **WORKS**: Do more and more for God. (Galatians 3:11-12; Ephesians 2:8-9)

3. **LITTLE TRANSFORMATION**: Appears to be very spiritual, but actually very shallow. Low level of dying to self to be transformed into a new creation in Christ. (Colossians 2:21-23)

4. **LITTLE LOVE**: Divisions, splits, bite and devour each other. (Galatians 5:15)

5. **LITTLE POWER**: Lots of talk but few miracles. (1 Corinthians 4:20)

A Birthright Butterfly's World

1. **THE CROSS**: The most important thing in my Christian walk is the crucifixion and resurrection of Christ and Jesus being my first love. (Colossians 1:15-20; Revelation 2:4)

2. **COMMUNITY**: We gather together in homes with believers who have a passion for the cross, in trusting and caring relationships. (Acts 2:42-47; Acts 4:32-35; Acts 20:20)

3. **TRANSFORMATION**: We are transparent with God and each other, in order to die to self and be transformed into new creations in Christ. (Romans 6:3-4; 2 Corinthians 5:17)

4. **RECONCILIATION**: As new creations, we are reconciled to the Father as sons and daughters, and to each other as brothers and sisters in Christ. We enter His relationship world of supernatural love, joy, and peace, even in the midst of trials. (Romans 8:15-16; John 13:34; 2 Corinthians 5:18-20)

5. **POWER**: In this world of love, we are fused together as one and God fills us with His supernatural power. We enter His rulership world of victory over sin, Satan, and curses to be blessed and fulfill our destiny to bless others. (John 17:20-23; Acts 1:4-8; Acts 2:1-4)

Now we have the answer to our two big questions, "Where's the love?" and "Where's the power?" We have little power because we have little love. We have little love because we have little transformation into new creations in Christ. Why? Because learning more about God and doing more things for God doesn't change our inner man much. But making Christ crucified the most important thing in our lives and being in transparent and trusting relationships with other believers who share that passion brings huge change!

I call the five-part Birthright Butterfly world "The Lost Secret Sequence." Think of the sequence like a five-pronged key that opens a treasure chest. Inside this treasure chest is God Himself! When we get God, we get love, joy, and peace even in the midst of trials. And we get power for victory over sins, Satan, and curses, to be blessed and be a blessing. Our lost birthright world of love relationships and rulership power has been found!

The Lost Secret Sequence

1. THE CROSS
2. COMMUNITY
3. TRANSFORMATION
4. RECONCILIATION
5. POWER

Since *The Lost Secret Sequence* represents the core message of this book, let's explore it further. First comes the cross. The crucifixion and resurrection of Jesus is how Christianity began—without it our faith would not exist. To this day, it represents the very essence of Christianity. That's why Christ crucified must be the most important thing for all believers and Jesus must be our first love. This truth is clearly confirmed in the following scripture:

He is the image of the invisible God, the firstborn over all creation. For by Him all things were created that are in heaven and that are on earth, visible and invisible, whether thrones or dominions or principalities or powers. All things were created through Him and for Him. And He is before all things, and in Him all things consist. And He is the head of the body, the church, who is the beginning, the firstborn from the dead, that in all things He may have the preeminence. For it pleased the Father that in Him all the fullness should dwell, and by Him to reconcile all things to Himself, by Him, whether things on earth or things in heaven, having made peace through the blood of His cross (Colossians 1:15-20).

But somehow the most important thing in Christianity is no longer the most important thing in the church. That somehow has a name—Satan! He stole the message of the cross and has been running for dear life ever since. He knows once he gets caught, and we get the message of Christ Crucified back, it's over for him!

Second comes Christian community. It's what we all long for, to be in real caring and trusting relationships. Right after Jesus ascended to heaven, we see this deep human need of love being fulfilled in the book of Acts. They met in homes, got to know each other, built trust, and were there for each other in times of need. This continued for hundreds of years. But shortly after the emperor Constantine legalized Christianity in 313 AD another change occurred. He began to build church buildings, and Caterpillar Christianity emerged. Soon, well-intentioned believers would brush shoulders every Sunday as they walked in and out of church. The sweet and intimate home fellowships they had enjoyed became a thing of the past. I'm not advocating shutting down all the church buildings. What I am

> TRANSFORMATION IS THE KEY ELEMENT TO ENTERING GOD'S WORLD OF LOVE AND POWER.

saying is we all need to make Jesus Christ crucified preeminent and have home fellowship with believers who share this passion (we will explore home fellowships further in chapter fifteen).

Christians who embrace the lost secret of the cross and community go on to experience number three, transformation—the key element to entering God's world of love and power. With a passion for the cross and trust in each other, we are able to be transparent with God and one another. We allow the Lord to shine His light inside of us, so we can die to self and be transformed into new creations in Christ—it's no longer I who live but Christ who lives in me (Galatians 2:20). Remember, I don't want to be God, I want God to be me! Adam and Eve tried to turn the Garden of Eden into a *how to* world of knowledge and works to become like God, and it didn't work. Transformation is not about learning how to do something, it's about dying to self so that God can do things through us.

Now comes the good part, number four, which is reconciliation. We are reunited with the Father as sons and daughters and each other as brothers and sisters in Christ. We go beyond just human caring to a world of supernatural love, joy, and peace—even in the midst of life's trials.

Number five is the grand finale...power! God's chosen method to release power in the natural world is through fusion—the thermonuclear explosion of a hydrogen bomb, which is the power of the stars. So it is in the supernatural world. The book of Acts says that when they were gathered together in one accord (fusion), the Holy Spirit came and filled them with power. It's the power for victory over sins, demons, and curses. It's the power that Satan fears!

A simple summary of The Lost Secret Sequence is this: What's missing in conventional Christianity is the cross and community. Together they transform us into new creations in Christ—a metamorphosis from Caterpillar Christians into Birthright Butterflies. Then the cry of our heart is answered, as we enter the lost world of God's love and power.

That's the world I want to live in, don't you? In this world, the truth that Satan isn't as big as we make him out to be will be understood. We will agree with Isaiah 14:16-17 which, talking about Lucifer, says, "Those who see you will gaze at you, and consider you, saying: 'Is this the man who made the earth tremble, who shook kingdoms, who made the world as a wilderness and destroyed its cities, who did not open the house of his prisoners?'" Satan, compared to God and Jesus in us, is very, very small. The biggest thing that gives him power is the fact he is *the great deceiver*.

Here's a final motivation for all of us to take those two swords out of Satan's hands and live in a world of power and dominion over the devil. The seed to write this book was planted at a restaurant, with a vision of

Jesus and God the Father looking at one another, saying, "Did We do this for nothing?" They were both very sad. Their hearts were broken. Now let's play out some real-life scenarios involving good intentions and offenses and see how we could break God's heart and not even be aware of it.

Here's one scenario. What if, even if my commitment is very sincere, my relationship with God and my Christianity develops into one based on how much I know and how much I do. What is that saying? "I can attain a righteousness based on knowledge and works, and I don't need You anymore. I'm this generator, and I'm cranking up my own righteousness." We don't think about it, but Jesus and the Father are real, live beings in heaven who hear and feel what we are saying. They are trying to tell us, "You're off on your little trip here, learning, learning, doing, doing, learning, learning, doing, doing; and what you're really saying without knowing it is, 'You died for nothing.'"

Scenario number two is represented by one of the deadliest things that a Christian can ever say: "That's just the way I am." A decision comes up in our life, and the Bible says, "For waging war you need…many advisers" (Proverbs 24:6), and, "In a multitude of counselors there is safety" (Proverbs 11:14), but we say, "I'm just not an input-oriented person!" The Bible says, "Give generously" (Psalm 37:21; Romans 12:8), and, "If you sow abundantly, you will reap abundantly" (Luke 6:38; 2 Corinthians 9:6, both paraphrased), but we say, "I'm just not a big giver." The Bible says, "Don't put your light under a bushel basket" (Matthew 5:15, paraphrased), and to live this out, the Holy Spirit prompts us to share something with a person, but we say, "I'm just a quiet person." The list goes on, and on, and on. The most famous—or infamous—words of every Christian are, "That's just the way I am."

THE MOST FAMOUS—OR INFAMOUS—WORDS OF EVERY CHRISTIAN ARE, "THAT'S JUST THE WAY I AM."

No one ever thinks, when we're saying those 'innocent' little words, that we're really saying Jesus died for nothing. However, when I accept the "false me"—my personality based on hidden idols and the demons attached—I'm really telling the Lord exactly that, "You died for nothing," and it hurts Jesus and the Father a lot.

EMBRACING THE CROSS
REMOVES SATAN'S SWORDS

SEARCH ME OH LORD

Deal With Offenses

The last scenario is when I'm offended by a brother or sister I love and I end that relationship. Do you know what I'm saying without knowing it? "Lord, what You did on the cross was not enough to cover this problem. In this situation You died for nothing." We don't know we're saying that; no one would knowingly say that. We all super-spiritualize breaking off relationships with people, but the reality of the fact is that when we do that, we are saying, "You died for nothing."

As I said before, there are some physically and mentally abusive situations that the Lord will tell us to get out of. But I can tell you, from personal observation, there are many Christians who claim they are in unbearable, abusive situations when that is not the truth. The reality is this, many times their idols were getting bumped into and they were being offended by Jesus, who is a rock of offense; but the devil and their emotions convinced them otherwise—it's always easier for us to blame someone else than to look inside and deal with our own junk.

Thank goodness, God is gracious, compassionate, and full of mercy. When He passed before Moses, He said, "The Lord, the Lord, the compassionate and gracious God, slow to anger, abounding in love and faithfulness" (Exodus 34:6). Thank the Lord He understands we are dust. The church never intended to get into the wisdom of the world system, right? No Christian ever intended on getting stuck in the caterpillar stage. Nobody ever wanted to get into idols, right? No one plans to end relationships with people they love. But, guess what? The *good news* is this. God understands that. He's speaking to our hearts, and what He's saying is, "Look, I have mercy on you. I understand you've been duped, deceived, and ripped off."

The Bible says that if we know the truth, the truth will set us free, and those whom the Son has set free are free indeed (John 8:32, 36). Jesus said, "The thief does not come except to steal, and to kill, and to destroy. I have come that they may have life, and that they may have it more abundantly" (John 10:10). That's the purposes of this book, to get the truth out, so we can live an abundant life. It gives us all the opportunity to make a choice—to embrace the cross and take those two swords out of Satan's hands. To say, "Search me, Lord, and expose all of my good intentions." To cry out, "You've forgiven me of my sins; how can I not forgive those who have offended me?"

We can embrace the vertical beam of the cross and remove the sword of good intentions by saying this simple prayer:

Father God and Jesus, I am so sorry I broke Your heart with my good intentions. I thought I was getting closer to You with all of my knowledge and works, but in reality I was getting farther away. And worst of all, without knowing it, my path of self-righteousness was saying You died for nothing. My false me being in control also hurt You. All the times I said "That's just the way I am," thinking it was a good thing, even though it went against Your Word. Again, without knowing it, I said You died for nothing. You didn't die for nothing—You died for me! And I accept all that You did on the cross for me and trade in all my good intentions for the only goodness that is real—the righteousness I have by putting my faith in You Jesus.

Are we now ready to embrace the horizontal beam of the cross and take the sword of offense out of his hand? We can, by saying this prayer,

Lord, I forgive the person (people) who offended me just as I have been forgiven by You when I have sinned and hurt people. I release them; their slate is clean. They don't owe me anything, because You alone are my source for everything. I remit the effect of their sin on me. I give all the pain, sorrow, anger, and hate to You on the cross so I don't have to carry any of the junk. I take the ax to any bitterness that is trying to take root in me; by the blood of Jesus, I cut it off and remove it. I repent for any judgments I had against that person and ask You to forgive me. And finally, I pray that You will help that person to see the error of their ways and how they are hurting people. I also pray that You either have them return to me or have me go to them to share the truth in love so that our relationship can be restored.

When we pray this prayer, we are putting a big smile on Father God's face. Remember, we are made in His image and likeness. Think about what it would be like if you were a parent and your children were offended and decided never to see each other again. Wouldn't that break your heart? But wouldn't you be overjoyed if instead they prayed this prayer and were reconciled? It's the same for our heavenly Father.

Did you pray these prayers? Were you sincere? If so, gaze at the closing painting for a while. Picture yourself as part of that scene, with the Lion of the Tribe of Judah victorious. Your smile will grow just as big as your heavenly Father's!

My Personal One-on-One Encounter With The Lord

Also for Home Group Discussion

How are the devil's two swords, "good intentions" and "offenses," connected to two of his names, Lucifer and Satan?

_____

_____

_____

_____

_____

Why has Satan so intensely swung these swords since the Garden of Eden? What does he have to gain or lose?

_____

_____

_____

_____

Do I understand the physics principle that nature abhors a vacuum? What does that mean when applied to spiritual things?

_____

_____

_____

_____

What's most important to me: is it learning more about God and doing more things for God—*or*—is it Christ crucified and real relationships in Christian community? What's my identity: is it knowledge and works, which produce achievements—*or*—is it dying to self and being transformed into a new creation in Christ, a wonderful prince or princess becoming a king or queen?

_____

_____

_____

_____

How, through my thinking and actions, have I unknowingly said to Jesus and the Father, "You died for nothing"? What are some of the examples of this in my life?

_____

_____

_____

_____

_____

What is the Lord showing me about how to make the lost secret of the cross and community part of my life, to be transformed into a Birthright Butterfly? Am I ready?

_____

_____

_____

_____

_____

Suggestion: Do you want to have power and dominion over Satan instead of vice versa? If you haven't read the scriptures at the end of the chapter three One-on-One Encounter, I would really encourage you to do so. Everyone who has, reports that it's been a life-changing experience.

REFLECTING ON THE ART

- In what way does the painting that opens this chapter speak to me?
- Did the sketch have an impact on me? If so, how?
- Can I now picture myself in this chapter's final painting titled *Triumph of the Lion of the Tribe of Judah?*

_____

_____

_____

_____

_____

A New Covenant
A New Heart—A New World

CHAPTER 14

A New Covenant

A New Heart—A New World

HOW WOULD YOU LIKE TO GET THE HEART of the Lion of the Tribe of Judah, who is standing victorious over Satan? We can! In fact, it's our God-given birthright to have dominion over the devil. God wants to give us that new heart, and the way He's going to do this is through a New Covenant. Through His Old Testament prophets Jeremiah and Ezekiel, the Lord spoke about a new and better covenant that He was going to bring to us. It's an incredible covenant because it was cut with the blood of His one and only Son.

As we've already talked about in this book, we often look at ourselves and the church and have to ask, "Where's the love? Where's the power?" If we're asking those two questions, then we're obviously not fully receiving everything that He has provided for us in the New Covenant, are we? I believe the Lord wants us to know how we can fully enter into this wonderful New Covenant—the new world of love, blessings, and fulfilled destiny that the lost secret opens up to us. The first part of the lost secret is that we *make Jesus Christ and Him crucified preeminent* in our lives. The logic of this is that if God the Father established the covenant through the crucifixion and resurrection of His Son, then any diminishing of that from its place of preeminence will weaken what we're going to receive out of that covenant. Sometimes we make things too complicated, but it really is that simple. As we load other things on top, and put them ahead of what—and Who—created the covenant in the first place, then we're diminishing the covenant. That's the first and simplest truth as to why we're not experiencing the fullness of the New Covenant. The number one secret to God's power has been lost.

To get a better understanding of the covenant and its promised blessings, we're going to address three questions. The first is, *What is a covenant?* We take for granted that we understand what a covenant is, but when we really study the meaning, there's more to it than most of us probably realize. The second question is, *Why is the New Covenant different and better than the Old Covenant?* And third, *How do we literally get this New Covenant inside of us—into our hearts?*

Let's dig right in. What is a covenant? The biggest mistake most of us make is to think of a covenant as merely an oath. We say, "I'm going to enter into a covenant with you. I'm going to give you my word, and we're going to make a pledge to do something." That's a very, very weak definition of what a covenant is; it's not God's idea of covenant. The first thing we need to understand is, God's idea is that a covenant governs relationships. It's all about relationships.

Genesis 15 sets up a covenant between Abraham and God. When we look at the actual word usage in that chapter, making the covenant meant "to cut." God *cut* a covenant with Abraham. Did you ever hear the term "cut a deal"? It came from here—from the word covenant. It means, in Hebrew, "to enter into a compact, a confederacy, an alliance, a league, made by passing between two pieces of flesh." It's a very visual concept.

How important is this covenant we're entering into? We're going to take an animal and cut it in half to symbolize two people. There will be blood shed—you can't give anything higher than life, can you? When that blood is shed, we're saying that those two halves are entering a league. They're going to enter an alliance, and they will walk together as one. That's way beyond a typical oath. Think of NATO, the North Atlantic Treaty Organization. That's a covenant, or an alliance. And what that commitment means is that if someone attacks one member of NATO, it is as if that someone has attacked all of the members. We will fight to the death to defend any country in NATO. That's what the word *covenant* means.

There are a couple of other root words in the Scriptures related to *covenant* that bear noting. In Genesis 1:1, when it says, "God created the heavens and the earth," the word *created* is a derivative of *covenant*. It literally means "to create by cutting." The idea is the same as when we cut down trees; we select and choose certain trees, in order to use the wood to create and form something else. It's a formative process.

The other root word for covenant is similar because it means "to select." But it also means "to feed, give meat, and render clear and manifest."

I never knew this before, but if we take all of those Hebrew words for covenant, and put them together, God is sending this message to us: *I want to make it clear to you that I have chosen you to enter into an alliance with Me, so I can feed you and bless you. I cut this covenant with you by the body and blood of My one and only Son, so that you and I, and your brothers and sisters in Christ, can be one. Will you let Me cut you in half, to divide the false you from the real you so that this false fleshly you can be put to death on the cross of My Son and you can be raised a new creation? Then you can enter into this New Covenant with Me, and I will fill you with all of My love and power so you can receive your promised blessings and be used by Me to bless others.*

> I WANT TO MAKE IT CLEAR TO YOU THAT I HAVE CHOSEN YOU TO ENTER INTO AN ALLIANCE WITH ME, SO I CAN FEED YOU AND BLESS YOU.

That is what those words associated with *covenant* mean. It gives the concept a whole different feeling, doesn't it? It's a very, very powerful message the Father is giving us—way beyond just giving us an oath or making a pledge. Now that we've learned what a covenant really is, there's a very simple truth we have to acknowledge if we're going to be joined together with a holy God. He cannot join together with a fleshly me, no matter how much He wants us to be joined. It is impossible. No matter how much we try to learn the difference between right and wrong, and no matter how hard we strive to do what is right, that will never put our flesh to death, and God can never join in union with our flesh. Therefore, *apart from the cross, no one can fully enter into the New Covenant.*

We make things very complicated, but it's really very simple. Holy God, sinful flesh. He says, "I cut a covenant with My Son so your flesh can be put to death. You can be raised a new creation, holy in the image and likeness of My Son, so that you and I can be one." That's the deal.

We've learned, though, that we have strayed. We start out at the cross when we're born again. We start out making a wholehearted commitment and dealing with our known sins, but then we get off on a tangent of trying to learn more and do more, and our flesh says, "Thank you very much, but I'm still alive and well." We wind up wondering, *Where's the love, and where's the power?* It's where it's always been, in the cross. Knowledge and works will never put our flesh to death.

That takes us right on into the answer to question number two: *How is the New Covenant different and better than the Old Covenant?* The Old Covenant was about man's works—my knowledge of right and wrong and what I do right. Guess what the New Covenant is about? What Jesus did on the cross! It's not about *my* works. Do you see the fork in the road? It comes up immediately; the Old Covenant goes one way, and the new takes off in a different direction.

What was the Old Covenant about? It was external, visual, and temporary. It had a temple; it had sacrifices; it had feasts. It had very visible, tangible elements; but the Bible clearly states in the New Testament that it is now obsolete. Hebrews 8:13 in the Amplified Bible says, "When God speaks of a new [covenant or agreement], He makes the first one obsolete (out of use). And what is obsolete (out of use and annulled because of age) is ripe for disappearance and to be dispensed with altogether." It was there as a placeholder—temporary.

What is the New Covenant? It's internal—we are the temple; it happens inside of us. It's invisible, and it is eternal. The New Covenant is a totally different thing, isn't it? It's a night-and-day difference. We're starting to understand how much better the new is than the old, but this is the jackpot of it all: relationships. Remember, a covenant is something that governs relationships.

Under the Old Covenant, if a person sinned it affected his relationship with his brothers and sisters, and with God, right? Very clearly, in Leviticus 20, the Bible lists certain sins that, if committed, would cause the person to be cut off from the assembly or even put to death. In this way, under the Old Covenant, my sin would dictate my relationships with others and with God. Guess what the New Covenant says? *Nothing we can ever do will sever our relationship with God or with each other because of the cross.* What do you think is a better way to govern relationships between people, and between people and God? Since I need lots of mercy, I'd pick the New Covenant every time. We all would, wouldn't we?

SINCE I NEED LOTS OF MERCY, I'D PICK THE NEW COVENANT EVERY TIME.

Why do you think Satan tries so hard to get us back to the Old Covenant? Because under the Old Covenant, relationships can end, can't they? And everybody has seen this happen—either to themselves or someone else: I'm learning a lot of things about God; I'm doing a lot of things for God, and all of a sudden something bad happens in my life. *Hey, what's up? There must be a problem with You, God, so I'm going to end my relationship with You.* Right? It happens all of the time.

Or maybe I'm in a relationship with you. I'm doing a lot of things for you, bending over backwards for you, and all of a sudden you do something inappropriate and nasty to me. Whoo! I'm going to end my relationship with you! It happens every day in the church. Why? Because we're not fully in the New Covenant.

That sort of severance in relationships is not a New Covenant activity. It's Old Covenant thinking. We paint it, spruce it up, and make it look holy. We actually think we have the right to sever from each other or terminate our relationships with God, but we don't. Not under the New Covenant.

The New Covenant says that nothing can separate us from the love of Christ—not nakedness, famine, peril, principality, or anything else (Romans 8:35-39). And *nothing* can sever our relationship with God the Father and the Holy Spirit, or with our brothers and sisters in Christ. That's why Satan wants so desperately to get us back into the Old Covenant of religion and super-spirituality, because under that covenant we can end relationships. Also, he knows what we've already discovered in this journey: There is power in relationships. When we fuse with God and with one another, we get power. Who is adversely affected by that power? The devil. This stuff is not rocket science; it's all very simple. God is now removing the scales off of our eyes so we can understand.

Now let's answer the third question: *How do we get this New Covenant into us—into our hearts?* When you read the scriptures from Jeremiah and Ezekiel about the coming New Covenant (they are listed in the one-on-one encounter at the end of the chapter), five distinct aspects of this covenant emerge. It's these five things the Lord wants to put into us to give us a new heart.

Do you know what the word *new* means? "A fresh new heart, cheerful and full of glad news." Sounds like the good news of the gospel to me! So let's imagine ourselves in the cocoon, and God taking a lump of coal, which represents our Old Covenant heart, and with great pressure and heat turning it into a raw diamond. He then cuts five beautiful facets into that diamond, and when He's done, He's going to step back and say, "I've created an absolute masterpiece."

> DO YOU KNOW WHAT THE WORD NEW MEANS? "A FRESH NEW HEART, CHEERFUL AND FULL OF GLAD NEWS."

When you read these Scriptures from Jeremiah and Ezekiel, there's a common thread through all of them: idolatry and harlotry. The number one sin—or flaw—we see is that man creates gods and wants to take over for God. That's the bad news. That's what has to be cut out. The good news is that through the cross of Christ, He can remove those idols and transform our divided heart into one heart. Jeremiah 32:39 says He's going to give us "one heart and one way." There will be no more affections divided between God and idols. Remember what we learned about having a divided heart—that we make Jesus our Lord, but we have hidden idols that vie with Him for control? We believe the Holy Spirit is our Counselor, but the demons that are attached to the hidden idols are always whispering in our ears. We believe God is our Father, but then Satan gets us into a joint custody battle, because he wants to be our father. We are divided—we have a divided heart—but the first beautiful facet is *one heart.*

Now comes the second facet. We learned in Psalm 115:4-8 that those who have idols become like them. What are idols made of? Stone. And stone is dull and stupid; it can't see, hear, or think. To make this point more clear, let's look at the story of the loaves and fishes in Matthew 15:29-16:12. Jesus has just performed the miracle of the loaves and fishes and fed the five thousand people. He gets on the boat with His apostles, and He says to the apostles, "Beware the yeast of the Pharisees." The apostles, who seem very dumb at this point, look at one another and ask, "Gee, did we forget the bread?"

And Jesus answers (paraphrased), "How dull are you? Don't you remember? Didn't you see with your eyes and hear with your ears when I multiplied the loaves and fishes?" They didn't because they had hard hearts. It was before the cross. Jesus had spoken earlier about this concept in Matthew 13:13-15. He said, "Isaiah prophesied, 'You see with your eyes but you don't see. You hear with your ears but you don't hear. You perceive with your heart, but you don't understand, lest you would turn and I would heal you.'"

Idolatry causes even whole-hearted disciples of Christ to have hard, dull hearts. Even the simplest things—perhaps especially those simplest things—we don't get. But He promises to give us a heart of flesh, soft and compassionate, and quick to understand (Ezekiel 11:18-21). I like that. It's a great exchange. I'm getting rid of my hard, dumb, stupid heart, and He's replacing it with a soft, moist *heart that can receive and be filled*. If we picture this master jeweler, He's cut the second facet.

The third facet is that He wants to put the reverential fear of God in our hearts so we will worship Him alone (Jeremiah 32:38-40). And this is worth saying again: God is jealous. He's telling us, "Don't put the things of man ahead of Me, the world system of knowledge and works or the idols from your father's house, people, or country. Don't even put the things of God ahead of Me. I'm going to put such a reverential fear in you that you will never even put My Word ahead of Me. You won't put worship ahead of Me; You won't put ministry ahead of Me. You will have reverential fear of Me." It's a worshipful, reverential fear because we know He's recreating and changing our hearts. We're at a place where we say, "I wouldn't think of putting anything above You. You are worth it."

That's a pretty powerful place to be, isn't it? It's a place of ongoing worship. Our hearts are always worshipping God, all of the time, and as we go through life, there's nothing we'll put ahead of God. Nothing is enticing enough for us to put it ahead of God—we worship Him and Him alone. It's the same place that Abraham was on Mt. Moriah, which, as we know, is Calvary—the place of clear vision. He didn't put his one and only son ahead of God, and that's why God said, "Now I know that you fear Me." Abraham had *reverential fear*. That's the third facet.

The fourth facet is that the Lord said He's going to put *His law and His Word into our hearts* (See Jeremiah 31:33). In the Old Covenant, the finger of God chiseled His law into stone; in the New Covenant, the finger of God chisels it onto our hearts. Like a master jeweler, He takes that diamond and He carves *love* into it. Romans 13:8-10 says that all the law and the prophets are summarized by one thing: love. Jesus reminds us to "love the Lord your God with all your heart, with all your soul, and with all your mind," then adds, "You shall love your neighbor as yourself," and states that "On these two commandments hang all the Law and the Prophets" (Matthew 22:37-40). In addition, He

> ## LIKE A MASTER JEWELER, HE TAKES THAT DIAMOND AND HE CARVES LOVE INTO IT.

gives us a new commandment, "As I have loved you...you also love one another" (John 13:34). He removes the external commands of the law to love, and then He writes the law of love into our hearts.

What does the cut of a diamond determine? How light is let in and how it goes out. As the Lord is carving these facets into your heart, picture it opening up to receive more of His light. It begins to shimmer and blaze like fire, and with every beat, every vibration, your heart is saying, "I love you, Lord, with all of my heart, all my soul, all of my strength. And, I love my brothers the way You love them. I'll never judge them; I'll never shun them; I will lay down my life for them as You laid down Your life for Me." As that spiritual heart beats inside of us, resonating with that message all of the time, it lets in more and more light. And we glow—we become radiant—and let more of His love out.

The fifth facet we also find in Jeremiah 31, this time in verse 34: we're going to *know God*. The word *know* here means "to know by experience." It's a marital word, as when we know one another intimately in marriage and become joined as one flesh.

What would happen if we knew—by experience—the Lord? Where would our level of faith go? We would *know* that God is light—that God is love—that God is one—and that God is Spirit and power (1 John 1:5; 1 John 4:16; Deuteronomy 6:4; John 4:24).

If something comes up—a need, a temptation—you know what? God isn't a theory anymore or a concept, but we possess Him inside of us and know Him by experience. We *know* He is light, which means that the words He speaks are true. We *know* that He is love and that He loves us. We *know* that He is one—the Father, Son and Holy Spirit are one—and we are one

Old Covenant Heart

LAW

1. Divided Heart – Idols

2. Heart of Stone – Hard

3. Lack of Reverential Fear of God

4. Our Thinking – Can't Obey

5. Don't Truly Know God

New Covenant Heart

LOVE

1. One Heart – No Idols

2. Heart of Flesh – Soft

3. Reverential Fear of God

4. His Words – Ability to Obey

5. Know God by Experience

with Him. And that out of oneness, His power is released and nothing is impossible for Him. He has the power to back up His word to me and His love for me. Our faith becomes internalized and organic because we know God and God lives inside of us.

Now I know that everybody is scared—we're always scared about going to the cross—and it is a scary thing to say, "Cut me in half." But imagine if we allowed God to do that, and allowed the master jeweler to fashion that beautiful, five-faceted diamond gem inside of us; would our lives ever be the same? It's a whole new world, isn't it? That's why it's called the *New* Covenant. It's not the old world of the Old Covenant. It's not about this world at all; it's about a new world that the cross opens up to us.

I encourage everyone to go deeper into this in the one-on-one encounter by reading the Jeremiah and Ezekiel scriptures, but right now let's just summarize them. There was an *abomination*. That's the word that is used. That abomination was playing the harlot with idols, by both the leaders and the flock alike. This abomination provoked God to anger, and when we do it today, it separates us from Him just like in the Old Testament. It brings us into captivity, curses, destruction and death. That's what happened to the Israelites, and it's happening to the church today.

When we choose to make Jesus Christ and Him crucified preeminent, we fully enter the New Covenant—cut with the body and blood of Jesus Himself. It brings God joy; He's not angry. He totally unites us with Himself and brings us blessings and life. That's our choice—it's life or death.

I believe God is wooing us back to Him, and I believe that at this point in the book He is saying, *Why don't you ask Me to enter into the fullness of this New Covenant relationship? All you have to do is ask. I stand ready to answer.*

Remember what was said earlier in the chapter, the message God gave about the New Covenant? Go back and read it. And then let's tell the Lord, "I want that!" He's interested in us; He's gone to a lot of trouble for us. He's ready to give us everything in the New Covenant—everything Jesus won for us on that cross. We've been seeking; we've been asking; we've been knocking—but on all of the wrong doors. And the Lord is saying, *Now that you understand what a covenant is, and how much different and better the New Covenant is—now that you see how I want to fashion your heart in these five ways, like a perfect diamond—ask Me. I will give it to you.*

If that is your heart's desire, you can use the following prayer as a guide to enter into this New Covenant with the Lord.

> *Father,*
>
> *I want You to cleanse me of the filth of my harlotry. I want You to purge me of all of my idolatry—my good intentions. I want You to cleanse me of that. I want You to give me one heart. I don't want a divided heart anymore. I want my heart to be totally and completely consumed with You. I want You to take out my heart of stone, my dull, hard, and stubborn heart, and replace it with a soft heart that's compassionate and quick to understand. I want You to put the reverential fear of God inside me, which is the beginning of wisdom, and I want You to write Your Word—Your law—on my heart. That law is love. Last but not least, I want to know You. I want to get You and possess You. I ask You to give me more of Yourself. Fill me with Your light so that I can shine forever like a diamond in Your hand.*
>
> *I am Yours, my Beloved. All of me. And now I receive You as mine—completely.*
>
> *Amen.*

My Personal One-on-One Encounter With The Lord

ALSO FOR HOME GROUP DISCUSSION

What is the difference between a covenant and a mere oath?

_____

_____

_____

As I read again of the Father's desire for me to experience all the riches of His covenant, do I long to be in covenant with Him?

I want to make it clear to you that I have chosen you to enter into an alliance with Me, so I can feed you and bless you. I cut this covenant with you by the body and blood of My one and only Son, so that you and I, and your brothers and sisters in Christ, can be one. Will you let Me cut you in half, to search you, so your carnal nature can be put to death on the cross of My Son, and you can be raised a new creation? Then you can enter into this New Covenant with Me, and I will fill you with all of My love and power so you can receive your promised blessings and be used by Me to bless others.

_____

_____

_____

_____

No one can experience this beautiful covenant with the Father without the cross. Am I now motivated more than ever to embrace the cross which is for me and not against me? What things may still be holding me back?

_____

_____

_____

_____

Do I understand the difference between the Old Covenant, which was external, visible, and temporary, and the New Covenant, which is internal, invisible, and eternal? Which one do I choose for my life?

_____

_____

_____

_____

Can I visualize my heart being transformed from a lump of coal into a flawless, fiery diamond because of what Jesus did for me on the cross?

_____

_____

_____

_____

Take the time to read these scriptures from Jeremiah and Ezekiel and see for yourself the five facets of the New Covenant that God, as a Master Jeweler, wants to carve in our hearts: Jeremiah 31:31-34; Jeremiah 32:27-44; Ezekiel 11:18-21; Ezekiel 18:1-32; Ezekiel 36:17-38

_____

_____

_____

REFLECTING ON THE ART

- In what way does the painting that opens this chapter speak to me?
- Did the sketch have an impact on me? If so, how?

_____

_____

_____

Love and Power
in a Home Group

CHAPTER 15

Love and Power in a Home Group

NO ONE CAN GO ON THIS SPIRITUAL JOURNEY ALONE. The experience is meant to be shared. Just as the original release of power came to a hundred and twenty people in the Upper Room, so it will be now. We need to be with others, persons whom God will place in our lives, in order to go through this process of transformation. Based on Scripture, I believe the ideal situation is a home support group.

Let's start by asking the question, "What was truly new in the New Covenant?" The word new in the Greek means *novel* or *fresh*, i.e. *unused*. Would the five majestic trees fit this definition? The Word, prayer, worship, fellowship, gatherings, and ministry all existed in the Old Covenant. They all moved forward into the New Covenant with some changes and additions. What two things, though, never existed in the Old Covenant? The crucifixion and resurrection of Jesus, and God's people meeting in homes. The church puts a lot of emphasis on the majestic trees, which is needed. But the core of Christianity, which was introduced in the book of Acts, is all but forgotten. The cross and community, the secret to unlocking God's power, have been lost!

We've spent a lot of time on the first part of the lost secret, the message of the cross. Let's take a closer look at the second part—believers with a passion for the cross meeting in homes.

There's something different about a home. A home is where people live, eat, and raise children. It's a place to rest, a place of family. A home is different than a building. Previous to the New Covenant, God's people went to the temple and synagogues, but they had never met in homes until the New Covenant. The concept of believers bonding together in small home groups started in the New Covenant church.

If anybody questions the importance of being together in a very tightly knit small group, the simplest way to prove it is this: before anything existed in the whole universe, there was a Trinity. That was the original small group. God the Father, God the Son, and God the Holy Spirit were working together as one. If the Lord ever intended for us to be loners—to be alone and on our own—there never would have been a Trinity. If God Himself chose not to go it alone, how much more should we sit up and take notice and realize that we've got to be in close relationships in order to experience transformation, reconciliation, and receive supernatural power? We all need these close relationships in order to fully experience The Lost Secret Sequence, to restore what's been missing in conventional Christianity.

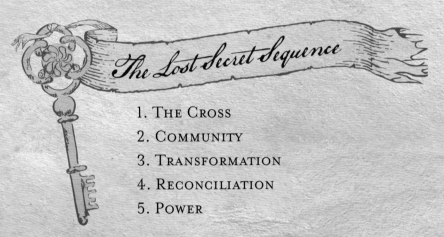

The Lost Secret Sequence

1. THE CROSS
2. COMMUNITY
3. TRANSFORMATION
4. RECONCILIATION
5. POWER

The second part of the lost secret, *community*, is what really creates momentum in this sequence, propelling us forward on our spiritual journey. Within Christian community we can encourage one another to enter the cocoon to be transformed into Birthright Butterflies. We then enter a world of supernatural love, joy, and peace even in the midst of life's storms. Once we are fused together as one, God fills us with supernatural power. A world of victory over sin, Satan, and curses, to be blessed and fulfill our destiny to bless others awaits.

Since Christian community plays such an important role to entering this world, we're going to look at what works, when we get together as Christians, and what doesn't work. We're not doing this to judge anyone or knock anything. The reason we're doing this is because, again, when we look at ourselves and the church, we have to ask, "Where's the love, and where's the power?" If what we're doing now was working to produce a lot of love and power, we wouldn't have to figure out anything different, right? So we're simply asking, "What do we need to do differently?"

Let's look at the first thing. Does going in and out of a church building on Sunday—picture a visual image of brushing shoulders with fellow Christians—does that produce enormous amounts of supernatural love and power in the church? It hasn't. I'm not advising ministers to shut down their churches. In fact, Acts 2:46 states that early believers went to the temple and met in homes. But to me it's obvious that we need more than just meeting in church services.

I know some people may say, "What about home Bible studies or home cell groups?" There's a lot of that in the church, right? But do we see that producing supernatural love and supernatural power? No. Why?

There must be a difference in the way we gather together and how they gathered together in the church of Acts. They had supernatural love. The Bible says that all the believers held everything in common, selling their possessions and distributing the proceeds according to each others' needs (Acts 2:44-45). Is there a lot of that happening in the church today? They also had supernatural power. The Bible also says that when they laid hands on the sick, people recovered. We don't see a lot of that happening, either. It's pretty clear they had something we don't. What was it?

There are three scriptures that tell us—three right in a row, in fact. And that's not an accident; God is trying to show us something. In Acts 1:14, the Bible says, "These all continued *with one accord* in prayer and supplication, with the women and Mary the mother of Jesus, and with His brothers" (emphasis added). That's before Pentecost.

Then, in Acts 2:1, it says "When the Day of Pentecost had fully come, they were all *with one accord* in one place" (emphasis added). Finally, in Acts

2:46, it says, "So continuing daily *with one accord* in the temple, and breaking bread from house to house, they ate their food with gladness and simplicity of heart" (emphasis added). The Bible uses the phrase *with one accord* in each of those verses. Do you know what *one accord* means in the Greek? "Unanimous passion." And what did these people have a unanimous passion for? Jesus Christ and Him crucified and raised from the dead.

WHAT DID THESE PEOPLE HAVE A UNANIMOUS PASSION FOR? JESUS CHRIST CRUCIFIED AND RAISED FROM THE DEAD.

A good way to illustrate this is if we think back to the 9/11 terrorist attacks. Before 9/11 the U.S. was a very divided country, but when an event far bigger than everybody in this country happened, it brought America together, didn't it? It brought the U.S. into unity. In the weeks and months after 9/11, there was nothing more important than that event. Many attempts had been made before 9/11 to unify the country. They involved people getting together to discuss areas of common ground, and projects and programs to bring about unity. They rarely work, but a 9/11-type event does bring unity. What happens, though, when the memory of the event fades? The unity soon disappears. But the cross was a 9/11 with a second phase. The people who were brought together in unity then died to self and were transformed into new creations. These people then cared more about others than their own selves and were able to stay in unity. That's the difference between man's attempts versus God's success at unity.

That's the way it was with the believers in Acts. When Jesus was crucified, it totally devastated them. Then when He was raised from the dead, all of their petty differences fell aside. Everything else in their life took second place—the most important thing in their lives was Jesus Christ and Him crucified and raised from the dead. They had a *unanimous passion*. Then, as they were transformed into new creations, they were able to sustain and even strengthen that unity. That's the first difference between our home gatherings and the church of Acts. The cross was the center of everything for them, but for us it's not. I'm not criticizing cell groups or Bible studies. They're good, and I'm not saying to stop having them. But is the unanimous passion for the cross of Christ the most important and unifying aspect of these home gatherings? Even home churches need to ask themselves this question.

The second difference between those earlier believers and us is *humility*. They were broken. The apostles left all and actually lived with God in the flesh 24/7 for three years. That's a very high spiritual experience. Then, however, because of the cross, their hidden inner problems were exposed. They got knocked off their spiritual high horse, right? These were people, like Peter, who said they'd never deny Him, but they did deny Him. People who doubted He was really who He said, or that He would really rise again. When they encountered the cross, they were humbled—given a reality check of what was really going on inside of them—transformed.

WHEN THEY ENCOUNTERED THE CROSS, THEY WERE HUMBLED—GIVEN A REALITY CHECK OF WHAT WAS REALLY GOING ON INSIDE OF THEM—TRANSFORMED.

These people were not only unanimously passionate about Jesus but broken as well. There's not enough of that in the church today. In the church today—and I know because I was one of them—there are many people who think they are super-spiritual. We think we're something that we're not. We're not humble.

So what was the church of Acts like? The cross was preeminent, they gathered together in homes, they were humbled and transformed, they had supernatural love to sell and share possessions, and they were filled with the power of the Holy Spirit. Guess what? They had the Lost Secret Sequence and were living in the world of Birthright Butterflies. I believe God is saying that He wants to start forming groups that have that flavor, that texture, that make-up that the church of Acts had. Then we'll start seeing a lot of love and power—the world that was lost will be found.

Here's a concept for small home groups that I believe the Lord wants us to consider:

God is gathering together small groups of Christians in homes.
No man will be the head of these groups; Jesus will be their only head.
Their primary focus will be Jesus—His cross and resurrection. These

groups will allow the Holy Spirit to show them the truth about the junk inside of them—the hidden idols that are competing with the Lordship of Jesus and controlling them. These will be safe places, cocoons where believers will be in trusting and transparent relationships. As these small groups of Christians interact within these cocoons, the glorious process of transformation will take place—dying to the false self and all of its good intentions, to be raised as new creations in Christ—the real me set free. They will become one with God, one with themselves, and one with each other, to be filled with power! Then they will emerge as Birthright Butterflies, to live a life of being blessed and fulfilling their destiny to bless others. The power of God Himself will emanate out of these groups, to multiply and expand His Kingdom.

There are several principles we can glean from this concept in order to understand it better. The first is that *God is gathering*. It is *He* who is gathering together small groups of Christians.

If we read Luke 6:12-13, we see that before Jesus picked the original twelve apostles, He went up onto a mountain and prayed all night. *Then* He chose the twelve. Who put that original group of twelve apostles together? It was God the Father through Jesus. They didn't choose who they would be with, God did! That's the principle.

> WE PICK SITUATIONS WE'RE COMFORTABLE WITH, BUT GOD PICKS SITUATIONS THAT WILL CHALLENGE US, TO TRANSFORM US.

As Christians, do we pick our church? Do we pick the people we have fellowship with? Or does God? I'm afraid we do. We shop for churches like we shop for cars. *This church has a great facility. I like this style of worship and preaching. It's so comfortable!* We do the same thing with Bible study groups. We pick the people we are comfortable with, but what God is saying to us is, "Why don't you try letting Me pick the people you're supposed to be with? Maybe you'll have more love and power." We pick situations we're comfortable with, but God picks situations that will challenge us, to transform us. It's a very subtle point but a big one. God is gathering small groups of Christians. Don't rush out after you've read this book and form your group. Instead, pray and ask God to form the group. He might surprise you.

The second principle from the concept is that *Jesus will be the only head* of the group. He was the head of the twelve apostles, and He should be the head of every group. This doesn't mean that there will be no human leader; God always works through leadership. These home groups have to have leaders, but the most important quality of a leader is whether he or she promotes the Lordship of Jesus Christ. Is there a passion for Jesus to be Lord of everyone's life? Paul said in 1 Corinthians 2:2, "For I determined not to know anything among you except Jesus Christ and Him crucified." Paul was not promoting his own leadership; He was promoting the Lordship of Jesus Christ. That's the job of a true leader. That's the criterion! If a person is leading from any other platform, well, he or she shouldn't be leading the group. It's a very simple test.

The third principle is *trust*. There has to be trust in a home group, because the bottom line is, eventually you've got to get to the point where you open up and spill your guts out to each other. If you don't open up and do that, then all of the junk just stays inside. However, trust doesn't happen overnight. It's going to take some time to build it in real relationships. We have to take time going out apart from our home groups, having dinner, doing recreation—whatever we can to develop relationships so we can actually trust each other. Without trust we'll never really open up with each other, and that's one of the most important things about being in a home group. Remember, being transparent is a key to transformation. Trust takes time. Transformation takes time. A ram-it-through project and program mentality doesn't work in this home group world.

Are you starting to see the difference between the world God has for us and the kind of experiences we're used to?

The fourth principle is that once trust has been built, we *choose to become accountable* to one another. We all have blind spots that we can't see without others helping us. Stand in front of a mirror and try to see the back of your head. Can you see it? Is there any way humanly possible for you to see the back of your head? Not without another mirror, or a couple of mirrors. That's what the people in a home group become to each other. We are mirrors, and as the group progresses and trust deepens, we start saying to each other, "I am seeking your input. I need your prayer. I'm choosing to be accountable to you."

That doesn't normally happen in a Bible study. Bible studies are generally about studying the Bible, which is great, but a whole new dynamic is introduced when people submit to one another in love and become accountable. It's not about controlling anyone else; it's a choice made by a free will. We say to one another, "I'm learning the Trinity principle. God didn't do it alone; I can't make it alone. I need you."

The fifth principle is that it all has to be *led by the Spirit* of God. Nothing is happening, nothing that matters, without the Holy Spirit. The way this works is that as we gather together, we open in prayer and totally submit ourselves and our time to Him. *Holy Spirit, take over whatever agenda I had; I'm laying it down. Whatever You want to accomplish, do it.* The leader of the group can't have the desire to be in control; instead he must promote the Lordship of Jesus and allow the Holy Spirit to be in control.

That's my prayer for this book as well. It's in the form of a map for a spiritual journey, and maps are good. The one-on-one encounters at the ends of each chapter are good, and they are designed for home group discussions. But the Holy Spirit has to be free to be in control of the journey. Each group is different, every person is different, and God knows what we all need. A home group—or this book studied in a home group setting—will never work as a formula. We have to get out of the way and let the Holy Spirit lead. I can't tell you how many times, as the leader of our group, the Holy Spirit had me drop my planned agenda for the evening. And every time that happened, our fellowship was rich and wonderful.

> A HOME GROUP WILL NEVER WORK AS A FORMULA. THE HOLY SPIRIT HAS TO BE IN CONTROL OF THE JOURNEY.

When we put these principles into place and let God be God, people together will be transformed into new creations in Christ. We will be reconciled with our true selves, with God, with each other, and we will become one. Then, through that oneness, God is going to release power—the power of the Holy Spirit.

To elaborate a little bit more on becoming one, here's a concept called The Greatest of the Greatest: Three Ways. The scripture that the concept is based on is 1 Corinthians 13, the very famous "love chapter." Paul writes a lot of things about love, then, at the end he says that there are three, faith, hope, and love. "But the greatest of these is love." And in John 15:13, Jesus says, "Greater love has no one than this, that he lay down his life for his friends." What those verses together are saying is this: Love is the greatest thing, and the *greatest love you can ever have is to lay down your life* for somebody—the greatest of the greatest.

What if we applied the "greatest of the greatest" three ways in a small group of Christians? Number one, we'd say, "Lord, I want to lay down my life for You. I'm going to let You split me open. I'm going to let You put the false me to death—I don't want any more idols controlling me. I want intimacy and oneness with You, for real." The first thing is that we love the Lord enough to lay down our lives to become one with Him.

The second thing is, if we have a mate, we say, "I want to lay down my life for you. I want to be one with you in the truest, most intimate sense." That's not just *phileo* love, which is brotherly love, and it's not just *eros*, which is sexual union. I'm talking about *agape* love, which is how God loves us. It's an all-consuming love. This is the love that says, "I'm laying down my life for you to become one with you."

The third way we'd apply this love in a group is to lay down our lives for the people in the group in order to become one with them—in order to have unity.

What would happen in a home group, if through the power of the cross people were actually living this out? It's very, very interesting. Do you know what a nuclear bomb explosion is? It's a chain reaction, a series of events, not just a single event. As that chain reaction begins and then gains momentum, it releases incredible power.

Using that as our analogy, the chain reaction would go like this. I become one with myself first. No more false me versus the real me; I am one. The next part of the chain reaction is that I become one with God… and one with my mate…and then I become one with the fellow members of my group…and that chain reaction produces power even stronger than a hydrogen bomb explosion: *the power of God*! How?

A Person

A Couple

A Group

Together Again

Remember earlier in the book where we asked, "Who is the real me?" We said that at the moment of conception, God takes a piece of Himself, puts it in the fertilized egg in the womb, and that's how people come into existence. Did you ever think that when God takes a piece of Himself out, that He's splitting? He splits off a little piece of Himself and puts it in you and me.

As this chain reaction occurs, do you know what God is doing? (This is cool.) He's putting Himself back together again. What do you think would happen if the God who created the whole universe, who had split off little pieces of Himself in order to create billions and billions of people, started to fuse Himself back together again? How much power would be released? That's power, right? He's taking all of the pieces, male and female, and He's fusing Himself back together. This sequence is visually depicted in the sketch on the previous page.

I believe that means God is reconciling the world back to Himself, and it's no accident. In Colossians 1:19-20, it says, "For it pleased the Father that in Him all the fullness should dwell, and by Him [Jesus] to reconcile all things to Himself, by Him, whether things on earth or things in heaven, having made peace through the blood of His cross." God's purpose in Jesus Christ is to reconcile all things back to Himself—to put Himself back together again. And then we are in Jesus, so "in Him we live and move and have our being" (Acts 17:28).

God fusing Himself back together again to produce power is an amazing concept. The whole idea is that the power of God Himself will emanate out of these home groups. It won't be about projects and programs, but God Himself touching people through people. That's a whole different paradigm than what exists, isn't it? Let's think about just how important it is—this *becoming one*.

Jesus opened up His public ministry with the Sermon on the Mount. He closed His ministry with His teaching at the Last Supper. But do you know the last words that Jesus said before He went to suffer and die? He said,

I do not pray for these alone, but also for those who will believe in Me through their word; that they may all be one, as You, Father, are in Me, and I in You; that they may also be one in Us, that the world may

believe that You sent Me. And the glory which You gave Me I have given them, that they may be one just as We are One...that they may be made perfect in one, and that the world may know that You have sent Me, and have loved them as You have loved Me (John 17:20-23).

Jesus says it again and again, "Make them one the way We are One." Watch out world! Watch out when that happens, because through the lost secret of the cross and community, there is now a way for people to become one with their true selves, with God, and with each other. The simple setting of a home group is the best place for this to happen. The book of Acts shows us that.

> JESUS SAYS IT AGAIN AND AGAIN, "MAKE THEM ONE THE WAY WE ARE ONE." WATCH OUT WORLD! WATCH OUT WHEN THAT HAPPENS.

This is kind of interesting: Do you think science could be used to prove this concept of power through oneness? There's always a big battle going on between science and the church, right? I'm going to explain further the science behind a nuclear explosion to prove this simple concept of home groups and people gathering together in one accord, bringing about the release of enormous power.

The most powerful force in the entire universe is a thermonuclear explosion. It's the power of the stars and the sun. Do you know where that power comes from? *Fusion.* It comes from little hydrogen atoms coming together as one, and it is the most powerful force in the universe. That's a scientific fact.

There's another nuclear reaction, also very powerful, called *fission.* Fission was used in the original nuclear bomb, and the way it works is that you take the element uranium and split its atoms. By splitting uranium atoms, you cause a great amount of energy to be released.

But *fusion*—fusing things together—is actually much more powerful than fission. When you take hydrogen atoms and fuse them together, you get a much bigger explosion than the original nuclear bomb. They say it's *three to four times more powerful*—that the amount of mass transformed into energy is that much greater in a fusion reaction than by fission.

More transformation occurs in fusion than fission, and that's one of our key words: *transformation*. We've learned that transformation leads to reconciliation, which releases power.

This is where the science gets really amazing. Scientific fact: Uranium is the heaviest thing. Uranium's atomic mass is 238; it's the heaviest substance on the face of the earth. Guess what hydrogen's atomic mass is? 1. It's the lightest thing in the universe, even lighter than helium. The least is actually the greatest—has the greatest potential for power.

If we look at the system of knowledge and works, it's heavy, right? *This is what I know; this is what I do.* Jesus said to the Pharisees [paraphrased from Luke 11:46], "You load them down with burdens, but you won't lift one finger." Sounds heavy, doesn't it?

What did Jesus offer? "Take My yoke upon you and learn from Me…for My yoke is easy and *My burden is light*" (Matthew 11:29-30, emphasis added). Do you know what being saved by "grace though faith" is? Total reliance on God—it's light. It's not about me, it's about Jesus.

> GUESS WHAT FUSION IS? IT'S TWO PEOPLE HOLDING HANDS LOOKING AT THE CROSS. IT'S NOT ABOUT ME OR YOU, IT'S ABOUT JESUS. WE'RE IN UNITY.

What does knowledge and works produce? When what I know about God and what I do for God is different than what you know about God and what you do for God, we get into a fight. What do we do? We split—we undergo fission. It causes a lot of energy to be released, because two very heavy people who think they are super-spiritual get into a fight and go separate ways.

Guess what fusion is? It's two people holding hands looking at the cross. It's not about me, or you, but it's about Jesus. We're in unity, because what we have in common is what *He* did, not what either of us knows or does. And that fusion will generate a lot more power than the fission of bickering over who's right or wrong.

Here's a final scientific comparison that illustrates another parallel with God's plan for home groups. There was an article in *National Geographic*, October 2001, and it was called *The Power of Light*. This is a true story. There is a project called the National Ignition Facility, or NIF, and it's being built in California. It's costing 3.2 billion dollars to fund it. There's a group of scientists working on this concept, and they have a very simple theory. They have a little pellet, smaller than a tootsie roll, and it's filled with gas. The pellet is inside a huge ball that weighs one million pounds, and that ball is full of lasers. The theory goes that if they can concentrate enough light from those lasers on that little pellet, they will create a miniature star. An NIF project physicist has proposed that "NIF will produce more power in a one-nanosecond laser pulse than all the power generated in the rest of the world at that moment."[1] What he's saying is that, if they can get enough light on the little tootsie roll canister full of gas to create nuclear fusion through the power of light, then they will create a miniature star. And that will generate more power in a nanosecond than has been created across the entire world at that same moment.

You know what I believe God is saying to us today? I believe He's saying that He wants to generate this power in small home groups. He wants to release His power in thousands and thousands of groups around the world. And how is He going to do it? He's going to put a small group of people in a little tube. You know what a tootsie roll tube looks like? A cocoon. It's a tight place, and He's going to bombard it with light. The light is Jesus—the vertical beam of the cross where we are transformed as we say, *Search me, O Lord,* to become one with ourselves and the Lord. The horizontal beam is where we become one with each other. So underneath all of that light—Jesus who is the Light of the World—we're going to be transformed into new creations in Christ so we can be fused together, and in this process God is going to fuse Himself back together. That will release enormous power!

If you think it can't happen, check out the Upper Room. There were 120 people there, most of whom were not even named. After they were transformed by their experience with Jesus—His death and resurrection— they were in one accord. Then the Holy Spirit came down with power and created a miniature star there in Jerusalem. And you know what? It changed the entire world! What's more, He's going to do it again.

Here's the question: Are we serious? Do we believe it? These people spent 3.2 million bucks at the NIF; that's how much they believe

---

1 Joel Achenbach, "Power of Light," *National Geographic* (October 2001): p. 10.

it. They believe it's possible to create miniature stars. God is saying, "I don't just *believe* it's possible, I *know* it is! I know by experience. I've already done it in the church of Acts."

God gave me a very interesting warfare concept for my own life that connects to this NIF project. He said to my heart, *You're a warrior like Joshua and David, and I've called you to fight.* I thought that was cool—and a little bit daunting. But then He said, *I'm going to give you a secret to getting the power you need for victory in battle. You need to be* simple *and* little. I didn't really understand what that meant.

> THEY BELIEVE IT'S POSSIBLE TO CREATE MINIATURE STARS. GOD IS SAYING, "I DON'T JUST BELIEVE IT'S POSSIBLE, I KNOW IT IS! I'VE ALREADY DONE IT IN THE CHURCH OF ACTS."

It took years, but when I finally studied what it meant to be *simple*, I discovered that the Biblical meaning is "unmixed." No more mix between the wisdom of the world—the knowledge and works system I was in—and the worldly system of hidden idols that was in me. No. He wants me unmixed, and He wants me to be pure.

You know what *little* means? "To become *less* and come to the *end of yourself*"—to be a person who has died to self. So a person who's simple and little is pure and light and easily fused—easily becomes one with God and his or her brothers and sisters in Christ—and out of that oneness will come power for victory in battle. Let's connect that with what the article on the NIF project went on to say:

> Here we come to one facet of the miracle of light. It has no volume. And photons have no charge, so in the process of being concentrated into a very small space [the tootsie roll size capsule], they don't repulse each other as negatively charged electrons do. (NIF will fit 4×10^{24} photons into the target capsule.) "They don't bother one another."[2]

What does the word *little* mean? To come to the end of yourself, to have no volume. What does the word *simple* mean? Unmixed, no more

---

2 Achenbach, p. 10.

negative charge from the worldly systems. A person who becomes simple and little through the cross becomes like light: They can come together in one accord in the cocoon of a home group and not bother each other. Then God's supernatural nuclear fusion can occur. Ephesians 5:8 says, "For you were once darkness, but now you are light in the Lord. Walk as children of light." And 1 Thessalonians 5:5: "You are all sons of light and sons of the day. We are not of the night nor of darkness." The miracle of light happened at Pentecost, through the cross and the Holy Spirit; those 120 people were transformed into children of light who were in one accord. The power of the Holy Spirit came and the rest, as they say, is history. But history is about to repeat itself in an even greater way during these end times.

This is all very heady stuff—miniature stars in homes, wow! But we need a reality check before we embark on God's NIF project. Here are three pieces of wisdom. First, *offenses* will come in your group. Cocoons are safe places, but they are not a perfect little world; they are a messy place too. When these offenses come, you will have a choice: bring them under the four-part Lordship of Jesus as described in chapter 9 or handle them on your own. If you bring them to Jesus, the dealing with offenses will accelerate the transformation process and make your group stronger. If you don't bring them to Jesus, they could rip your group apart. God's NIF project is not a joke; it represents a serious Kingdom advancement that will bring serious opposition from the devil, who happens to be the accuser of the brethren, the master at causing offenses. So know ahead of time, offenses will come to your group! But ultimately that's what makes the cocoon a truly safe place—taking care of all offenses at the cross.

The second thing is *control*. Sincere group members with good intentions will be tempted to control the leader. What's more, sincere leaders with good intentions will be tempted to control the group. Therefore everyone must remember that no man is head of the group. Jesus is, and the Holy Spirit is in control. If this control issue rises up and causes offenses, you again must make a choice to submit it to the four-part Lordship of Jesus to resolve it. If you do, dealing with control will speed up your transformation process of dying to self and the group will become stronger. If you don't, control could rip the group apart.

Finally, with the power will come *persecution*. Jesus said in Matthew 10:24-25 that no student is above his teacher, and if they called Jesus

Beelzebub, how much more you or I. You may not be welcomed with open arms by your family, friends, or the church. Look what happened to the apostles in the book of Acts: They were beaten by the authorities, but they rejoiced and considered it an honor to suffer for Jesus' namesake. When we face these trials in our groups, we must have the same attitude.

To summarize, remember the painting Satan's Field of Slaughter, with his two swords? He will come at your group with offenses and the good intention of control, but take heart, Jesus has defeated him at the cross. And when you start experiencing persecution, rejoice, because that's a sign that you have and are spreading the real, full-strength gospel.

Speaking of real, you may be wondering how these home support groups work in real life. After three years, here's what we have to report from our group. One of the biggest things is a sense of family. Many of us have experienced splits within our natural families. As humans, we all have a strong need to be part of a family. God promised in Psalm 68:5-6 to place orphans in families, and He has with us. We may not be a family based on natural blood, but the blood of Jesus has turned us into a family that is just as real. Maybe better.

How about trials? One night, the Holy Spirit showed us that a strong attack of the enemy was coming and we needed to *circle the wagons*. We did and the attack came—health, marriages, finances, you name it. But because we circled the wagons and didn't try to fight alone, we achieved victory over every attack. We talked about it after, and we were all convinced that the home group concept was a key to making it through.

Next comes answered prayer. When Jesus Christ crucified is the most important thing in your life, your prayers have power. Why? Because Jesus is the power of God! And when you really know someone and care for them, your prayers go to a higher level. The other factor was group members weren't just asking for prayer; they sought advice also. And it really worked. One couple who had been living together got married. (That may not sound real churchy, but it's the real world and God used the group to make things right). Another had a calling to buy houses, fix them up and then sell them. After many failed attempts, the first house happened! One member lost his job and the Lord placed him in a new and better one. We now have a prayer and praise journal.

We all list things to lift up in prayer, and when the Lord answers, we move it to the praise side and add another one.

Should we be surprised? God's ways really do work.

In closing let's consider this. We are all familiar with the book of Genesis in the Bible. It means the beginning, the creation of something. Did you know there is a *Genesis part two* in the Bible? It's chapter two in the book of Acts. It's the beginning and the creation of the New Covenant church. What does it say? 120 people with a unanimous passion for Jesus and the cross were gathered in an upper room. The Holy Spirit fell and filled them all with power. The sound was so loud that people in the streets heard it and came to see what was going on. Peter shared with them, and 3,000 people accepted

FROM THE UPPER ROOM TO LIVING ROOMS, THE CROSS AND COMMUNITY WOULD MULTIPLY AGAIN AND AGAIN AND AGAIN!

Jesus as Lord and Savior that day. And those people who now, too, had a unanimous passion for Jesus then began to break bread and fellowship in their homes. From the Upper Room to living rooms, the cross and community would multiply again and again and again!

The start—the beginning—the creation—of Christianity involved these two things, the cross and community. They are still the core of our faith today. This is the lost secret that will truly transform us into new creations, so we can enter God's world of supernatural love and power. This world is available to us right now, just as it was to them! *For the promise is to you and to your children, and to all who are afar off* (Acts 2:39). Our cry to God of "Where's the love?" and "Where's the power?" has been answered. The only thing left is our decision. I pray that many worldwide will make it.

My Personal One-on-One Encounter With The Lord

ALSO FOR HOME GROUP DISCUSSION

As a believer, do I long for real relationships with my brothers and sisters in Christ, to be part of Christian community? Why do I feel this way?

_____
_____
_____
_____

Do I understand that the crucifixion and resurrection of Jesus, and believers meeting in homes are the two new things in the New Covenant? Are these two things, which make up the lost secret, missing in my life?

_____
_____
_____
_____

Would I trust God enough to pray and ask Him to place me in a home group, or use me to form one? How important is being in one accord (fusion) to receiving God's power?

_____
_____
_____
_____

Have I discovered that a home group is different than a Bible study or church cell group? Do I understand that even a home church, without the preeminence of Jesus Christ and Him crucified, is different than the home group concept shared in this chapter?

_____
_____
_____

Do I realize that home groups are not perfect little worlds, and that cocoons are messy places? Will we choose to take our offenses and the good intentions of control to the cross, to truly make our home groups a safe place?

_____

_____

_____

QUESTIONS FROM THE LOST SECRET SEQUENCE

1. THE CROSS: Is the most important thing in my Christian walk the crucifixion and resurrection of Christ and Jesus being my first love?

2. COMMUNITY: Do I gather together in homes with believers who have a passion for the cross, in trusting and caring relationships?

3. TRANSFORMATION: Am I transparent with God and my group members, so I can die to self and be transformed into a new creation in Christ?

4. RECONCILIATION: To what degree have I been reconciled to the Father as a son or daughter, and to other group members as brothers and sisters in Christ? How much supernatural love, joy, and peace am I experiencing even in the midst of my trials?

5. POWER: How much supernatural power am I experiencing for victory over sins, Satan, and curses, to be blessed and fulfill my destiny to bless others?

_____

_____

_____

_____

_____

REFLECTING ON THE ART

- In what way does the painting that opens this chapter speak to me?
- Did the sketch have an impact on me? If so, how?

_____

_____

_____

_____

Christianity Reduced to Its Simplest Form

Philip Howe

CHAPTER 16

Christianity Reduced to Its Simplest Form

SO FAR OUR SPIRITUAL JOURNEY has been about us making the cross the most important thing in our lives and gathering together with believers in homes who share this same passion. That's the micro-view. Now we're going to switch gears and take a macro-view. Let's look at the bigger picture of the church today and how to get the worldwide revival that we all desperately need.

There is a scientific principle—*simplicity*—which says that if you can understand things at their simplest, most basic level, you can do amazing things. Chemists understand this. Once they discovered the basic periodic table of the elements, they've been able to do combinations and accomplish incredible things in chemistry.

Medical professionals understand it. Once they broke the genetic code and began to understand the DNA double helix, a whole new world opened up to medical science.

And physicists understand it. When they unlocked the secret of the atom and understood things at an atomic level, they were able to release and harness nuclear power. Sometimes this knowledge has been used for destruction and sometimes for good, but that's the principle of simplicity.

What if *we* could reduce Christianity to its simplest form? What could the church—the body of believers—do with that? We're going to ask two questions: "Who is God?" and "What's His plan to save mankind?" It doesn't get any simpler than that.

A good place to start is by scripturally exploring who God is. A first scripture to examine is 1 John 1:5, which says that *God is light.* A neat thing here is that it doesn't say God *gives* light; it says He *is* light. So literally, if you could go inside of Him, you would see that He is made up of light. He is a body; He is a being of light. His supernatural molecules are light.

The second scripture we can look at is 1 John 4:16, which says that *God is love.* Again, we've got to take note of this: it doesn't say that God merely *loves;* it says He *is* love. If you went up to Him and stuck your arm inside of Him, it would be like sticking your arm inside a river of liquid love. He *is* love. Your arm would just be in this amazing environment of love. That's who He is, through and through—love.

The next scripture we can check out is Deuteronomy 6:4, where the Bible says that *God is one.* The amazing thing is that there are three divine persons—the Father, the Son, and the Holy Spirit—and somehow these three separate divine persons are one. They are actually distinct *and* one in the same being. That is a supernatural quality. Only God can do that.

The final verse to examine here is John 4:24, where it says *God is Spirit.* When the Bible says *God is Spirit,* it's saying *God is power.* He's not limited to the natural power of this world…He has supernatural power.

> LET'S LOOK AT THE LOGIC OF THIS SEQUENCE—THERE'S AN INCREDIBLE PICTURE THAT COMES OUT OF IT: LIGHT, LOVE, ONENESS, POWER. "THAT'S WHO GOD IS!"

Let's look at the logic of this sequence—there's an incredible picture that comes out of it: light, love, oneness, power. First, without light, it's impossible to have love. If there are accusations, lies, or any other darkness between people, there is no way to have love. There's *no way to love each other when we're in darkness*—it's just all confusion. Misinformation rules and reigns, and it destroys any possibility for people to love one another.

The second principle that emerges from this logic is that *without love it's impossible to be one.* Why is that? Because we've got to love each other unconditionally to be one. Everybody is going to make mistakes; everybody is going to blow it. If our oneness depends on perfect performance, no one will ever be in unity, because no one is perfect. We must deeply love in order to stick it out through the hard times. We have to have *agape*—unconditional love—to be one.

The third principle is, *without oneness there is no power.* Whether we like it or not, and whether we agree with it or not, God has chosen a way to release power in the universe. That way is fusion. It's the power of the stars, the power of the sun. When He fuses hydrogen together, it makes a thermonuclear explosion, and that is the greatest power in the entire universe. So the third principle of oneness produces the fourth principle of power. When we put all four together, we get this sequence: He's light—to produce love—that produces oneness—that produces power. That's who God is.

Now let's explore the second big question: *What is God's plan to save mankind?* He instituted that plan two thousand years ago, again with four parts. Number one was *God with us*—Emmanuel. That's Christmas. The book of John is very clear. It says Jesus was *the light of the world.* So, when God came down to be with us, He was the light of the world, and the very first thing that Jesus did was what? Teach. Even when He was a young boy in the temple, He taught. And they couldn't imagine where He got His teachings. Here's an interesting fact: in church history, the earliest major feast or celebration day was actually Epiphany, on January 6, not Christmas. It was the day marking the arrival of the Wise Men. Epiphany means a *flash of light*, and it celebrated the coming of the Light into the world.

What's the next thing in God's plan? *He died for us and was raised from the dead.* That's Easter. And John 3:16 says what? *God so loved the world that He sent His only begotten Son to die for us.* Then, in John 15:13, He said, "Greater love has no one than this, than to lay down one's life for his friends." God's second act was to die for us, because He loved us that much.

The next thing God did was to *make us one.* His group of followers who were arguing, contentious, and debating who was the greatest—all of a sudden the division was gone. The Bible says "they were all with one accord in one place" (Acts 2:1). Why? Through the power of the cross, they were made one. Just as God was one—Father, Son, and Holy Spirit—they became one with Him and with each other.

What was the fourth thing that happened? *God filled them* on Pentecost—as He fills us. The Holy Spirit came down when they were in unity and filled them. What did Jesus distinctly say? He said, "Tarry in the city of Jerusalem until you are endued with power from on high" (Luke 24:49). What were they filled with? *Power.*

God's plan to save mankind involved light, love, oneness, and power. *So who God is and His plan to save mankind are one and the same.* That's a very simple yet profound truth. What is more, once that truth has been opened up for us, I don't believe we'll ever read the Bible the same again. We're going to see that sequence—its truth—repeated over and over again in the Bible.

> SO WHO GOD IS AND HIS PLAN TO SAVE MANKIND ARE ONE AND THE SAME.

We said earlier that if you could take the simplest elements and understand them, then you could do amazing things. What is the amazing thing that all sincere Christians are looking for, praying for, and crying out for? We want revival to come to the earth, right? I believe what the Lord is saying to us today is that, "I have explained Christianity in its simplest form, which is who I am and what My plan is to save mankind. I did it to give you insights on how to get this amazing thing that you have been seeking without very much success, which is revival."

Remember, the theme of the chapter is *simplicity.* What if the Holy Spirit is saying, "I know how interested you are in revival, so why don't you look at how the original one happened two thousand years ago?"

If we think of it from a consumer point of view, everybody wants the original. There's an original formula, an original recipe, and nobody wants the imitation version, right? So the Holy Spirit is saying, "Why don't you guys check out how the original revival happened?"

What if we take the four elements and make it simpler yet? Let's reduce the four into three by looking at *kyros* time (*kyros* being a Greek word for time). It's different than *chronos,* which is a stretch of time. *Kyros* is a specific time, like the day you were born or the day you got married.

Here is how we can simplify those four elements by using *kyros.*

Two thousand years ago there was a three-part, *kyros*-time, sovereign move of God to bring revival to the earth. Number one was God with us—Emmanuel. That's Christmas. Number two was God dying for us and being raised from the dead. That's Easter. Now let's

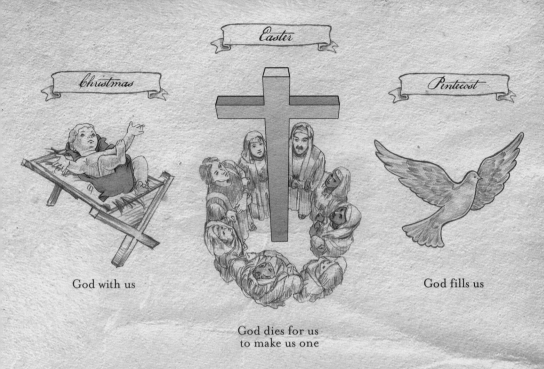

Christmas

Easter

Pentecost

God with us

God dies for us
to make us one

God fills us

combine Easter with the third thing, which was when everyone was brought together in one accord through the cross. Number three is Pentecost, and they were filled with the Holy Spirit. Do you know what the word *Pentecost* means? That time in the Jewish calendar was the customary feast of the harvest, and what happened immediately after the third sovereign move of God occurred? Three-thousand people were brought into the church. *That's* a big harvest in one day!

I KNOW HOW INTERESTED YOU ARE IN REVIVAL, SO WHY DON'T YOU LOOK AT HOW THE ORIGINAL ONE HAPPENED TWO THOUSAND YEARS AGO?

If we look at the sketch, we notice a few things. The cross is the centerpiece of the three elements. That's because Jesus is the Capstone, the Chief Cornerstone. He's to be preeminent. Do you think the centerpiece of these three elements would have something to do with revival coming? Or do you think it would be possible to skip over the centerpiece and still get revival?

The answer's pretty obvious. You're never going to be able to skip over the centerpiece. Somehow, though, the most important thing in Christianity that can bring revival is no longer the most important thing in the church. That's a big clue God has given us as to why we're not having revival.

Did you know that several years ago, Bill Bright, founder of Campus Crusade for Christ, mobilized 100,000 people to fast and pray for revival in the United States? He was led by the Holy Spirit, and God told him the U.S. desperately needs revival. It wasn't a regular thing. It was a forty-day fast, and many of the people actually just drank water for those forty days. What if God's answer to that fast was totally unlikely—and stunningly simple? What if the answer was not God sending down revival from heaven, but God sending down instead an explanation of how the original revival happened. What if He said, "Make Jesus Christ and Him crucified preeminent in the church. As a result, have believers with that passion gather together in homes—to be transformed into new creations in Christ and become one. Then I will send the Holy Spirit from heaven with power for revival." That's not what we'd expect, is it? But God is the God of the unexpected, isn't He?

So let's think about that. If we're waiting for a second visitation from heaven to come to bring revival to the earth, we may be waiting a long time. The second step for the Lord to bring revival into the earth is not a visitation from Heaven; it is a decision and a choice based on an event, the crucifixion and resurrection of His Son. It's wild isn't it? But study the original.

In the original revival two thousand years ago, there was a visitation, God with us. There was a second event, God died for us, and people had to decide at the time whether they accepted it or not. The ones that did became one, and then the next visitation came: they were filled with the Holy Spirit and with power. So this is a clarion call to the church: *If you want revival, understand how the first one happened!*

Did you ever hear the saying, *I've got good news and bad news for you?* I believe God is saying that the bad news is this: He's not going to fall from heaven in the next step and magically bring revival onto the earth. That's the bad news. The good news, however, is this: *We no longer have to wait—the lost secret has been found.* We can make the decision right now to make Jesus Christ and Him crucified preeminent again, to get together with small groups of believers who share that passion, to be transformed into new creations in Christ, and become one. Then guess what? We'll be gathered together in one accord and praying, just like Jesus told the original small group of 120 disciples to do. Then the second visitation will come. The Holy Spirit will fall on us with power, and it will be a much greater power than the church knows now, because the cross will once again be preeminent and believers will be in one accord. And with that power will come revival. That's pretty good news, isn't it? We don't have to wait anymore; we can take action now.

Let's look at what God started with 120 people in the Upper Room—the church of Acts. In light of what the early church *didn't* have, how do you think they accomplished what they did and produced such great fruit? They did not have the Bible as we know it; the New Testament wasn't even written yet, and the Old Testament was still on scrolls. People did not have the individual Bibles we have today and most would not for many centuries. They didn't have study Bibles; they didn't have a *Strong's Concordance*—none of that.

What is more, once they got kicked out of the temple and dispersed, they had no big public buildings, no specialized facilities or meeting rooms. They certainly had no sound systems, books, tapes, CDs, DVDs, radio, or television, right? They didn't have choirs or orchestras or worship teams. They had none of that stuff. Yet how well did they spread the gospel and bring about revival, even without all of those things? A lot better than we do.

WE ARE SPIRITUALLY SOPHISTICATED, BUT THEY WERE SPIRITUALLY ADVANCED.

Why? There are two important concepts we need to explore: *advanced* versus *sophisticated*. There's a big difference between being spiritually sophisticated and being spiritually advanced. We are very spiritually sophisticated, but they were spiritually advanced.

During this teaching my wife said, "You know what? We Christians today think we're very powerful because we look at our buildings and our facilities and all of the resources we have. We look at all of that sophistication, and we genuinely think we're very powerful and advanced. But the reality is that when a real problem comes, where is the love? Where's the power?"

When an offense comes, or somebody bumps into somebody else, are we loving, or do we split? When somebody is in need of a healing, do we lay hands on the sick and see them recover? Not too often. We appear to be powerful because we are mixing up spiritual sophistication with being spiritually advanced. However, God says, "I'm not interested in how sophisticated you are. I told you to become like little children." He wants us to *keep it simple!*

This real-life story illustrates it better than anything. There was a missionary in India named Hillary Harrison. There are relatively few Christians in India; they are persecuted, and the women especially are treated poorly.

There was a particular Christian woman whose husband had died, and she had no protection. She was persecuted unmercifully in her village. People threw rocks in her windows and egged her. She was looked down on because of her sex and hated because of her faith, and she had nobody to defend her.

One day the missionary, Hillary, went to the lady and asked, "What scriptures are you hanging onto, to help you deal with this horrible persecution you're going through?"

The woman looked at Hillary very sincerely and answered, "Hillary, I just want you to know that I don't have a scripture because, first of all, I don't have a Bible. Second, if I did have a Bible, it wouldn't matter because I can't read. Who I *do* have is Jesus Christ." That is all she had, and He was more than enough.

> THAT LADY WAS AS ADVANCED AS THEY COME. SHE WAS A SPIRITUAL GIANT. AND DO YOU KNOW WHY? SHE HAD JESUS!

Now I'm not knocking the Bible; I'm a Bible teacher. But the principle is this: we can be very spiritually sophisticated and not be spiritually advanced. That lady was, in my view, as advanced as they come. She was a spiritual giant. And do you know why? She had Jesus!

There's a guy in Scripture who also illustrates this point very well. His name was Saul—Rabbi Saul. Here's his sophistication résumé, found in Philippians 3: "Circumcised the eighth day, of the stock of Israel, of the tribe of Benjamin, a Hebrew of the Hebrews; concerning the law, a Pharisee; concerning zeal, persecuting the church; concerning the righteousness which is in the law, blameless" (vss. 5-6).

What did sophisticated Saul find out?

> *But what things were gain to me, these I have counted loss for Christ. Yet indeed I also count all things loss for the excellence of the knowledge of Christ Jesus my Lord, for whom I have suffered the loss of all things, and count them as rubbish, that I may gain Christ and be found in Him, not having my own righteousness, which is from the law, but that which is through faith in Christ, the righteousness which is from God by faith; that I may know Him and the power of His resurrection, and the fellowship of His sufferings, being conformed to His death, if, by any means, I may attain to the resurrection from the dead (vss. 7-11).*

He goes on to say in verse 15, "Therefore let us, as many as are mature, have this mind; and if in anything you think otherwise, God will reveal even this to you."

What is Paul saying? It's an oxymoron, isn't it? Whoever is mature in the faith, have this mind: to take all of your sophistication and throw it out the window. In verse 8 he tells us whatever we thought was gain and great to count them as rubbish, which in the Greek literally means dung—to look at all of our so-called sophistication as cow manure. Then, knowing this, to trade it all in—*for the sake of knowing Christ.* And here's a pretty wild fact: the Hebrew word for *idol* actually meant dung ball! So all of our sophistication, our knowledge and works, our good intentions, and our idols, actually had the worth of a dung ball compared to knowing Christ!

Paul happened to write a huge portion of the New Testament. He was a major force for getting a lot of the Gentile world saved at that time. It's safe to say, then, that he's a person we'd want to emulate, right? You know what Paul said? "I resolved to know nothing while I was with you except Jesus Christ and him crucified" (1 Corinthians 2:2 NIV). Saul was spiritually sophisticated, but Paul was spiritually advanced. There's a big difference. Paul also said one more thing we need to take note of. In his world there was a lot of competition going on. People were claiming to be super-apostles, saying this and that, and he responded to them in a very blunt way: "The kingdom of God is *not a matter of talk* but of power" (I Corinthians 4:20 NIV, emphasis added). That wouldn't apply to the church today, would it? Ouch.

This could be another ouchy one. Back to what my wife said about thinking we're powerful because of our buildings. Look at the Old Covenant. God's people in the Old Covenant were very intrigued with buildings. Not just the Pharisees, but even Jesus' own disciples. They said, "Jesus, look at this temple! Look!" You know what His response was? "A time is coming when not one stone is going to be left on another stone" (Matthew 24:1-2, paraphrased).

In the New Covenant, it's not about buildings anymore, is it? *God doesn't inhabit a temple; He inhabits people.* Caterpillar Christians, if we're honest, are very interested in buildings and facilities, and projects and programs to carry out ministry. We're very addicted to that. Right?

Butterfly Christians have a different focus. Their focus is *getting God, and giving God* to other people. The focus is people, not buildings. God is far more interested in people than He is in buildings, and He can be far more effective in spreading His kingdom through people than through buildings. Why is that? Because *people need other people.* There is no substitute. Computers will never replace people, robots will never replace people, and machines will never replace people. People who are in trouble need other people to come up beside them, look at them, touch them, and love them. That's the way God's supernatural power transfers between us.

> PEOPLE AREN'T INTERESTED IN WHAT I KNOW ABOUT GOD, OR THE PROJECTS AND PROGRAMS I'M DOING FOR GOD. THEY WANT GOD HIMSELF, BECAUSE THEY DESPERATELY NEED HIS LOVE AND POWER.

But think of a truly needy person who has a health problem, a financial issue, a marriage problem, etc. That person isn't interested in what I know about God or my pet projects and programs. They desperately need God Himself. If I'm not really carrying a lot of God with me, I can't really help them, can I?

With that thought in mind, let's refer back to our spiritual journey map. At the end of the map there is a treasure chest at the foot of the cross—think of it as the vault that we've been talking about, that the combination in the Lost Secret Sequence opens up. Here's what's in that treasure chest. It's not worldly blessings. It's not what you think it might be. *It's God Himself.* The promised land for God's chosen people is no longer a place. It's a person, and that person is God Himself. The cross is our way to get to this promised land. Jesus is saying, "I actually died for you, not just to tear the veil of the Holy of holies, not just to give you access to God, but to actually give you the opportunity to have God as your personal possession, your personal treasure." *That's* the ultimate power of the cross. But think about it, when we get God we get everything—love relationships and rulership power. It's like borrowing money versus owning the bank. Which is better? Now when we go to minister to a person in need, we have a lot to give them. Like the apostle Peter, who said, "Silver and gold I do not have, but what I do have I give you: In the name of Jesus Christ of Nazareth, rise up and walk" (Acts 3:6). And that, my friends, is a different ministry paradigm than what we're used to—get God then give God.

> **THE PROMISED LAND FOR GOD'S CHOSEN PEOPLE IS NO LONGER A PLACE. IT'S A PERSON, AND THAT PERSON IS GOD HIMSELF.**

Let's close with a final thought on this restoration-revolution God is bringing about. Picture a puzzle that God is putting together. Let's start with the five majestic trees. He's brought the Word back to a very high level. Intercessory prayer has dramatically increased. Praise and worship are far more enthusiastic. There are many types of gatherings and fellowships now available. And now ministry has been expanded to include the prophetic and other gifts of the Spirit. How about the fivefold ministry that existed in the original church? Ephesians 4:11-12 says, "And He Himself gave some to be apostles, some prophets, some evangelists, and some pastors and teachers, for the equipping of the saints for the work of ministry, for the edifying of the body of Christ." It's not just pastors and evangelists anymore; the offices of teacher, prophetic, and apostolic are now being restored. But the Lord has saved the best for last. The last piece to be

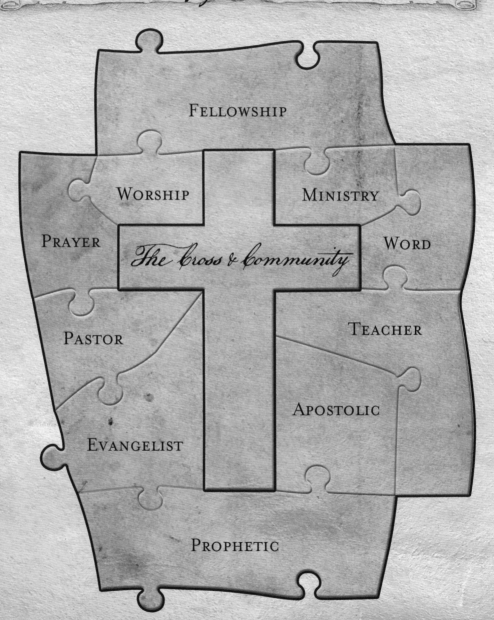

FELLOWSHIP

WORSHIP

MINISTRY

PRAYER

The Cross & Community

WORD

PASTOR

TEACHER

EVANGELIST

APOSTOLIC

PROPHETIC

restored is the centerpiece, the cross and community. When that happens, watch out! Incredible power will flow into the five majestic trees and the fivefold ministry. Why? Because Jesus Christ crucified is the power of God, and God's chosen method to release power is through fusion. It's a double dose of power!!

When this happens, the end time revival will actually surpass the first one in the church of Acts. The Scripture says that the latter rain will be greater than the former (Joel 2:23-29). It has to be because the Gospel must be preached to the four corners of the earth, and the church must be without spot or blemish for the return of Christ. That's a greater revival than in the church of Acts, and we get to be part of it—if we choose to make Jesus Christ crucified preeminent and share that passion in a home group, to be transformed, reconciled, and filled with power!

So there we have it, Christianity reduced to its simplest form. *Who God is, and His plan to save mankind, are one in the same.*

ONE. God, who is light, came down to be the light of the world—we celebrate that as Christmas.

TWO. God, who is love and one, died for us on the cross to make us one with Him and each other—we celebrate that as Easter.

THREE. God, who is Spirit, which means power, filled the 120 people who were in one accord with the Holy Spirit and power—we celebrate this as Pentecost.

To close this chapter, let's look at a simple history of man. God created Adam and Eve and gave them a birthright—to have a face to face relationship with Him in love, joy, and peace, and to have rulership over the world and Satan in order to be blessed and be a blessing. At the Fall, that birthright of relationship and rulership was lost, stolen through a deception of the devil. The process of restoring our God-given birthright was begun with Abraham. It was completed by Christ on the cross, who was then raised from the dead. But by the end of the fourth century, Satan had stolen our birthright again. The time has now come for every human being to get their God-given birthright back, once and for all!

Do you want *your* God-given birthright back? If your answer is yes, you can join God's cross and community restoration revolution today.

My Personal One-on-One Encounter With The Lord

Do I understand the four parts of who God is? Do I understand His four-part plan to save mankind? Do I now see that who God is and His plan to save us are one and the same?

_____

_____

_____

Can I now simplify the four to three? What is the simple message of Christmas? Easter? Pentecost?

_____

_____

_____

_____

Have I been praying for and seeking revival? Do I now realize it will involve a choice based on an event, joining with other believers to make the crucifixion and resurrection of Jesus Christ the most important thing in our lives?

_____

_____

_____

_____

What is the difference between being spiritually sophisticated and being spiritually advanced? Based on this, do I see what the church of Acts had that we don't have today? What are some of the ways that I may be spiritually sophisticated?

_____

_____

_____

_____

Have I come to the end of the map, now knowing that inside the treasure chest is God Himself? Do I realize that when I get God, I get everything? Is my new ministry paradigm this: Get God, Give God?

_____

_____

_____

_____

Am I ready to join God's end-time restoration revolution involving the cross and community? What might my first few steps be to join this restoration revolution?

_____

_____

_____

_____

REFLECTING ON THE ART

- In what way does the painting that opens this chapter speak to me?
- Did the sketches have an impact on me? If so, how?

_____

_____

_____

_____

What Will Happen
When God Restores the
Cross and Community?

What Will Happen When God Restores the Cross and Community?

In the days of King Josiah, Hilkiah the high priest found the Book of the Law among some rubbish in the temple. A long-lost treasure had now been found! When it was brought before the king, he tore his clothes and assembled all of the priests and the people. He ordered the book to be read, and afterward the king and all of the people repented and renewed their covenant with the Lord. Then they cleansed the temple and the entire land of idols (2 Kings 22 and 23).

So it is with us today—or can be—as we uncover the meaning of the riddle on the map: "Lost and Found to Be Unbound…Up Then Down to Get My Crown." Something very old and very valuable that was lost for 1,600 years, has now been found—the lost secret of the cross and community. When we make Jesus Christ and Him crucified preeminent in our lives and gather in homes with other believers who share this passion, we fully embrace the New Covenant again and are unbound. Then, as Caterpillar Christians, we go down into the cocoon to be cleansed of our idols and transformed into beautiful monarch butterflies—kings and queens who get our crowns.

This transformation takes place as we experience the Lost Secret Sequence. Think of this sequence as a five-pronged key that unlocks a treasure chest that's filled with God Himself and His world of love, power, blessings, and fulfilled destiny.

The Lost Secret Sequence

1. **THE CROSS:** The most important thing in my Christian walk is the crucifixion and resurrection of Christ and Jesus being my first love.

2. **COMMUNITY:** We gather together in homes with believers who have a passion for the cross, in trusting and caring relationships.

3. **TRANSFORMATION:** We are transparent with God and each other, in order to die to self and be transformed into new creations in Christ.

4. **RECONCILIATION:** As new creations, we are reconciled to the Father as sons and daughters, and to each other as brothers and sisters in Christ. We enter His relationship world of supernatural love, joy, and peace, even in the midst of trials.

5. **POWER:** In this world of love, we are fused together as one and God fills us with His supernatural power. We enter His rulership world of victory over sin, Satan, and curses to be blessed and fulfill our destiny to bless others.

What's been missing in conventional Christianity has now been restored—the cross, community, and the transformation they bring about. Now the cry of our hearts for God's love and power has been answered. This sequence isn't a how to formula; it's a Holy Spirit-led process that is personalized and different for every individual and group. The Lost Secret Sequence is for every church, every minister, and every believer—in fact it is for every person on the face of the earth! It's low tech, with no need for facilities or finances, so this world of supernatural love and power is available to everyone. This sequence is one of three major concepts shared in this book. The second big concept is this:

CATERPILLAR CHRISTIANS MUST DIE TO SELF

Christianity is not about doing; it's about dying and being raised a new creation in Christ. If it was about doing, Jesus would have been born into a royal family. He would have been sent to the best schools and then headed up various positions in the kingdom for further training. He would have ruled as a king for a long time and instituted many huge projects and programs. Instead, He was born to a lowly family. He lived a nondescript life and worked as a carpenter until age thirty. His public ministry lasted for just three years. Then His true mission occurred. He died for our sins and was raised from the dead. Caterpillar Christians who are very much into doing must come to realize this truth and begin to focus on dying to self. The third major concept is this:

No One Can Make this Journey Alone

We all need to die to self, but we can't do it alone. In a small home group, we help each other with our blind spots. We support each other through our trials. Together we are transformed into new creations in Christ. The lost secret of the cross and community has been found!

I believe God's decision to restore the cross and community represents a restoration revolution that will reform the church and bring revival to the whole world. Do you want to be part of it? Jesus' hand on the cover of the book is sending a universal message, inviting everyone to make that choice. To the born-again believer, it's saying, "Stop! I love you. Return to Me as your first love." To the minister it's saying, "Stop! I love you. Remember what's the most important thing for you and those I've called you to minister to." To the person who is not born again, it's saying, "Stop! I love you. Come and get to know Me."

> GOD'S DECISION TO RESTORE THE CROSS AND COMMUNITY REPRESENTS A RESTORATION REVOLUTION THAT WILL REFORM THE CHURCH AND BRING REVIVAL TO THE WHOLE WORLD.

If you've never accepted Jesus into your life, you can get to know Him right now by simply saying from your heart, *I need You, Jesus. I believe You personally died for me on the cross and were raised from the dead. My name is written on Your hand. I'm sorry for my sins. Forgive me, and come and enter my heart. I make You both Lord and Savior of my life.*

Now we can all look at this last painting, entitled "First Love," and see ourselves in it. At the foot of the cross, with Jesus as our first love, there is rest. The lie that God is not good and we're not good enough is gone. It's replaced by the truth that God is good and we're wonderful. The lust for the law, to use knowledge and works to take care of our own problems and succeed to gain self-esteem, is gone. It's replaced by faith in Jesus and what He did on the cross. The law of the Spirit of life in Christ Jesus has set us free from the law of sin and death. A river of life now fills us with supernatural love, joy, peace, and power. Now we can all say, "Jesus, You did not die for nothing!"

One final thought. Sixteen hundred years is a long time for the two core keys of Christianity to have been lost. That represents a lot of momentum for entrenched human traditions, so it's going to take lots and lots of God's grace and mercy for this restoration revolution to happen. Fittingly, the book started with a parable of grace and will close with a prayer for grace. If the Lord has put a fire in your gut for the lost secret to be restored, join with me in prayer. Let's pray like Daniel did during Israel's captivity in Babylon (Daniel 9:1-19). His heart-felt cry was heard, and I believe ours will be also.

O Lord, we have sinned. We have left You, Jesus, as our first love. The great sacrifice of Your cross is no longer the most important thing in our lives. We don't gather in homes in loving, trusting, and caring relationships. We got caught up with the wisdom of the world and have become enamored with knowledge and works. We harbor many hidden idols that vie for our affections and compete with Your Lordship. We fight with each other and easily end relationships. We know that all of this breaks Your heart. We are sorry. Forgive us.

O Lord, we need another kyros-time sovereign move of Your grace in our generation. We know this is the only way that this restoration revolution will happen. Open our eyes to the cross and community. Enable us to be transparent, to be transformed. Then pour Your supernatural love and power into us so we can spread the sweet fragrance of Jesus to a lost and dying world. It's not because of our righteousness that we ask this but because of Your great grace and mercy. O Lord, hear! O Lord, forgive! O Lord, listen and act! Do not delay for Your own sake, my God, for Your church and Your people are called by Your name , and the whole world is waiting for You!

Let the journey continue...

About the Author:

Rick Suarez was the son of a blue-collar worker who achieved great business success at a very young age. As a wealthy atheist, by God's grace, he experienced a dramatic conversion to Christianity. Because of his wealth and wild lifestyle, he struggled to make a wholehearted commitment to the Lord. Through God's strength, he finally dedicated his life totally to the Lord. Then something unusual happened. Instead of his life getting better and being blessed, things got worse! He went through a long period of very fiery trials and suffered great loss. God used this time to show him the junk that was still inside of him (hidden sins and idols he knew nothing about). The conventional Christianity he knew and lived came to an end, being replaced by a Christian walk with the cross and community as his primary focus. He was transformed by this experience, as were other members of their home group. Rick is the founder of Fresh Start Ministries. His passion now is to share the freedom, intimacy, and blessings that are available to all through the cross and community. He has been married to his wife Lu Ann for 32 years. They have four children, a son-in-law, a daughter-in-law, and a grandson.

How To Obtain Art And Receive More Teachings:

The painting below and some of the art in this book are available as posters, or as prints that are suitable for framing. There are also other life-changing teachings by Rick Suarez that are available. To learn more about the art, teachings, or having Rick speak to your church or organization, use the contact information below.

F O R   Y O U

Contact information:

Web: www.lostsecret.org

Email: info@lostsecret.org

Mailing address: The Lost Secret
                                    P.O. Box 35217
                                    Canton, Ohio 44735

Continue Your Journey On Our Website

www.lostsecret.org

- Share your thoughts on *The Lost Secret* and see what others are saying
- Read the author's blog
- Communicate with the author at rick@lostsecret.org
- Go inside other home groups around the country and the world
- Get a behind the scenes look on how the book was created
- Order additional copies of *The Lost Secret* at bulk purchase discounts

Sharing The Secret

Many people who have been touched and transformed by *The Lost Secret* give it to family and friends. It makes a wonderful gift because it's a beautiful art-filled book that also contains a life-changing message. Others use it for ministry in churches, youth groups, counseling sessions, battered homes, and prisons. Bulk discounts are available for purchases of five books or more. This book has been self-published by a small ministry, so your help in getting this message out would be greatly appreciated. Here are a few ideas: You could talk about the book on your e-mail lists or other places that you interact with people on the Internet. We suggest not making it an advertisement, but just to simply share how the book has touched and transformed you. If you have a website or a blog, consider sharing how the book impacted you. Don't give away the lost secret, but recommend that they read it and then give them the link www.lostsecret.org. If you own a business, consider putting the book on your counter for resale. We offer wholesale prices for retail sales.

Acknowledgments:

Please don't give me credit for this book; it truly was the Lord's doing. I didn't even know these concepts and principles existed until the Lord shared them with me. The Holy Spirit worked through an entire creative team to produce this book and even gave "downloads" for art ideas through family members of the team. In doing so, the Lord modeled a powerful principle for us: it really is Him making things happen through a body of believers. So know that it was the Lord touching you as you were reading this book, not me.

I thank my wife, Lu Ann, for standing by my side during my twenty-one year experience of nonconventional Christianity, which I neither understood nor handled very well at times. I thank my children for doing the same: Ricky, Kristin, Elisha, and Mary. I thank our home group: Wayne, Kay, Shawn, Lisa, Steve, Janet, and Aaron, who for three years listened, interacted, and prayed as the book was being taught. A very special thanks to my dear brother in the Lord, Julius Toth, God's businessman who sponsored the first printing of this book.

I also want to thank the entire creative team for their passion for this project: Jason Rovenstine, the creative director who connected me to many members of the team; Gwen Faulkenberry, who worked with me on the rewrites and became a true sister in the Lord in the process; Philip Howe, an established artist who did many of the oil paintings; Lisa Wood, an up-and-coming artist who also did oil paintings; Richard Carbajal, an established illustrator who did all of the sketches; Janice Manuel, who did the final edit.

And a special thanks to you, for getting to know my best friend better…Jesus.

CREATIVE TEAM CONTACT INFORMATION:

Here is the contact information for the members of the creative team that I mentioned in the Acknowledgments on the previous page:

Jason Rovenstine   *email:* info@roverhaus.com

Gwen Faulkenberry   *email:* gfaulkenberry@hotmail.com

Philip Howe   *web:* www.philiphowe.com
                                   email: philip.howe@verizon.net

Lisa Wood   *web:* www.lisajacksonwood.com

Richard Carbajal   from Deborah Wolfe LTD,
                                   web: www.illustrationonline.com

Janice Manuel   *email:* manuel1941@aol.com

Dedication:

TO JESUS CHRIST AND HIM CRUCIFIED,
WHO ALLOWED US TO TORTURE AND MURDER HIM,
IN ORDER TO SAVE US.

PRAYER:

For I resolved to know nothing (to be acquainted with nothing, to make a display of the knowledge of nothing, and to be conscious of nothing) among you except Jesus Christ (the Messiah) and Him crucified. And my language and my message were not set forth in persuasive (enticing and plausible) words of wisdom, but they were in demonstration of the [Holy] Spirit and power [a proof by the Spirit and power of God, operating on me and stirring in the minds of my hearers the most holy emotions and thus persuading them], so that your faith might not rest in the wisdom of men (human philosophy), but in the power of God.

1 Corinthians 2:2, 4–5
Amplified Bible

Notes:

Notes: